April 2000

W9-CFG-647

The Complete
SIAMESE

SALLY FRANKLIN

HOWELL
BOOK HOUSE

New York

HOWELL BOOK HOUSE
A Simon & Schuster / Macmillan Company
1633 Broadway
New York, NY 10019

MACMILLAN is a registered trademark of Macmillan, Inc.

Library of Congress Cataloging-in-Publication data

Franklin, Sally.
      The complete Siamese / Sally Franklin

                    p.   cm.
                ISBN 0–87605–941–8
                1.Siamese cat. I.Title
            SF449.S5F73 1996   95–40659
            636.7'25 – dc20   CIP

Manufactured in Singapore

10 9 8 7 6 5 4 3 2 1

CONTENTS

Chapter One: THE HISTORY AND CHARACTER OF THE SIAMESE   **6**
Legends; Early history; Origin of varieties; The source of the Siamese breed; The Siamese in the UK; Appearance; Personality; Differences between colours; Voice; Intelligence and interaction; The standard of points (1892); A cult figure.

Chapter Two: CHOOSING A SIAMESE   **17**
Making the choice; The personal commitment; The family commitment; The right surroundings; Giving your time; Financial considerations; Preparing your home; Safety measures; A suitable Siamese; Kitten or cat? Male or female? Breeding plans; Finding a Siamese breeder; Assessing stock; Vaccinations; After-sale service; The final decision.

Chapter Three: PREPARING FOR YOUR SIAMESE   **25**
Finding a veterinary practice; Outdoor or indoor pet?; Outside runs and pet doors; Cat-proofing the home; Equipment; Collecting your Siamese; Arriving home; Early training; Getting to know each other.

Chapter Four: NUTRITION & FEEDING   **35**
Dietary development of the cat; The concept of life-cycle diets; Types of food; Dry foods; Wet foods; Dyes and chemicals; Label analysis; The merits of mixed feeding; Prescription diets; Feeding guide.

Chapter Five: GENERAL CARE AND MAINTENANCE   **41**
Cleaning the ears; Checking eyes; The nose; The chin area; The mouth; Claws; Declawing; The tail; Grooming the coat; Hair balls; Bathing your Siamese; Fleas; Ringworm; Internal worm infestation.

Chapter Six: THE BREED STANDARDS   **57**
Siamese registration policy; The GCCF Standard; Preliminary standard of points for cinnamon, caramel and fawn point Siamese and their associated colour varieties.

Chapter Seven: THE AMERICAN SYSTEM   **70**
Early American cat shows; Early American Siamese; American Cat organisations (The American Cat Association; The Cat Fanciers' Association; The Cat Fanciers' Federation; The American Cat Fanciers Association; The American Association of Cat Enthusiasts; The Traditional Cat Association; The International Cat Association); The classification of Siamese; Showing in the USA; The TICA Standard.

Chapter Eight: SHOWING YOUR SIAMESE   **80**
To show or not to show? Is your cat good enough? Entering shows; Show preparation; Entry to the show hall; At the show; Ring judging.

Chapter Nine: SEAL POINT SIAMESE   **86**
The early days; The turn of the century; 1911–1920; The twenties; The thirties; The forties; The fifties; The sixties; The last twenty-five years.

Chapter Ten: BLUE POINT SIAMESE   **97**
The first examples; Champions and opponents; Achieving recognition; Post-war problems; Colour concerns; Worthy champions; The seventies; The eighties; The nineties; The Blue Point in the USA.

4

Chapter Eleven: CHOCOLATE POINT SIAMESE   **104**
First references; Debate about colour; The struggle for recognition; The German connection; Developments in the thirties and forties; Defining the chocolate point line; Gaining recognition: Decline in colour; Grand champions; Colour concerns.

Chapter Twelve: LILAC POINT SIAMESE   **110**
Controversial beginnings; USA recognition; UK recognition; The source of the colour; A breeding programme; The variety develops; Problems arise; Breeding recommendations; American viewpoints; Lilac point champions.

Chapter Thirteen: TABBY POINT SIAMESE   **117**
Origin of the variety; Naming the variety; Recognition; First champions; The last 25 years.

Chapter Fourteen: THE SEX-LINKED SERIES OF COLOURS   **123**
The sex-linked gene inheritance: Investigations into breeding; History of a Red Point Siamese; Breed registrations under AOV; The Penarwyn prefix; Applying for recognition; Formation of a new cat club; Early lines and champions; The early Tortie points; Prominent prefixes; Other sex-linked varieties; The Colourpoint, Rex coated and AOV club; New classification; Cream point Siamese; Other varieties.

Chapter Fifteen: GENETICS OF THE SIAMESE   **132**
By Roy Robinson, F.I. Biol.
The four basic colours; Genetic inheritance; Phenotype and genotype; The genetic importance of Tabby points; Extending the genetic principles; Sex-linked heredity; Identification by breeding behaviour; Epistasis relationship; General genetic inheritance.

Chapter Sixteen: BREEDING   **154**
Responsibilities of breeding; Finding homes; The costs; Registration of the breeding queen; Condition of the breeding queen; Breeding age; The cyclical pattern of breeding; The oestrus cycle; Timing of mating; Finding a suitable stud; The health and condition of the stud; The stud cat's quarters; The stud fee and contract; Medical tests; The timing of the litter; Preliminaries to mating; Mating; Post-mating.

Chapter Seventeen: PREGNANCY AND BIRTH   **161**
The stages of pregnancy; Delivery kit; First stages of labour; Normal birth; The breathing kitten; The umbilical cord; The placenta; Breech birth; Difficult births; Moving the kittens; Clearing up; Checking for defects; The first few days; Feeding kittens in an emergency; Identification; Potential Problems; False pregnancies.

Chapter Eighteen: KITTEN DEVELOPMENT   **171**
The first week; The second week; The third week; The fourth to sixth weeks: the weaning process; The sixth to eighth weeks; The eighth to tenth weeks; The tenth to twelfth weeks; The thirteenth week.

Chapter Nineteen: RECENT DEVELOPMENTS   **177**
Cinnamon and fawn; The English development; The Dutch development; Linking of the van Mariendaal and Twinkle Star's line; The Salste Connection; Caramel and apricot; The Scintilla line – apricot; The Scintilla line – caramel; Other Siamese lines; Possible USA caramels; Silver pointed Siamese varieties.

Acknowledgements

I am deeply indebted to many friends for providing me at often very short notice illustrative material and information to help me complete this book which I hope will give many Siamese pet owners a great deal of pleasure over the years. I am pleased to acknowledge and thank:

Harry and Rosie Meekings for proof-reading all the text at its various stages, answering many questions and providing copy pedigrees of named Siamese cats. Special thanks to Rosie who as The Honorary Secretary of the Siamese Cat Association allowed me to borrow Association Journals and library material, giving me permission on behalf of the Association to quote from these Journals. Kevin and Gail Dean, Jean and Don Franklin for additional proof reading.

Roy Robinson, F. I. Biol., for providing the chapter on Genetics.

Paddy Cutts, of Animals Unlimited, for allowing me to use many pictures from her excellent Library free of charge as a personal favour for this book.

Other photographs by Marc Henrie, Steve Franklin and the author, or as credited in the book.

Brenda Watson for the Line Illustrations.

Lesley Pring, Secretary of the GCCF and her assistants, T. Scott and Pip Allen for queries and for permission to reproduce the GCCF Standard of Points and Registration Policy and Klaus Dessauer for information relating to the Siamese Joint Breed Advisory Committee.

The Honorary Secretaries of the GCCF Clubs for responding to my requests: The Siamese Cat Club; The Siamese Cat Society of the British Empire; The Seal Point, Blue Pointed, Chocolate Pointed and Red Point & Tortie Point Siamese Cat Clubs; Midshires Siamese Cat Association; The Northern Siamese Cat Society and The Balinese & Siamese Cat Club.

My Veterinary Surgeon, Roger Till, for answering numerous questions and correcting my spelling on veterinary terminology; Phil Richards, Laboratory Manager of Redland Minerals; The Cat Association of Great Britain; Ken Kerr and Monica Goddard (prefix Kerrimon) for information and support; Pat Turner (Caramel and Apricot sections) and Dr David Summers of Martin Technical, Canada, for checking the Nutrition chapter.

Brian Doyle, Peter Embling, and the CATS magazine team for research material and support.

Cat Associations from all over the world and their members who have kindly forwarded information and sent pictures for this book: Yvonne Craane and Maria Falkena-Rohrle (Holland); Marie Holmes (New Zealand); Helen Shevchenko (Russia); Daphne Negus, Phil & Mary Anne Magitti, Diane L. Fineran (USA).

The Independent Cat Association; The American Cat Fanciers' Association; and The American Association of Cat Enthusiasts.

And finally no acknowledgment would be complete without mentioning my Editor, Anne Smiley (now a friend and owned by one of our kittens, Salstekaneel Felicity), and my husband Steve who took on the unpaid jobs of housekeeper and Salste cat minder whilst I wrote the text.

Chapter One

THE HISTORY AND CHARACTER OF THE SIAMESE

One of the best known and most easily recognisible of cats is the Siamese, which has been described as combining "the grace of a panther, the fleetness of the deer, the softness of down, the strength of the lion, and the affection of the dog in one charming bundle". Siamese have a special attraction because of their aristocratic attitude, their talkative and intelligent personalities, and their very distinctive coat pattern and colouring.

LEGENDS

Many legends surround the Siamese cat, and there is one particularly endearing myth which associates the creation of the Siamese with the journey of Noah's Ark.

In a story from a book entitled *Animals and Man*, by George Cansdale, a description was given of the boredom of the animals in the Ark during their long journey, and of their ways of alleviating it. The Siamese, it says, originated through interspecies mating, with the ape falling in love with the lioness who then produced the first cat. This type of mating leaves much to imagination but, so the story goes, it gave birth to the character of the Siamese, which is said to have the "attributes of an ape and the bravery of the lion".

Until the latter part of the nineteenth century very few people outside Siam, as it was then known, had actually seen a Siamese cat. However, visitors to that country, now called Thailand, would have been told of this animal, which belonged exclusively to the Royal Family and to favoured members of the Siamese aristocracy. This exclusivity, together with the unusual Himalayan appearance, personality and voice of the Siamese, would have ensured the transformation of any tales or myths into full-scale legends.

Written records reveal that Siamese cats, in their country of origin, were venerated as guardians of the temples. When a person of high rank died, it was usual to select one of these cats to receive the dead person's soul. The cat was then removed from the royal household and sent to one of the temples to spend the rest of its days living a ceremonial life of great luxury, with monks and priests as its servants.

These cats were reputed to eat the finest foods from gold plate and to recline on cushions made of the most opulent materials, which had been provided by the departed one's relatives in an attempt to receive good fortune and blessings. Once they became temple cats, they were supposed to have special powers and could intercede for the soul of the dead person.

Years ago features such as crossed eyes and kinked tails were looked on as characteristic of the breed and many legends exist as to their origin. It was said that a Princess of the Royal House of Siam used her cat's tail as a ring-stand while she was bathing. The kink in the tail prevented the rings from falling off and being lost.

Another legend accounts for both the cross-eyed feature as well as the development of the kink. Once, when all the men of Siam left their homes to defend their kingdom, just two cats – one male Siamese, Tien, and one female Siamese, Chula – remained in order to guard Buddha's golden goblet in the sacred temple.

The male cat became pretty restless and, after mating the female Siamese, left her in order to find another priest to look after the temple. The female, apparently, was so overwhelmed by the responsibility of guarding the Buddha's treasure that she never once glanced away from the goblet, wrapping her long tail around its stem to prevent theft in case she should fall asleep.

As time passed by waiting for Tien to return with a new master, she could no longer forestall the birth of her kittens, who all arrived with the physical characteristics that she herself had acquired during her period as watchguard – a kinked tail and crossed eyes. Just occasionally, even today, kittens are born with these features – so the legends are kept alive.

Siamese cats have also had regal connections in the past in the UK. Cat shows in the late 1800s received a great boost when it was known that Queen Victoria was an enthusiast and she and her family attended some of the early ones. There are photographs of Queen Alexandra on the Royal Yacht holding a Siamese. Queen Elizabeth II was given a Seal Point Siamese kitten, who became known to her as Timmy, to celebrate the occasion of her marriage to Prince Philip, Duke of Edinburgh. The kitten was officially registered as Corsham Royal Boy. Princess Michael of Kent has also been photographed with her Seal Point Siamese.

Famous film stars have also owned Siamese cats. James Mason, with his wife Pamela, were given their first Siamese, called Gamma, the night before their wedding in the 1950s by a friend. Vivien Leigh took her Siamese, New, with her when filming *Anna Karenina*. Other Siamese have actually featured in films, one of the most notable being the Walt Disney film, *That Darned Cat*, starring Hayley Mills, and the cartoon film *The Lady and the Tramp*!

EARLY HISTORY
Studies indicate that the cat evolved from small mammal-like reptiles who were given their chance to develop with the disappearance of the dinosaurs. One of the groups was classified as Carnivora, which included large species of cats such as lions, tigers and cheetahs, and the smaller species including the lynx, margay and ocelot.

Cats developed into a species that depended on other live animals for their food, and

Carnivora Margay: Maria Falkena said of her Margay, Buenn: "She was the most beautiful living creature that I ever met in all my life." Photo: Maria Falkena.

physiologically they grew to be strong, muscular, fast-moving hunters, with sharp teeth which became well-adapted to shearing and cutting meat. By the time of the emergence and development of 'man' into the superior species, there were varieties of Felidae in existence, similar to those seen today, which included the group known as Felis, the smaller cats.

It is not known when man first attempted to domesticate the Felis group but it has been attributed to the period around 2,000 BC. It is certain that by 1600 BC the cat was treasured as a sacred animal, a hunter and pet. Ancient Egypt was primarily a rural community with farming as its mainstay and, inevitably, the growth of crops must have attracted rodents. The Eygptians soon found that they could train cats to catch these pests and also to retrieve birds and other small mammals.

Gradually the cat became revered as a sacred animal. Its divinity was attributed to the way its eyes reflected light; the cat was regarded as the "guardian of light". The cat goddess Bast, also referred to as Basht or Pasht (perhaps the origin of the word Puss), was depicted with a cat's head in various forms; some heads were dressed to resemble Pharoahs whilst other cats held musical instruments or shields. Other statuettes held children, some had kittens at their feet. A city by the name of Bubastis became a centre for pilgrimage, with the temple to the goddess housing sacred temple cats. Their Latin name was Felis Lybica Bubastis. After the sacred temple cats died, their remains were buried with the ancient Egyptian Pharoahs and nobility.

It is known that the ticked agouti-coat, similar to that of the present-day Abyssinian, appeared in the depictions of Felis Chaus, together with the smaller mackerel-striped pattern of the tabby, Felis Lybica. The worship of the goddess Bast died out after nearly 2,000 years and was finally banned by an Imperial decree in 35 AD – which coincided with the dawn of Christianity, but probably too soon for it to be the result of Christian influence.

ORIGIN OF VARIETIES
The cat that had been associated with the working man, Felis Lybica, spread throughout the world to the Middle East, India and China, with evidence of the Phoenician traders bringing them into Italy, and the Roman legions then introducing them into other parts of Europe. St George Mivart indicates in his book *The Cat*, written in 1881, that the cats brought into Britain by the Romans would have mated with the wild cat, Felis Sylvestris.

There have been many recorded accounts of matings between Felis Sylvestris and the domestic cat over the years, including a relatively recent occurrence associated with the origin of the Cinnamon and Fawn colours of the Dutch Siamese and Oriental breeds. The Dutch breeder, Maria Falkena-Rohrle, founder of the Van Mariendaal line, discovered that hybrids of a mating between a member of the Felis Sylvestris Rubidae species and a domestic cat can be tame.

Genes mutated over a period of time, producing variations in coat length, colour and patterns over the breed spectrum, and adding to the domestication of the cat population as the hazards of fighting for survival in the wild diminished, thereby allowing different breeds to evolve naturally into what can be classified as two extremes of shape – the heavily-built chunky cat and the slender, lithe, foreign type of cat. In between these lie many categories. Over a period of time, artificial selection has played a part in the evolution of the different breeds which appear in both long-haired and short-haired forms.

THE SOURCE OF THE SIAMESE BREED
The antecedents of the Siamese breed have been lost in the mists of time and there has been much speculation as to its origin. In one of the earliest books on the subject, *The Siamese Cat,* the writer, breeder and judge, Phyl Wade, stated that she had little doubt that the ancient Egyptian cat was the

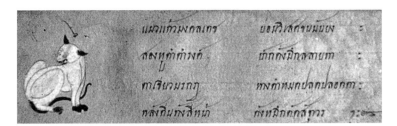

From the Smud Khoi of Cats, in the Thai National Library, Bangkok:The Wi-Chi-an Maad Siamese.

Photo: Daphne Negus.

ABOVE: Wi-Chi-an Maad (Diamond Siamese).

LEFT: Full length Smud Khoi of Cats. Smud Koi are books that are concertinaed rather than bound or rolled as a scroll.

Photos: Daphne Negus.

ancestor of the Siamese. It is thought that she based her theory on the fact that the body and skull structure of the Siamese breed appeared to resemble those of the thousands of mummified cats that were found in Egypt in the early part of this century and sold off as fertiliser. There is evidence that this slender, foreign-type structure of cat was not specific to Egypt; it appeared in cats of varying coat patterns in other parts of the world.

The Thai National Library in Bangkok houses manuscripts from an ancient city known as Ayudha, which was the capital of Siam until 1767. One of these manuscripts is called the Cat-Book Poems, Smud Khoi, and it is illustrated with a pale-coated Seal Pointed Siamese, with less pointing than the Siamese of today. Part of this manuscript describes the cats as having black tails, feet and ears, together with white hair and reddish eyes. The blue eyes of Siamese still reflect a reddish glow, especially when photographed!

Further evidence of the existence of the breed in the eighteenth century is thought to have been found in the illustrations of cats resembling Siamese in Plate 1 of the English edition of *Travels through the Southern Provinces of the Russian Empire in 1793-4* by P. S. Pallas, published in

London in 1802. The cat referred to was described as having much darker colouring than the examples in the Cat-Book Poems. Although the points were similarly black in colour, with denser covering on the extremities compared to the Ayudha Siamese, the body was covered with chestnut brown hair, with dorsal black shading on the backbone. On the face "a black streak runs along and surrounds the eyes and ends in front of the forehead." The illustration revealed the heads to be rounded in shape, more like the 'Apple-headed' Siamese that are currently being bred by a few traditionalists in the USA, in an attempt to re-create the 'old-fashioned' Siamese type of the turn of the century. The dark colouring would probably occur because the temperatures around the Caspian Sea area of the southern, independent countries that were once part of the USSR are cooler than those of the Malaysian Peninsula and it is known that the development of pigment in the coat of the Siamese is temperature-dependent: the cooler the temperature, the darker the colour. If the cat described by Pallas was a Siamese, then there is no evidence indicating how it reached the Caspian Sea or whether the breed developed naturally within this area. However, the Caspian Sea was close to the Great Silk trading route which passed through Turkmenistan and its capital Ashkabad into Uzbekistan, with the old cities of Bukhara and Samarkand at the foothills of the Himalayas, and on to Kazakstan, with its capital Alma Ata, and finally went from Mongolia into China. Perhaps traders brought these cats with them from Siam, whilst trading on this route, to protect perishables from rodents.

The Complete Book of the Siamese Cat, written by the Denhams, referred to an article written in 1951 by Professor F. E. Zeuner on the origins of the domestic cat, who made it clear that there were two strong arguments in favour of the Siamese having originated from the Malaysian Archipelago. One was the Siamese pointed coat pattern – he referred to the Himalayan rabbit, which had the same coloration. The other is the Siamese tail, which is certainly different from the tails of other breeds. Some Siamese tails were either kinked at the end or could be described as truncated which, according to Lilian Veley, who was an influential owner of Siamese at the turn of the century, was an excessive development of the kink.

Many of the first Siamese imported to the UK had kinked tails. It was recorded that Champion Wankee had this characteristic. Two of the cats given by the King of Siam to Miss Forestier-Walker also had kinked tails. These were not regarded as a fault in Siam, but in England breeders had declared a preference for the straight tail.

In *Our Cats* of February 1952, a Mr P. M. Soderberg made his views known quite strongly

Many of the first Siamese imported to the UK had kinked tails.

Photo: Paddy Cutts.

regarding the problem of judging the kinked tail. The Standard of Points in existence then said: "The tail should be quite straight or slightly kinked at the extremity." Obviously, it was very much a subject under discussion and the author's thoughts on the matter were very explicit: "If I had my way no Siamese would have a kinked tail, but people who have far greater experience are most anxious that the kink should be retained because they regard it as a characteristic of the breed. Whatever we may feel about this question, no judge has the right to put a cat down because it has a slight kink, but the word 'slight' can be interpreted in many ways." He finally suggested that the official Standard should be more explicit on this point.

Lilian Veley declared that she would never breed from a cat with an excessively kinked tail, which she called a "bob-tail", when she was describing the different types of kinked tails in her Foreword to Volume Two of the *Siamese Cat Register*, produced by the Siamese Cat Club in the UK. Charles Darwin had noted that the kinked tail was a very common feature in all kinds of cats living in the Malaysian part of the world. There is no definite account of how it developed within the Siamese breed and he intimated that it could either have been passed to the Siamese breed by interbreeding with non-Siamese cats, or it may have been a feature of the Siamese breed passed on to the ordinary cat population.

THE SIAMESE IN THE UK
The Siamese breed has now been known in the West for about one hundred and twenty years. The January 1960 edition of the magazine *Our Cats* referred to an interesting exchange of facts, dating from May 1959, about the arrival of Siamese cats in England. In it was published a letter from Raymond D. Smith, from Pittsburgh USA, who was the publisher of the American *Cats Magazine*. He mentioned Sam L. Scheer of Florida who had been following this interchange of correspondence.

Sam Scheer, who had an extensive library of cat books, was able to confirm from these sources of reference, that Lady Neville's Siamese "Poodles", listed in the 1872 Crystal Palace catalogue, could be identified as one of the earliest known Siamese cats existing in Britain.

He referred to Harrison Weir's *Our Cats and All About Them,* which was published by Houghton, Mifflin Co. in 1889:

"Among the beautiful varieties of the domestic cat brought into notice by the cat shows, none deserve more attention than the Royal Cat of Siam. In form, colour, texture and length, or rather shortness of its coat, it is widely different from other short haired varieties; yet there is but little difference in its mode of life or habit. I have not had the pleasure of owning one of this breed, though when on a visit to Lady Dorothy Neville, at Dangstien, near Petersfield, I had several opportunities for observation. I noticed in particular the intense liking of these cats for the woods, not passing along the hedgerows like the ordinary cat, but quickly and quietly creeping from bush to bush, then away in the shadows...

"Lady Dorothy Neville informed me that those which belonged to her were imported from Siam and presented to her by Sir R. Herbert of the Colonial Office. The late Duke of Wellington imported the breed, also Mr Scott of Rotherfield. Lady Dorothy Neville thought them exceedingly docile and domestic, but delicate in their constitution; although her ladyship kept one for two years, another for over a year, but eventually all died of the same complaint, that of worms, which permeated every part of their body.

"From the foregoing it will be seen how very difficult it is to obtain the pure breed, even in Siam, and on reference to the Crystal Palace catalogues from the year 1871 until 1887, I find that there were fifteen females and only four males, and some of these were not entire. I have always understood that the latter were not allowed to be exported, and were only got by those so fortunate as a most extraordinary favour, as the King of Siam was most jealous of keeping the breed entirely in Siam as royal cats.

"The cat exhibited by Lady Dorothy Neville had three kittens by an English cat; but none showed any trace of the Siamese, being all tabby."

These excerpts were taken from a much longer chapter, all of which clearly indicated that the name Siamese was applied to the pointed coat pattern as long ago as 1872. Thus, through the effort of Sam Scheer and Raymond Smith, the Editor of *Our Cats* stated that he believed the date of the first Siamese in England could be attributed to 1872 at least.

It has been suggested that the early entries to cat shows described cats by the country of origin rather than by their breed, but the Daily Telegraph commentary on the Crystal Palace show in 1879 recorded the cats owned by Mrs Cunliffe-Lee as having a type of Siamese pointed coat pattern.

The fact that Harrison Weir referred to the Crystal Palace catalogue of 1871 could pinpoint the existence of the Siamese breed in Britain to as far back as 1870-1871. It has been well recorded that Siamese were described as 'an unnatural nightmare kind of cat' at this show, which was regarded as the fore-runner of the cat show that is known today. An engraving of the Siamese cats who were exhibited in 1871 showed one of them as having white paws.

APPEARANCE

The Siamese coat pattern is most striking and consists of darker colouring on the 'points' of the face, ears, feet and tail. The neck and slender body carry a very light tint of the pointed colours, which visually produces a dramatic contrast of light and dark colour. This, as has been said, is referred to as the pointed, or Himalayan coat pattern. Kittens appear white when born, and it is only after a few weeks that the colour of their points emerges. As they grow older they become darker, and this is one of the features that adds to their mystique.

The Siamese coat should be soft and close in texture. When they walk, their deliberate, panther-like movement is enhanced by the firm muscular build and long whipped tail which can be swished from side to side with great aplomb.

Many Siamese fanciers regard their almond (oriental) shaped blue eyes as their most striking feature. In certain lights they appear to glow red; we usually notice this with our Siamese when dusk falls. They vary in their depth of colour across the whole range of colour points, owing to the gene responsible for Siamese pigmentation. The blue colour has often been likened to various garden flowers, including delphinium and forget-me-nots, and also to the sapphire gemstone which, to be of good quality, should be a very clear blue colour. Apparently, in the early days, the eye colour was not so deep as it can be today. Some current pedigree lines now produce kittens which show deep blue eyes from about three to four weeks of age.

In 1881 St George Mivart wrote in his book, *The Cat*, that: "The Royal Siamese cat is of one uniform fawn colour, which may be of a very dark tinge. There is a tendency to a darker colour about the muzzle – as in pug dogs. It has also remarkable blue eyes, and sometimes, at the least, two bald spots on the forehead. It has a small head."

PERSONALITY

The individuality and uniqueness of the Siamese is also reflected in its most affectionate and sociable nature, with some traits that are peculiar to the breed. They appear quite dog-like in their characters and show particular attachment to humans. They need to have continuous contact with people from a very young age and often become extremely possessive over one person within a family. My own Seal Point Siamese likes nothing better than to drape himself over my feet and

Siamese Seal Point: Ch. and Pr. Beaumaris Alexander. Siamese cats are sociable and affectionate, with a great attachment to humans.

Photo: Paddy Cutts

objects vociferously if I have to get up when it does not suit him to move, even if it is to prepare his next meal. A lot has been written about life with Siamese and one of the most fascinating was the forerunner of all books devoted to the Siamese as a character, as opposed to a factual book published on the breed. The title was *Charles*, which appeared in 1943. This particular Siamese, otherwise known as Charles O'Malley, was a great character who lived for thirteen years. The book was reprinted ten times in three years and the author was Mr Michael Joseph, the publisher.

One of the most humorous articles written about the unique personality of the Siamese was by Dana Learn, which first appeared in the American *Cat World Magazine*, entitled 'What is a Siamese Cat?'

"Between the innocence of not owning a cat and the dignity of not admitting that you own one, you will find a delightful creature called a Siamese cat. Siamese cats come in assorted sizes, weights and colors, but all Siamese cats have the same creed: To enjoy every second of every minute of every hour of every day and to protest with noise (their biggest weapon) when the last minute is finished and we pack them off to another room.

"Siamese cats are found everywhere – on top of, underneath, inside of, climbing on, swinging from, running around or bumping into. Some fools love them, a lot of people hate them, our husbands and children tolerate them, our visitors try to ignore them, and Heaven protects them! A Siamese cat is truth with a smudge on its face, beauty with oftentimes a kink in its tail, wisdom with one of your good stockings in its paws, and hope of the future with a choice piece of dinner in its mouth.

"When you are busy a Siamese cat is an inconsiderate, bothersome, intruding jangle of noise. When you want him to make a good impression, he always does something like emptying the ash tray and playing with it.

"A Siamese cat is a composite – he has the appetite of a horse, the digestion of a sword swallower, the energy of a pocket-sized atom bomb, the lungs of Adolf Hitler, the shyness of a violet, the audacity of a steel trap, the enthusiasm of a firecracker, and when he wants to be graceful, can oftentimes cross an empty room – and if there is a match on the floor stumble over it.

"Nothing else is so noisy or so loveable. Nobody else gets so much fun out of trees, bugs, or just being ornery. Nobody else can pile up into one corner a piece of cellophane, a half-eaten cracker, a balloon, a piece of weed and a genuine cockroach – dead and repulsive.

"A Siamese cat is a magical creature. You can keep him out of the closets – sometimes – but you can't keep him out of your heart. You can get him out of the bathroom – but you can't get him out of your mind. Might as well give up – he is your captor, your jailor, your boss and your master – a dirty-faced, pint-sized, dog-chasing bundle of noise. But when you come in at night, with only the shattered pieces of your hopes and dreams, he can mend them with the magic sound – 'Meowrr'."

The personality of a cat, whether it is Siamese or the 'good old moggie', is just as much dependent on the understanding and interest of the owner as on the cat's pedigree lines. It is difficult to determine the intelligence of any one cat, but it can be said that ownership is very important in bringing out the individual characteristics. A cat who is uninterested in life is a very sorry sight indeed. What makes the Siamese character so appealing and unique is that its personality and behaviour is like an exaggeration of all the well-known feline characteristics.

DIFFERENCES BETWEEN COLOURS
There is speculation that the four basic colours of Siamese – Seal, Blue, Chocolate and Lilac – have slightly different personalities. Whether this can be put down to the different colour genes is questionable but, nevertheless, it is a very interesting hypothesis.

Where Seal Points are concerned, it has been said that they are far more aristocratic – the most Siamese of the Siamese breed. They are self-confident, even to the point of tolerating grooming, in comparison with the other colours, and very possessive of their owners. A most interesting observation is that they dislike change in their lives.

The Chocolate Point Siamese are held to be the most extrovert and affectionate of the four colours, whilst the Blue Point Siamese tend to be more thoughtful and quiet – if that is at all possible for the Siamese breed. It is said that the Lilac Point Siamese react to events with a more artistic and melodramatic type of temperament.

These character generalisations are fun to note but, perhaps, should not be taken too seriously, as character and personality surely derive from inheritance from the pedigree lines and also the effect of environment.

VOICE
Although all cats express their sentiments vocally, it can be said that the Siamese is the most talkative of the feline breeds, and you, as the devoted owner, will soon learn what is being communicated to you.

The miaow of the Siamese is deep and melodious and, on occasions, it can be loud. They use their voice to great effect by changing their tone and pitch to express their demands and thoughts. They have a unique range of their own. Having developed a very special relationship with one person, they can monopolise a conversation with their owner, making it clear that they thrive on being talked to.

The female Siamese, when calling, can be likened to a singer during musical scale practice and this remarkable range of notes has often been the prelude to a girl being neutered quickly or being sent out to stud! In full-scale call, her voice develops into a yell that can be heard quite some distance away from your own home.

The male Siamese is usually talkative at any given moment of the day but, if there is a calling queen around, his tone of gentle conversation changes to shouting at his intended as if she is the latest 'pop star' to grace the scene. A very different sound is made when, for example, our stud, Jamie, watches squirrels come into the garden and run up the trees. His deep throaty miaows change into a clucking sound, which is also heard when the birds sit in safety on the ledge of his pen and tease him with their unavailability.

All Siamese are individual characters and, as such, have very different voices.

INTELLIGENCE AND INTERACTION

The writer Sir Compton Mackenzie was a great admirer of Siamese cats and was President of the Siamese Cat Club for a time. In 1934, he contributed a delightful introduction to the book called *The Siamese Cat,* written by Phyl Wade. In one of the most well-known passages regarding the character of the Siamese he wrote: "Siamese cats are jealous, greedy, and I suppose I must add destructive, for any piece of fine embroidery only exists in their fancy as a suitable toy for their claws. But, what are their faults compared with their virtues – with their sense of humour, their fidelity, their dauntless courage (except of the unknown), their playfulness, their conversational powers, their awareness of themselves, their honesty (by which I mean they will take a lobster off a table in front of you), their continuous passionate interest in all that is going on around them, and their depth of affection, which they are so able to show in so many exquisite ways?"

He also wrote that the Siamese has "for so many hundred of years been accustomed to attention that it expects at least as much intelligence in human beings as it possesses itself."

Many other authors have waxed lyrical over the intelligence of the Siamese cat and, whatever superlatives are used to describe or define this intelligence, it is a definite fact that many Siamese quickly adapt to elementary training, such as being taken for a walk on a lead and harness to view changing scenery and smells. Some Siamese will even respond to basic commands, having learned the responses in a very short space of time. Others carry out basic tasks and will fetch and carry for their owners on command.

As a breed they demand a great deal of attention from their owners and it is no good having a Siamese if all you want is a docile chocolate-box kitten. Unless you are prepared to give your Siamese your time and develop a mutual sense of fun and adventure, which can express itself through training your new friend, then you might as well choose another breed of cat. All Siamese have a healthy enjoyment of life, and training your little friend can bring you, as owner, so much pleasure.

THE STANDARD OF POINTS (1892)

The great cat fancier and show judge Harrison Weir wrote a Standard of Points in 1892. It is interesting to note some of the features which were apparent then.

Royal Cat of Siam

Head (10 points)

Small, broad across and between the eyes, tapering upwards and somewhat narrow between the ears; forehead flat and receding, nose long and somewhat broad, cheeks narrowing towards the mouth, lips full and rounded, ears rather large and wide at base, with very little hair inside.

Fur (10 points)

Very short and somewhat woolly, yet soft and silky to the touch and glossy with much lustre on the face, legs and tail.

Colour (20 points)

The ground or body colour to be of an even tint, slightly darker on the back, but not in any way clouded or patched with any darker colour; light rich dun is the preferable colour, but a light fawn, light silver grey or light orange is allowable; deeper and richer browns, almost chocolate, are admissible if even and not clouded, but the first is the true type, and the last merely a variety of much beauty and excellence; but the dun and light tints take precedence.

Markings (20 points)
Ears black, the colour not extending beyond them, but ending in a clear and well-defined outline; around the eyes and all the lower part of the head, black; legs and tail black, the colour not extending into or staining the body, but having a clear line demarcation.

Eyes (15 points)
Rather almond shape, slanting towards the nose, full and of very beautiful opalesque colour, luminous and of a reddish tint in the dusk of evening or artificial light.

Tail (5 points)
Short by comparison with the English cat, thin throughout, a little darker towards the base, without any break or kink.

Size and Form (10 points)
Rather small, lithe, elegant in outline, and graceful, narrow and somewhat long; legs thin and a little short than otherwise; feet long, not so round as the ordinary cat; neck long and small.

Condition (10 points)
In full health, not too fat, hair smooth, clear, bright, full of lustre, lying close to the body, which should be firm and hard in the muscles.

A CULT FIGURE

It can be said that Siamese cat owners all over the world belong to a unique cult that has lasted well over one hundred years. Features of this manifest themselves when two owners meet and exchange experiences based on the sheer joy of owning members of this breed.

An article written in July 1960 in *Our Cats* by Beryl Greatorex, tries very hard to define the cult of the Siamese, which is much more than an advertising gimmick used to promote the sales of things associated with prosperity and good living.

"It's long been known that actresses without a Siamese to cuddle stand less chance of making the best gossip columns. It's this aristocratic air that furthers the link between Siamese and the supertax class. While their numbers may increase, these cats seem unable to forget their ancestry. I've heard it said that Siamese owners conspire to give the breed a scarcity value. They don't. The fact that most Siamese kittens today fetch between five and eight guineas, and that you can't get one for less than four, is a sheer triumph for the cult of personality practised by the breed. Such is the impact of the Siamese family's personality that the breeder feels honour-bound to screen applicants for kittens for character and reliability. Thus Siamese more or less pick their owners before completely mastering them. In the strange status of the Siamese, there's a lesson for all animal-lovers."

The later decades of this century have seen a strong commercial element develop in the cult of the Siamese. Devotees can satisfy their fanatical feelings by buying decorative wall plates, stuffed toys, rolls of material, child and adult clothing, tights, stockings and socks. The list is never-ending. One of the most exclusive limited edition items of all is the twelve-inch high model of The Siamese Cat, produced by Sandra Soper whose prefix is Leolee, which can be made to match the colour of the model's points to the exact shade of those of your own Siamese and to finely tune the colour of the blue eyes to resemble those of your own pet.

It is no wonder that the Siamese cat, with its unique character and appearance, has mesmerised owners the world over for well over a century.

Chapter Two

CHOOSING A SIAMESE

In recent years surveys indicate that the cat has outstripped the dog in popularity both in the UK and the USA. Because of the increasing pace of life and demands both at work and at home the cat, being so easy to live with, is now the most popular animal companion.

MAKING THE CHOICE

The first decision you have to make when wanting to join the ranks of those owned by a cat, is which breed to choose or, indeed, whether to have a 'moggie', a cat whose ancestry is unknown. This decision will take some time, and may involve visiting shows or rescue organisations to ensure you choose the cat best suited to your environment and situation. For example, if you live a very busy life it may be better not to have one of the long-haired breeds which requires daily grooming. This chapter poses the sort of questions you should ask yourself if you are thinking of acquiring a Siamese, but please do not think this is an exhaustive list; take every step you can at the outset to ensure that you and the cat or kitten you finally take home will be mutually happy.

THE PERSONAL COMMITMENT

You have to be certain that you are ready to take on all the responsibilities involved with the care of your Siamese over a period of possibly fifteen years or more. There are no laid-down ground

Before you take on a Siamese, you must be confident that you can take on all the responsibilities of caring for a cat.

Photo: Paddy Cutts.

rules to guide you on what is right; this decision has to be based purely on your honest assessment of what you realistically need and can give. It should be recognised, however, that the relationship between you and your Siamese is going to be a very long-term and loving one and that there will be some bad times as well as the good ones.

Apart from considering the joys of looking after your pet and the pleasure the cat can bring you, there may also be days when the animal is not too well. As an owner you will need to bring yourself to cope with this, which can involve clearing up diarrhoea and sickness. Your vet may on occasions ask you to spend time nursing your Siamese and this could include special feeding and giving eye-drops and tablets.

THE FAMILY COMMITMENT
Buying a kitten or cat has to be a family decision. Children have to understand that an animal is entitled to be loved and respected and must not be teased or abused. Owning a loved family pet can be a very rewarding experience for all members of the family over the years, providing everyone is committed from the outset.

THE RIGHT SURROUNDINGS
If you live in rented accommodation you will have to be sure that the landlord or landlady will allow pets to live on the premises. Likewise, if it is possible that sometime in the future you will move to further rented accommodation, you will need to be sure that pets are allowed in the new premises. Changes in marital status and jobs are also reasons for once-loved pets to be passed to rescue organisations. Owning a pet is a lifetime responsibility and many breeders have been approached to take back the kittens they have bred because this type of situation has arisen.

GIVING YOUR TIME
When weighing up the equation of whether to buy a kitten or cat one of the most important factors is time. This needs to be given freely to the newcomer, especially in the early days, so that a close personal relationship can be formed which will develop over the years. This involves playing with the kitten, combined with training, grooming and general maintenance on a daily basis.

The question of time involves making a further decision about whether your new pet will rely purely on human friendship or have another cat companion for interactive skills. Siamese enjoy company and can be most demanding. Most breeders are happy to sell litter companions together, and the bond that has been developed from the beginning can help them get over the first few difficult days until they settle down together in their new home. Some breeders may give a small discount on the second kitten at the time of purchase.

FINANCIAL CONSIDERATIONS
Apart from the initial purchase costs of your new kitten, there are many expenses that will be incurred on a long-term basis. You should consider whether your budget will allow you to give your pet the life that he or she will need. In practice the cost may be more than you expect – very often pets live a more pampered existence than their owners. Likely costs will include:–

Food and litter: the cost of cat food over a year is a major consideration and will vary enormously depending on the type of food used. Another major item is cat litter. You may think that a cat will always go outside when the toilet is needed, but certainly in the early days a litter tray is essential and some cats continue to prefer this. There are several different types on the market at a range of prices.

Vet's fees and vaccinations: at some time in your pet's life you will need to consult a Veterinary

Surgeon. Apart from the routine yearly vaccinations and health screen, there are bound to be the occasional health problems which will probably involve both consultation fees and the cost of treatment.

Insurance: there are a number of insurance companies specialising in cover for pets. Policies are available to cover veterinary fees, which may include hospitalisation, physiotherapy and medication. Some policies will also offer cover for complementary medicine such as acupuncture, herbal and homeopathic medicines. Cover is also offered against death from accident or illness up to a maximum age limit. Depending on the policy chosen, cover against boarding cattery fees in the event of an owner's illness, a holiday cancellation, or advertising and reward payments in the case of loss by theft or straying may also be included.

Boarding and Holidays: looking after your cat during your own holidays will also have to be taken into account, with the cost of a boarding cattery while you are away. It is worth considering if your next-door neighbour is able to help care for your Siamese. Multiple cat households often get a friend or relative to live in while they are away, and we are beginning to see the advent of professional cat and housesitters. If a professional cat sitter is used, you will need to think about informing the insurance company that there is a change of resident in the event of damage.

PREPARING YOUR HOME

Once you have decided you can afford a cat, you then need to think about the effect the newcomer will have on your home and, equally important, the effect your home can have on the new Siamese. Owning an animal of any description involves wear and tear on the home and its contents. A point to bear in mind is that many household insurance policies specifically exclude damage caused by pets, so you should check this carefully if it could be a problem for you.

SAFETY MEASURES

The health and safety of your Siamese should feature in your initial thought processes. Your home will need to be cat-proofed and all members of the household will need to become 'cat-conscious'. You will have to decide which areas are forbidden to your Siamese and then practise closing doors. It is not uncommon for a new kitten to escape because someone forgot to close a door or window, sometimes with tragic consequences.

A SUITABLE SIAMESE

Having decided that a Siamese is the breed for you, there are some other questions to ask in order to identify the right kind of Siamese. Although you may be able to answer some of these yourself it is often helpful to talk to some Siamese owners.

Prices for pet, breeding or show-quality categories of kittens may vary from area to area; likewise kittens that are six months old and young adults will sometimes cost less than a young kitten of thirteen weeks. The GCCF recommends that kittens are not rehomed until they have had their full course of vaccinations and certainly not before twelve weeks of age. The price is also affected by the pedigree of the kitten. One that contains many titled cats in its antecedents, or which has a particular feature in its background, will probably cost more than an unknown line.

Most breeders assess their kittens in one of three categories; pet, breeding and show quality. Prospective owners usually start by considering a Siamese as a pet but often, when talking to breeders, the options of breeding from, or showing a Siamese, will also be discussed. Whatever you decide, always remember that your cat will be your pet and friend for life. Anything else is a bonus, if you want it. A pet-quality kitten may be considered undesirable for breeding or showing because of some small factor such as a kinked tail or round eyes. Alternatively, the kitten may be

Check that the eyes are bright, the coat is clean, and the ears are not red inside.

Photo: Paddy Cutts.

very good but the breeder just wants it to go as a pet. This tends to be the lowest price category. Some breeders stipulate that these kittens will automatically be registered on the Non-Active register of the GCCF to prevent them being used for breeding. Usually, it is recommended that such kittens are neutered at six months of age or whenever the vet advises.

A show or breeding quality kitten is likely to be more expensive. However, at twelve weeks of age no breeder can predict with certainty that a kitten will do well in future shows and may sensibly remind the purchaser that success in competition cannot be guaranteed. Kittens in this category have to conform closely to the Siamese breed standard.

You are likely to find it difficult to buy a top quality kitten – they are few and far between. Many breeders keep these for their own use, or they are offered directly to other established breeders and show exhibitors. Often breeders are reluctant to sell breeding queens or stud cats to people who have not owned one before. This is because of their concern for the welfare of the animal – breeding can be very difficult for the cat and the owner.

KITTEN OR CAT?

The prospective owner also has to consider whether they would like to have an adult Siamese instead of a kitten. Kittenhood is a very short period in a cat's life, although it is a most appealing and playful stage. Adult Siamese still play but, relatively speaking, may be much quieter and more understanding. The advantage is that an older cat is usually more settled in its ways and would perhaps suit a home with a quieter lifestyle. You can also miss out the potentially more destructive kitten stage. One disadvantage is that you, as the owner, will miss seeing your Siamese mature. It can also take longer to settle the older cat into your home. Whatever the reason behind the rehoming, the new owner has to be extremely patient with the newcomer. Once the animal is confident, secure and happy in the new surroundings, the owner is rewarded with a close relationship with the cat.

It is advisable in the early stages of rehoming to keep some control over all movements until satisfied that the cat has completely settled in. There are always stories in the press that some cats have found their way back to their original home by roaming over miles of countryside.

It is possible you may hear about an older Siamese whose show or breeding career has finished. These cats may have been neutered by the breeder. When they are offered for rehoming, it is quite likely they come with all their prizes and certificates. It can be quite a strong talking point that your newly acquired pet comes complete with a title!

MALE OR FEMALE?

Another important decision is whether to have a male or female kitten or cat. Generally speaking, the female Siamese is smaller than the male, who will be more muscular in appearance. If you decide on a male kitten, then, unless you are intending to keep him at stud, it is best to consider neutering him between the ages of six to eight months. Each Siamese matures sexually at a different age so some are ready to be neutered earlier than that. The best people to guide you on the correct time are probably your vet and the breeder of your kitten. Castration is a painless procedure carried out under general anaesthetic. An incision is made into the scrotum and the whole testicle is removed. Some soluble suture material is used to ligate the vas deferens onto itself; there is no need to suture the scrotum sac.

If a male kitten is allowed to mature into an adult without being neutered, then a different type of behaviour will develop. Most male cats lay claim to the territory they consider is theirs by right, and scent-mark this by swishing the tail in rapid movements and spraying urine. Although this behaviour is normal it can prove a little unpleasant in an owner's home. The male is also announcing his presence to fertile female cats of any breed, and warning any other un-neutered male cat on his territory that he will fight to preserve his dominance.

If the female Siamese is not neutered she will cry or call out at periodic intervals, making sounds very akin to a young baby crying. This is known as 'calling' and is accompanied by her adopting a

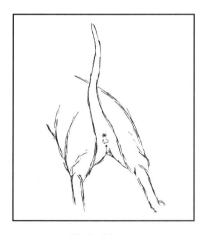

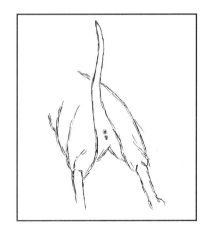

Male kitten.   *Female kitten.*

Drawings: Brenda Watson

characteristic mating pose, where she will crouch on her front legs, raise her rear end, tread her paws and present her genitalia for all to see. She will raise her tail in a sideways position. Some female cats will also spray at this juncture. The calling will last from one day to a few days, or even beyond a week, and will follow a regular cycle. If she escapes, a litter of kittens, fathered by one or more unknown male tom cats, will appear between sixty-three and sixty-nine days later. It would be wiser, therefore, to consider having your male or female pet kitten neutered before allowing them to mature, unless you wish to breed from them. Odour from cat urine within a house can be rather pungent, to say the least, but with careful thought and planning, there is no reason for any cat odour in your house. Like you, the cat loves to be clean and to live in a clean environment. There are two methods of spaying the female, one being to make a midline incision into the abdomen through the linea alba and, with a spaying hook, fish out the reproductive organs. Some veterinary surgeons make an extra charge for this type of spaying. It is usually employed if the animal is known to be a showcat or kitten. The more usual method is through a small incision in the flank. Early spaying is also recommended on health grounds, as continuous calling can result in cystic ovaries. After the operation, the female Siamese will usually no longer call and will settle down to a carefree life.

BREEDING PLANS

There is an "old wives' tale" suggesting that a female cat should be allowed to have one litter of kittens before she is neutered. Most vets will tell you that this is not true, and owning a family pet should certainly not be regarded as a means of teaching the children of the household the facts of life through allowing the pet to have a litter of kittens. Prospective owners may not realise that there are so many intrinsic costs in raising a litter – worming treatment, vaccinations to give protection against common diseases including the more recent ones of Feline Leukaemia and Chlamydia, advertisements for finding homes (which itself is usually a very difficult activity) and the ongoing supply of food, litter, bedding and toys as well as your time for training the youngsters. Certainly having kittens is not a way of raising money! One only has to look at the newspapers to see advertisements from animal welfare charities appealing for homes for unwanted cats, kittens and young mothers nursing kittens who, through no fault of their own, have been abandoned. Why add to the problem?

FINDING A SIAMESE BREEDER

By this stage you will probably have already made contact with a Siamese owner, which is likely to be the best place to start your search for a cat or kitten. It can sometimes be very difficult to find what you want, particularly if you have set your heart on a specific colour. Be prepared to make many telephone calls, and probably several visits, before you find the perfect partner.

Cat Shows: Many prospective cat owners start by visiting a cat show to look at specimens and to talk to exhibitors – most of whom are only too pleased to spend time talking about their cats.

Breeders: Breeders know other breeders, so if they do not have the kitten you want, they will always be able to direct your enquiry elsewhere, or to Cat Clubs.

Advertising: Classified advertisements in area newspapers can also provide avenues to explore, as can breeders' advertisements in cat publications.

Cat Clubs: Cat Clubs usually have a Kitten List, often held by the Secretary of the Club.

Welfare organisations: Welfare organisations specialising in cats often have Siamese in their shelters requiring homes. Most cat clubs also have a welfare section and are only too pleased to hear of potential homes for Siamese cats. Breeders will be able to pass enquiries over to the welfare officer.

Pet shops: It is not advisable to buy your Siamese kitten from a pet shop. Apart from the risks of infection, they will certainly not have liked being confined to a very small space. You will have no chance of seeing and examining the kitten's mother or, probably, any of the litter brothers and sisters. It is also quite likely that you may not receive all the necessary paperwork that should accompany a pedigree kitten. If you do see any Siamese kittens or litters being sold in this way, contact one of the specialist Siamese Cat Clubs, who may take up the matter.

ASSESSING STOCK

You have now come to the point where you can actually start enquiring to see if the kitten or cat you want is really for you. You will have made some contact with a likely source, but now you have to talk to the breeder or rescue organisation to satisfy them that you will be a good owner, and also to see if you and the potential Siamese 'hit it off' personally.

The first visit: It is always advisable to prepare a list of questions in advance. This initial excursion is very much a two-way process, and you should also be prepared to answer detailed questions. Naturally, you need to be assured of the kitten's home and breeder, but you must expect to be assessed as to your suitability to provide a long-term and loving home for the kitten.

One of the questions to ask is about the health of the kitten or cat and its pedigree antecedents or 'line'. Find out if there are any congenital problems such as cleft palate, cardiomyopathy, eye problems or club feet, especially if there is any possibility of breeding with the cat. Further questions concern any predispositions to conditions in its pedigree line, such as Feline Urological Syndrome (crystals in the urine – more usually found in male cats) or Cystitis (a component of FUS) in females. Ask if the breeder knows anything about the longevity of the kitten or cat's antecedents. Not many breeders own a household of several generations of one line, but it is likely they will be aware of other breeders' comments on the various pedigree lines within the breeding and showing world.

Handling the young kitten: Try to check for signs of flea and ear-mite infestation. When checking for fleas, ruffle the back fur backwards. Any signs of black flecks indicate flea dirt. Ear-mite infestation could be indicated if there is any coating of dark brown ear wax inside the ear or wax clumped within the folds of the ear. Normal ear wax is a lighter brown colour. If the skin on the ears appears 'reddened', this could indicate that the ears have been cleaned prior to your visit. Some breeders do this quite naturally so the kitten is seen at its very best. If the young kitten scratches its ears or shakes its head, these actions could be quite innocent, indicating that the youngster has just undergone ear-cleansing or, not so innocently, treatment for ear-mites.

Assessing the cat: There are two pictures to bear in mind when assessing the health of the kitten or cat. A Siamese in top condition is alert and responsive to commands, taking an interest in events and movements surrounding it. The fur will look clean, shiny and flat if adult. If you are looking at a kitten, there will be a certain amount of kitten 'down' but the coat will still be clean and shiny. The eyes will be bright and clear with no protruding third eyelid and there should be no discharge around the eye or nose area or evidence of diarrhoea around the rear end. On being handled the body should feel firm, with no evidence of protruding vertebrae.

By contrast, a Siamese in poor condition may be recognised by a coat which could be 'open and staring', dull and lifeless, possibly with dandruff particles on the surface. The youngster may look miserable, smell, lie with its forefeet close to its chest so that its elbows stick out, and take very little interest in the proceedings or visitors. The eyes might look downcast and dull and the third eyelids can appear over part of the eyes. There may be a discharge from the eyes, nose and the rear end. The youngster may even sneeze over you, and its abdomen look swollen. When held, the body may feel slack, with protruding vertebrae.

Personality of the Adult or Kitten: This is really a subjective assessment, because all Siamese are individuals with their own quirks of personality as well as the general characteristics peculiar to the breed. It depends whether you warm to the youngster and, equally importantly, if he or she takes to you. Rearing and environment also play their part in determining character. If the breeder has had a very close relationship with the mother cat and been trusted by her to handle the youngsters from as early a time as possible, there is a very good chance that they will all grow up with outgoing and loving personalities. It is also quite possible that the kitten will 'choose' you as its owner, rather than vice versa. When you visit a breeder and a kitten sits on your lap and goes to sleep, it is very difficult to resist!

VACCINATIONS

With the purchase papers of the kitten will be the vaccination certificate. All breeders whose kittens are registered with the GCCF should sell them with at least a minimum vaccination for feline rhinotracheitis and calicivirus (the 'flu part) and feline panleukopenia (the enteritis part). A few breeders will also include the leukemia vaccination within the purchase price of the youngster, on the grounds that this is a disease that few cats or kittens will survive. The vaccination can be carried out at the same time as the flu and enteritis vaccinations, but will be separately injected into a different site. If a breeder's household is not vaccinated against leukemia, most responsible breeders will test their breeding and showing stock at regular intervals for the disease, especially if their breeding queens go out to stud or attend cat shows. Some breeders will also vaccinate against chlamydia, although this is not so common, as it is not usually a fatal disease and is treatable.

AFTER-SALE SERVICE

In the UK it is common practice among reputable breeders to offer insurance cover with the kitten. The main aim behind this is to protect the purchaser against unexpected veterinary fees for illness, or compensation for death within the first few weeks in a new home – usually the most vulnerable time. This is not customary in the USA. Most breeders will offer an after-sale service, answering questions by telephone, or by visiting where possible. Many friendships have been formed between breeders and those who have their kittens.

Breeders may also agree to take the kitten back if a greater problem occurs. Some make it clear that this extends throughout the life of the kitten that they have brought into the world, for they would rather take back the kitten themselves than have it dumped on welfare organisations or, worse still, thrown out into the street. Usually a kitten is subject to being retested for feline leukemia and feline immunodeficiency virus before being brought back into the breeder's home. Depending on the reason for the return, the vet may advise a blood profile to be undertaken to eliminate any other source of infection or disease.

THE FINAL DECISION

A cat breeder friend once told us many years ago that when you sell a kitten you change someone's life. That initial interview between you, as the proposed purchaser, and the breeder can last at least an hour. Some breeders will actively encourage you to go away before making your choice, to give you some breathing space. It is so easy to make a decision based on the 'halo effect' as the youngsters play before you. Remember, owning a Siamese should be a commitment to that cat for life.

Chapter Three

PREPARING FOR YOUR SIAMESE

After you have agreed to have a kitten there are a number of preparations to make before the actual day of arrival. Some breeders will let you visit on a regular basis, if there is time before the kitten is ready, so that you can begin building up a relationship. This will help the new kitten adjust more easily to your house.

FINDING A VETERINARY PRACTICE

When you choose your cat, it is important to know who your vet is going to be – do not wait until an emergency occurs to find one.

Location: This is, together perhaps with cost, the most important consideration of all. Ideally, the vet should be close enough to home to get there quickly in case of extreme emergency, and certainly close enough so that travel to the surgery should not prove a problem, with or without a car.

Veterinarian interest: Most practices deal with a variety of animals but there are some which obtain a reputation for handling and treating felines. They are to be treasured and word soon gets around when a particular vet stays abreast of new advances in feline treatment. If the practice specialises in other species such as horses or farm animals, this should not present any problem as the vet has undertaken feline medicine as part of the rigorous training and should be prepared to refer your Siamese to a University Veterinary Department if there is a really obscure problem that needs investigation. The most important thing is that the vet has the time during consultation to explain procedures and conditions to you and, ideally, also be open to suggestions and comments from you as you learn about your cat.

Recommendation: One good way to find a vet is to talk to other local cat owners. All will have some stories to tell of their vet, and will be pleased to help you make a good choice.

OUTDOOR OR INDOOR PET?

When you agree to purchase a kitten from the breeder, it is likely that you will be asked whether you intend to let the youngster have the freedom of the garden and immediate environment outside your house. Nowadays some breeders specify as part of the 'contract of sale' a clause indicating that the kitten will be a 'house cat'. This is because they worry that the youngster could be run over by a car, stolen by unscrupulous people who do not share your love of cats, or be attacked and killed by a wild animal. Even the boundaries of city areas hold no limits for foxes nowadays.

Apart from the external dangers, there are also the problems of various feline viruses such as Leukaemia and FIV that can be easily transmitted to your pet. One school of thought believes that a cat can build up its own immunity to a virus if challenged by a cat who is healthy but is a virus

A cat that is allowed the freedom of the garden will be exposed to certain dangers, so you should give careful thought as to whether your Siamese should be an indoor or an outdoor pet.

Photo: Paddy Cutts.

Sumfun James Trueman enjoying the fresh air and sunshine, in his outside run.

Photo: Paddy Cutts.

carrier. The sad truth is that this is not always the case. It is thought that at least ten per cent of the feline population is infected with the leukaemia virus and it has been established that this is one of the most frequent causes of death amongst cats.

Cats that are not restricted to the house are also likely to get into fights with other cats and animals who are running loose. Cats who are strangers to each other, regardless of breed, will not greet each other as long lost friends – they can end up with cuts and abscesses that will need treatment. If you live in a country area, a farmer (or even your neighbour in town) may spray the ground with insecticides and fertilisers which may not be poisonous to the human owner but may be lethal to the cat.

A cat that has never been used to the outdoors will be at great risk trying to cope with all these dangers, let alone an unfamiliar environment. Cats and kittens who have never been let out by their breeder or owner usually do not even try to leave their home, providing they have a clean litter tray and access to some fresh air and sunshine.

OUTSIDE RUNS AND PET DOORS

Many owners naturally want their pet to have the benefit of fresh air and sunshine and buy a small run and shelter or attach a run to some part of the house. Before deciding on this option it is wise to check the deeds of your house in case there is a restrictive covenant preventing such an external structure. If you live in rented, Housing Association or Council property, check the rules and regulations.

Some cat owners erect a six foot fence (or whatever maximum height is allowed by their local Planning Department) around the garden, with a 'lid' attached, usually in the form of an angled netting top to the fence, which the Siamese cannot climb through or over. This gives a pet safe area.

Many owners then insert a cat flap in one of the house doors so the cats can move freely from there to the safe haven outside. These come in a variety of sizes and materials. They range from a four-way lockable flap, which is ideal for glass doors, to an electrical pet door powered through a transformer, to a de-luxe cat door with tunnel suitable for neat and easy installation. Others contain a two-way magnetic action to prevent other neighbourhood cats from taking up residence in your house. Colours vary, ranging from white, green, black to grey as well as woodgrain effect. It does not take a young Siamese long to learn how to operate one and this training experience can be most entertaining.

Other owners install a perch on the window sill which enables the pet to obtain fresh air if the window is on the latch. Many window sills are not wide enough to take a fully grown Siamese stretched out taking a sun bath, so a piece of carpeted or cloth-covered shelf is attached to the existing window sill to give the necessary space.

CAT-PROOFING THE HOME

This is not so awesome as it sounds and can actually provide a chance for all of the family members to contribute in welcoming the new arrival. A young Siamese, when settling in to a new home, cannot resist the chance to explore all the nooks and crannies and to smell, touch and taste any obstructions. You can guarantee that no space will be sacrosanct: your home will become the home of your Siamese, who will eventually find the way through all your personal belongings in every cupboard and drawer.

You, as the owner, have a duty to inspect every room for potential problems and make your home as 'bombproof' and as hazard-free as possible, to prevent any untoward accidents. Some cat breeders take a great deal of time with prospective owners explaining the need to cat-proof a home. One of the first questions asked is whether the home has a chimney. If the answer is yes, then the prospective owner is advised to place some chicken wire up the chimney to prevent cats and kittens from climbing up there.

Poisons: many household cleaning items can be poisonous to cats. Always check the label first before buying any item. Poisons that can cause problems to young children, let alone your Siamese, include Battery Acids, Alcohol, Anti-freeze, Prescription Drugs, Chlorine (Bleach), Phenol (present in many disinfectants), Slug and Snail Poisons, Rat Poison – the list is surprisingly large. A cat naturally grooms itself by washing and licking its fur, so any residual product, powder or solution can be ingested when the cat does this.

Greenery: Further potential poisons lie in wait for the Siamese newcomer with the current popularity of houseplants and dried flower arrangements. Established locations of plants may have to be changed to possibly less favourable places. One cat breeder I know has solved her problem by using macrame hanging baskets, which keep the plants in the correct place for light as well as out of the way of little paws and mouths. Some of the dangerous houseplants are daffodils and hyacinths, the foliage of which is extremely poisonous to cats, and many different types of ivy. With dried houseplants and arrangements a new owner has to be very careful of the type of chemicals and preservatives used to make some of these arrangements aesthetically pleasing to eye and nose. Plants in the garden that can cause problems are philodendron, christmas cherry, mistletoe and, of course, ivy, just to name a few.

To a young Siamese a plant is a toy, with hanging leaves providing the main source of attraction. Large pots of plants can double up as an additional litter tray. It is thought that Siamese, like many other cats, eat grass mainly as a purgative to clear their systems and remove hair balls and they are not too fussy whether the greenery being eaten is catnip, a pot of grass or your best plant.

If your Siamese is to be an indoor cat then there are specialist pots of grass and catnip that can be bought from your local petshop or cat show that will serve your cat's purpose. Other greenery that can be given safely includes lettuce leaves, broccoli tops and even peas and beans. These items will add interest to your Siamese's diet.

Other hazards: These include pins, threaded needles with cotton still attached, rubber bands that come as a free donation with letters in the mail, Sellotape, Christmas tinsel, cooking foil, cling film and metal lids from food cans or food wrappers. Although most pet food manufacturers now sell their product with easy-to-remove metal lids, even these have been known to cut cats' mouths when they try and lick off the drops of food that remain on the tin lid.

Larger hazards include washing machines, ovens, microwaves, dish-washers, tumble-dryers and even the lavatory. Many a young kitten has fallen into the lavatory when the owner has forgotten to put the seat down. Any items that you do not want your Siamese to sample must be stored or locked away.

EQUIPMENT

Beds: From the very first day, identify a draught-free space that you intend to use for your cat's bed, food and water bowls and litter tray. There are all sorts of beds that you can buy; the main factors determining your choice will be cost, warmth, softness, durability, and whether the bed is washable, easy to maintain and provides a safe haven. It will need to be large enough for an adult Siamese, though some owners buy a smaller one for their kitten which is replaced by a larger model when necessary.

Litter Trays: These come in a range of styles, from a simple rectangular pan to one with an enclosed hood complete with an air ioniser which works electrically to reduce urine and faecal odours. Some hooded litter trays include charcoal filters which reduce these odours.

Ideally the litter pan needs to be strong enough to hold a two-to-three inch depth of cat litter. There should be no angled corners and it must stand up well to being disinfected or bleached to kill off all germs. Many cat owners have at least two trays, so that as one is being cleaned, the other is in use. A cat should never be given a clean tray that is still damp with disinfectant or bleach. Even if you intend to let your Siamese go outside when settled in, you will still need an indoor litter tray, especially on cold, windy nights.

All cats have individual ways of using a litter tray, some squat in the litter having dug a hole for themselves whilst some stand and spray within the hood. Mothers train their young kittens from about the age of four weeks, or at the weaning time, to use a litter tray. Young kittens will

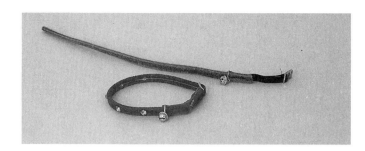

A bell on the collar will help to prevent your Siamese bringing home unwanted 'presents'.

Photo: Paddy Cutts.

A selection of feeding bowls.

Photo: Paddy Cutts.

A fold-down cat carrier. Cat carriers are made in many different materials, and the type you choose is a matter of personal preference.

Photo: Paddy Cutts.

A disposable cat carrier can be obtained from most veterinary surgeons.

Photo: Paddy Cutts.

*ABOVE: A wicker cat carrier is favoured by the
traditionalists.*

　　　　　　　　　　　Photo: Paddy Cutts.

*BELOW: Kerrimon Sumfun Jamie, pictured as a
kitten, investigating his new, leather carrier.*

　　　　　　　　　　　Photo: Paddy Cutts.

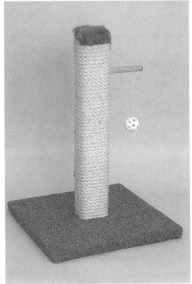

*Scratching posts come in a
range of different sizes to suit
all homes.*

　　　　　　　Photo: Paddy Cutts.

discharge their bladders several times during the day, following their feeding pattern, whilst adults will use the litter tray for the same purpose twice a day on average.

Whatever their personal preference, all cats like a clean litter tray in an accessible place. Some cats visit the litter tray as soon as they know there is a clean pan and clean litter just to give themselves a dry bath. The clay-based litters aid in this grooming technique by absorbing any excess grease in the fur.

Litter: Start by using a litter that the young Siamese is familiar with. Your breeder will certainly give you details of the one used in the breeding home and will most probably give you a sample to use for the first few nights. If you change to a different litter too soon during a stressful period, you can upset your kitten or cat's security. You can gradually move on to the litter you prefer by mixing the two and then phasing out the old one.There are many different forms of litter on the market ranging from natural lightweights to synthetic litters to heavyweights. The choice of litter in the end will depend on your preference and how you evaluate the absorbency factor.

Controlling odours: A wide variety of commercial products are available for controlling odours from litter trays. These include products available in a liquid or powder form which are sprinkled onto the litter in the pan. Removal of soiled waste is best carried out by a plastic litter scoop which can be easily washed and disinfected. There are metal scoops available but the chrome covering is likely to rust on continuous contact with the cat's urine.

If your new cat or kitten uses another area of the house, not the litter tray, one way to prevent this is to place some food on the spot. A youngster will rarely soil an area containing some favourite food. Another reason for cats soiling an area away from the litter tray is that they can object to the smell of the disinfectant being used by the owner, particularly if it is one of the heavier floral ones. Always use a disinfectant which is cat-friendly and user-friendly.

Finally, it is advisable to place the litter tray on a plastic tray which can be cleaned, or something washable such as a tumble-twist rug. If the cat has an accident outside the litter tray then these measures will protect the floor-covering from additional odours and from litter, which can be scattered around a small area.

Feeding and Water Bowls: Other basic necessities include feeding and water bowls which should be situated away from the litter tray. For extra cleanliness they can be put on a plastic tray or mat, which will prevent food from being dropped and trodden into the floor-coverings and are very easy to keep clean with a quick wipe of a disinfected cloth. My male Siamese loves to pick his food out of his bowl and eat it while standing over his plastic tray. It is advisable to choose water and food bowls made of ceramic materials or glass. Water bowls should be high-sided, whilst food bowls should be flat with only a small rim. These are available in all sizes and most owners start with small ones, changing over to larger bowls when the cat is fully grown. There are also many sizes and colours of plastic bowls available on the market.

Carriers: There are many reasons why it it is important to have a good-quality carrier. An owner should never take a cat or kitten into a car without using one, however much you think you or your passenger can control your pet on your lap. The squeal of another car's brakes can cause your cat to leap onto the floor of the car and get underneath the foot pedals or even jump up into your face, obliterating your vision. Also, if you were involved in an accident then your cat would almost certainly escape, and might never be found again. If stopped by the police whilst driving with a cat on your lap, or roaming around in the car, you could be charged with an offence. There are several types of carriers available, ranging from disposable cardboard boxes with ventilation holes and carrying handles to brightly coloured vinyl models suitable for airline travel. Whilst the cardboard variety may be sufficient for the once-a-year trip to the vet for vaccination, most people will want a more permanent plastic or wire one.

Scratching Posts and Toys: A scratching post in your home prevents damage to your household furniture, curtains and wallpaper. It is easy enough to train a youngster to use one. Simply by being placed on it, your cat will soon learn that this is the place to scratch. An additional training tip is to spray the post with a light covering of cat-nip spray which is available from shows and pet shops.

Cat toys are also being designed with varying degrees of sophistication. However, Siamese can have endless hours of fun with old socks, especially if there is a used crisp bag inside them, ping pong balls, scrunched up paper and even playing in front of household mirrors.

COLLECTING YOUR SIAMESE

Paperwork: When you are ready to take your Siamese home, the breeder will give you a large amount of paperwork. Under GCCF rules, registration papers must be provided at the time of sale, including at least a three-generation pedigree, transfer form and current vaccination certificate. Most breeders include information on settling the kitten into the new home, dietary advice, sometimes samples of food and litter that the youngster has used and information regarding the breed and breed cat clubs.

Make sure that you have the agreement of the breeder to telephone or call for advice at least for a few months following your purchase. Most breeders welcome this contact and many have made lasting friendships in this way.

When you go to collect your kitten or cat, do remember to take a suitable carrier with you. Some breeders will allow you to take a blanket in to them a couple of days previously so that your Siamese can start to acquire the smell of your household. If there are other pets in your household, it might be an idea to let them sit on this blanket before taking it over to the breeder. You can ensure that your Siamese will start to absorb the smell of your household on the journey home by placing this blanket in the carrier. Your kitten will also be very scared, and an excitable Siamese in a car can be very dangerous. The carrier gives security as well as protecting you. Drive carefully on the way home, and talk gently and reassuringly to the kitten.

ARRIVING HOME

The main point to remember is that the lovely, playful kitten or young cat you have seen and observed at the breeder's home will probably not be the same little character for the first few days after stepping over your threshold. The kitten will be confronted with strange people, pets, rooms, furniture and smells and have no mother cat to run to for protection. Although you and your family will be anxious to help your Siamese settle down quickly, you will have to ensure the cat's security and safety take preference over your own feelings. When thrown straightaway into a family atmosphere, your Siamese may hide under the first large object that presents itself, staying there for hours or even days without using the litter tray or eating or drinking.

Whatever the age of the new addition, it is best to let the cat come out of its carrier in its own time to get over the initial fright of changing environment. It is not advisable to deluge the youngster with welcoming arms, laps, the noise of the television, presents and all its new equipment within the first five minutes of entry into your house.

Place the carrier in an area or room that you have designated will belong to your pet, who can then start to absorb the new surroundings, and, if you can, close the door. The litter tray, food and water bowl need to be in close proximity to the youngster, with the litter tray a few feet away from the eating area. A small area to start with will make for a much happier Siamese and make integration into the rest of the household a much quicker affair.

Let the cat become used to one member of the family at a time and associate that person with affection, food, water and clean litter. The Siamese will slowly unwind, with your encouragement, and start to eat and to sit on you. Ensure that the rest of the household and any other pets are as quiet as possible and, in the first few hours or days, it is usually advisable to restrict other pets to another room. Even though it will appear that this introduction stage can be fraught with problems, it all depends on how quickly your Siamese can adapt. There is no hard and fast rule; many youngsters will need help, whilst a few bold spirits will adapt quickly, as if they have known your family and pets for years. Even if you bring in litter-mates together, the fact that they have been reared together and are related will not necessarily mean the same responses to a new home environment. Each Siamese has its own personality regardless of its upbringing.

Introducing existing pets: When you are satisfied that the newcomer has settled in sufficiently to be able to cope with introductions to your existing pets, you will need to manage the situation carefully. They can be interested enough in each other to become the best of friends very quickly, with your help as referee, or, at worst, they can actually fight each other.

There are a few simple measures that you can employ to assist integration. It is often best to let pets sense, see and smell each other with some form of barrier in between them. This can take the form of the pet carrier – at least your new pet will associate it with security – or a kittenpen that will be large enough to take a small litter tray and a bed, or an enclosed box which will again provide security and food and water bowls. The barrier will prevent fights and give both the existing pet and the new pet security as they establish the "pecking order" or hierarchy between them. Interestingly enough, an older cat will often accept another adult cat more quickly than a kitten.

At least by purchasing a Siamese (whose known character will be one of the reasons why you chose this breed) you will know that once initial introductions are made they can interact quite happily with other young cats and dogs. There is no laid-down time factor that will give you guidance as to when your pets will become friends; suffice to say most do, sooner or later.

Food and drink: Your kitten will have been vaccinated, wormed, fully weaned and litter-tray trained but is likely to be subject to some degree of stress on changing homes, which should only last a day or two at the most. It is quite likely the kitten will not want to eat for the first twenty-four to forty-eight hours. This is quite normal unless there are obvious signs of illness which you would need to refer to your veterinary surgeon. One way of encouraging a youngster to eat is to provide the same food that the breeder did. If using 'wet' food, place a little on your finger and let the youngster lick if off. It is a great way of getting to know your new pet. A twelve-week-old kitten's stomach is no bigger than a walnut and will not require a three-course banquet. Little and often is the way to feed a kitten, and patience at this stage will reap dividends. It is also possible you will find the faeces a little loose, but this should clear up within twenty-four hours. If diarrhoea carries on longer than this you need to seek advice immediately so it can be treated without delay, otherwise dehydration and other problems can develop. Many new owners arrange to take their new pet to the vet as soon as they leave the breeder's house so that a complete check-up can be made.

EARLY TRAINING

The transition into your home will go far more smoothly if you take advantage of this period to carry out some initial training. Your kitten's mother will already have given training in the basics of life – keeping clean, using a litter tray, feeding and drinking regularly and playing with siblings. Your kitten may have also learned some bad habits. Your youngster will not know what habits are acceptable to you. It is no good chastising the kitten or shouting about unacceptable behaviour; you will need to deal gently, using a quiet voice, until you are sure that your Siamese has accepted you as a trusted friend. A clean water spray, used sparingly, is a good training tool to start with. Later on your cat will know when you raise your voice in a firm manner that you are annoyed by some action. Never smack your Siamese, who will only be confused by being hurt by you. Training needs to be carried out in a systematic and repetitive fashion; it is no good allowing a piece of meat to be pinched off your plate one day, then chastising your cat another day for carrying out the same action. You will know when you have succeeded with training, because the cat's behaviour will indicate that lessons have been learned and will show an eagerness to please.

Very often any break in your Siamese's good behaviour is down to either the owner or illness. If your Siamese has an accident on the bed then it may be caused by something so simple as the litter tray, or scratching post, having been moved to a new position, or an infection may have developed. Siamese are very much creatures of habit and any change to their routine can offend their sense of order and behaviour.

GETTING TO KNOW EACH OTHER
However you decide to introduce your new pet to your household, it will help if you can spend as much time as possible with the newcomer. Many new owners arrange to collect their new pet either on a Friday evening or over a holiday period from work to ease the transition period. As Greta Hindley once wrote: "To anyone who wishes to buy a Siamese kitten but cannot give it plenty of loving companionship, my advice is 'Don't'."

Chapter Four

NUTRITION AND FEEDING

There is a saying that "you are what you eat" and nowhere is this more truly demonstrated than with Siamese cats. Feline nutrition is an evolving science which has its roots in research carried out more than fifty years ago. Respected feline food manufacturers realise that cat breeders are becoming more interested in dietary management, and they are now producing aids in the form of kitten and cat care packages, instructional leaflets and seminars that are frequently attended by breeders. Even advertisements that appear in magazines are becoming more educational in the message they are trying to impart.

DIETARY DEVELOPMENT OF THE CAT
Cats are carnivorous by nature and through their physiological development are strong, muscular, fast-moving hunters. They have the features of a carnivore, including sharp teeth designed for cutting. A cat living in the wild is attracted to its prey by movement. The hunting instinct is enhanced by the senses of sight, smell, hearing and touch. Cats' eyes can be likened to a photographer's wide aperture lens which, in effect, absorbs the maximum amount of light possible over a short focal length. The ears are positioned to detect sounds outside the auditory range of humans, and can, with amazing accuracy, pinpoint the source of any noise made by their prey at a distance or when hidden from view. As a hunter their claws are designed to secure their "kill". These instincts are still apparent with the house-bound Siamese who is fed commercially-prepared or home-prepared diets. We have all seen or heard of Siamese stealing the Sunday lunch and surreptitiously dragging the meat away to eat it in an undisturbed corner of the house.

Manufacturers have taken notice of these characteristics, particularly those of smell and taste. There are many pictures of cats who appear to be savouring the air with their mouths open; what is happening is that the cat is both smelling and tasting the air at the same time. If a cat cannot smell its food, then it will not eat, and nowhere is this more apparent than when the cat is ill, so a manufacturer will prepare a diet to appeal to the cat's sense of smell as well as of taste. The palatability of a diet is governed by taste, texture and temperature of the food. The cat's preference for a particular type of food does not mean to say that it is the best for the cat's nutritional needs at a particular time.

THE CONCEPT OF LIFE-CYCLE DIETS
Feline dietary requirements change markedly during the different stages of a cat's life, such as pregnancy, weaning, adulthood and old age.
Adult feeding requirements: Recommendations for quantities to feed are usually found on all products. If you are feeding two foods mixed, remember to use half the daily quantity for each

There are many varieties of dried, complete feline diets on the market, and your Siamese will probably develop a preference.

Photo: Paddy Cutts.

one. It is often said that a cat can monitor its own intake but I have seen Siamese who eat as if they think there will never be another meal in their life.

One of the best guides of all is the appearance of your pet, who should look in good condition with close-lying fur covering a svelte-shaped body. You should not be able to feel the vertebrae, see hollows in the abdomen, or an open, dull-looking coat. On average a fully grown Siamese female weighs between six and nine pounds whilst a male weighs between eight and eleven pounds. The size of your Siamese is dependent on many factors, such as pedigree line, body frame and health. The weight of your cat can be monitored at home by you standing alone on the scales, then standing on the scales holding your cat. The difference in weight is the weight of the cat.

Kitten Feeding Requirements: A cat is regarded as a kitten until at least nine months of age. Some dry food manufacturers often make a suggestion in their feeding guides that, once a kitten has reached at least ninety per cent of expected adult body weight and frame, then switch over to the adult formula. If the youngster is slow developing, then it is recommended that kitten food be used until the age of twelve months before switching over to the adult formula. A young kitten is incapable of ingesting large quantities at restricted, timed intervals; therefore young kittens should be allowed free access to food and water at all times.

Pregnant and Lactating Queens: Female cats in the last trimester of pregnancy, and lactating queens, should be allowed free access to a diet that is rich enough in calcium, phosphorus and the other elements to support the extra demand for nourishment. Provided responsible and adequate nutrition has been given, there should be no problems with primary or secondary uterine inertia at the time of giving birth. Good-quality cat foods contain adequate calcium and do not need to be supplemented for lactating queens.

The Elderly Cat: A cat at this stage of life has special dietary requirements. Although there is no life-cycle diet currently being marketed for the elderly cat, nevertheless the owner can provide an adequate diet. An ageing cat is definitely less active and needs fewer calories to maintain the optimum level of nourishment. There are some low calorie diets available for neutered cats and these can be used successfully with an elderly cat.

TYPES OF FOOD
The two main kinds are 'wet' food, usually available in tins or small prepacked containers, and 'dry' food, normally available in boxes or larger sacks. Wet food may be either a paste-like

For feeding requirements, a cat is regarded as a kitten until it is nine months of age.

Photo: Paddy Cutts.

consistency, or chunks of meat in a 'gravy' sauce (sometimes even with vegetables). Dry food comes in a variety of different shaped biscuits, varying between manufacturers.

Some dry foods are considered 'complete foods', meaning that a cat can be fed on these alone and get all the required nutrients in the correct balance. The other type of biscuits are often termed 'mixers', meaning that they are suitable for mixing with other food, often increasing its palatability, but should not be fed as a main diet since they do not contain the correct balance of nutrients for a complete diet.

There is also a semi-moist form around on the market, but generally speaking this is not so popular. One of the reasons may be the higher level of the preservative, propylene glycol, which prevents the food (which can include animal tissues) from drying out. In America the use of this preservative has now been banned. Many cat breeders are becoming interested in obtaining a diet that has very few or no added preservatives.

When feeding your Siamese always make sure that there is an adequate supply of fresh water available and that a well-balanced quality diet is eaten in the correct amounts to meet the cat's energy needs at any stage in its life-cycle.

DRY FOODS

The main advantage of feeding a dry diet is convenience. A cat naturally feeds between ten and twenty times a day in the wild, depending on its size and activity level. High energy dry food can be left down for the domesticated cat who is restricted to its immediate environment. This encourages free-choice feeding without the danger of bacteria growing on the food, because there is too low a water content for them to survive. Another advantage is improved dental hygiene because the cat has to crunch the dry biscuits. There may also be a cost advantage to feeding a dry diet. On average it is approximately half or even a third cheaper than feeding a canned or moist food of a similar quality. The disadvantages of a dry diet are few. However, there are certain points, the most important one being the need for extra water. Always make sure that there is an adequate supply available at all times. There is also a question about whether dry feline foods play any part in causing Feline Urological Syndrome (FUS). As the name "syndrome" implies, this is a group of conditions which includes cystitis in the female cat and urethritis in the male cat. With both sexes the cat may strain to urinate at frequent intervals, and in severe cases with the male, his back will arch in his attempt to pass urine, which may reveal traces of blood. What actually happens is that the urinary tract may be partially, or completely, blocked by crystals, which can belong to one of five different mineral structures, and which, singly, may not be larger than a grain of sand. A few years ago it was assumed that all minerals were the cause of this problem, until further research identified that an excess of one mineral in particular, magnesium, contributed to the development of these crystals.

All dry foods should be labelled with an expiry date and it is advisable not to purchase a bag of dry food with a limited shelf life unless you know for certain that the contents will be used within the period stated. The nutritional and vitamin content can only be guaranteed by the manufacturer for a certain period of time. Dry feline foods must also be stored carefully. Generally speaking, there is usually a guaranteed shelf life of a year, although this can be shorter if the temperature-level and humidity in the air are high. All manufacturers, therefore, include antioxidants to delay the deterioration process. Cats can be fickle in their feeding habits, and whilst most cats will happily accept dry and wet foods, there are a few who genuinely prefer one to the other.

WET FOODS
Many cat breeders choose to feed 'wet' food, which is either canned or food cooked by the manufacturer in foil trays. Unlike dry feline foods that only have dried ingredients in their formulation, wet food can have both wet and dry ingredients including animal flesh and cereals. The fat content of these foods tends to be higher and will provide more calories when energy requirements are likely to be increased. Because of the nature of these foods, they are extremely advantageous in tempting an anorexic cat to eat.

There are different kinds of wet food. Many of the 'premium' food manufacturers make canned cat food that is 'concentrated'. The main difference is that the cat needs to eat less in volume of this food than the 'normal' foods and therefore, although the price may initially seem expensive, it is still good value because the can will last longer. Generally speaking, canned and tray food can be stored for long periods because the high temperatures involved in cooking the food create a sterile environment. Like human food when cooked at high temperatures, there is a certain degree of loss of vitamin and other nutrient content, but nutritionists have adjusted the formula of these foods to take this into account. Because of the high palatability, cats can develop a fixed preference for one variety if this is fed exclusively for a period of time. Training a cat to change feeding habits can take a great deal of time and patience.

An owner will need to check whether the food given is a complete diet as opposed to a complementary diet. Long-term feeding of complementary diets can give rise to dietary deficiencies which will cause disease. They should be given in conjunction with another formulation to provide a nutritionally sound product or on a "treat" basis. As there is more moisture in these foods the cat will not need to drink as much as those who feed solely on a dry diet.

DYES AND CHEMICALS
If you decide to feed dry food as a complete meal or part of a mixed diet, try and avoid those that

have artificial colours or flavourings. Food dyes are not nutrients. As in human food, for example celebration cakes, colourings are added to make the food pleasing to the human eye. Some manufacturers also add colourants to make the food look appealing to the owner as part of the marketing process. Cats do not need fancy-coloured food. Natural canned foods are a brown colour not red.

Food allergies in cats can sometimes be caused by the chemicals in the food. This form of hypersensitivity is uncommon but nevertheless exists. One way it may be seen is if your cat pulls out large chunks of fur. (Another cause of "plucking" is hormone levels.) If you suspect there is a food allergy problem, then get your vet to recommend one of the Prescription Diets that are available.

LABEL ANALYSIS

It is interesting to note that there is a difference in the degree of information given on cat food labels in the North American market, which is more extensive than that normally seen in the UK. You need to know what is the healthiest food you can provide for your Siamese as well as how to decipher intelligently the information on the label.

All products have two main areas of information, the Guaranteed Analysis and the List of Ingredients. The Guaranteed Analysis provides a guarantee that some amount of the nutrients named actually appear in the food. Figures given may or may not be preceded or followed by the words, 'minimum' or 'maximum'. These are the limits as defined by the American National Research Council (whose scientists determine nutrient requirements for cats besides carrying out other functions). So, in comparing two similar types of product, the amount of a specific nutrient can actually vary by as much as five hundred percent and yet be permitted as passable because it lies within the NRC tolerance. This is because the small levels of differences in moisture and nutrient content between foods can result in larger differences in the overall balance of the food.

The List of Ingredients is usually printed in descending order by weight. However, it can become a little difficult to follow when it is not made clear which ingredients are dry and which are in a moist form. Another form of listing to be aware of is giving a single ingredient several different names. An example of this is 'chicken' followed by 'poultry by-product meal'. The image is of moist, succulent chicken followed by a very ordinary ingredient. What the label is really saying is that there is chicken in the product twice over, the latter ingredient in reality being the whole of the chicken excluding the feathers!

The owner of the Siamese needs to be alert to both of the lists and recognise that as their pet is a carnivore, an animal protein source needs to be one of the first two ingredients in a moist cat food and one of the first three ingredients in a dry cat food. It certainly pays to be aware of the statements and figures that are found on pet food labels.

THE MERITS OF MIXED FEEDING

It is amazing that something so basic as feeding your Siamese involves a great deal of thought and consideration. There are so many diets on the retail market nowadays, all easily available through supermarkets, pet shops and Veterinary Surgeries. A housebound Siamese is totally dependent on the choice you make, while indicating any preferences for a diet which is dry, wet or contains both. You, of course, will have to think about the cost of feeding your kitten or cat, whilst pandering to tastes and dietary needs. Once you have a clear idea of your pet's requirements, the only problem you then have to solve is the daily quantity, especially if you decide to feed a mixed diet.

Generally speaking, choose a good-quality product that has been proven effective and nutritionally sound within feeding trials. Any responsible pet food manufacturer will be glad to furnish you with details if requested. Very few cats are nowadays fed solely on a home-produced diet, purely because owners are aware that they could be giving their cat an unbalanced diet which will need to be supplemented with vitamins and minerals. Although offal is cheap to purchase it is not a good idea to feed it as a main daily dish, as cats can become addicted to various types which, over a period of time, will lead to dietary deficiencies and disease.

It is a myth that cats prefer fish, as few cats are able in reality to catch it for themselves in the wild. However, it will not cause your Siamese any harm if you give an occasional meal of cooked fish, egg or liver as a very special treat.

PRESCRIPTION DIETS
Some Veterinary Surgeons have started to run dietary advice clinics, for which there is a definite need, as there are many obese pets, or pets with clinical problems that can be improved, or alleviated, by the use of the correct Prescription Diet. However, the palatability factor needs to be considered because, however correctly formulated the food is for the condition in question, if a cat will not eat it then the diet cannot perform its role in aiding the treatment of the disease. Prescription Diets are available in wet and dry form and are more expensive than non-Prescription Diets to feed.

FEEDING GUIDE
It is recommended that the adult Siamese should be fed at least twice a day and that food should not be restricted unless the cat is under medical supervision or overweight. Owners should ensure they follow the feeding guide for particular kinds of food. Water should be available at all times. Kittens will need feeding more often: four times a day is common in their early months. Again, be careful to follow the appropriate feeding instructions. And remember, some Siamese are extremely clever at manipulating their owner's affections for more extra food above the daily requirement!

Chapter Five

GENERAL CARE AND MAINTENANCE

As Siamese are a short-haired breed their coats will not require much grooming. This, however, is only one part of general care and maintenance, which extends to keeping your pet free of worms and fleas, checking eyes for any irritation and foreign bodies, keeping ears, chin, teeth and gums clean, clipping nails and bathing.

CLEANING THE EARS
Starting from the top of your Siamese, check the ears, which cats cannot reach for themselves, at regular intervals; some owners will do this once a week, others twice a month. There is no definitive rule as each cat is different – some have greater secretions of wax than others. There are ear wipes available in an airtight container, or use cotton wool balls which can be dipped in baby oil. Cotton buds, used very carefully, are ideal for cleaning away wax in the folds of the ear. The only part of the ear that needs to be cleaned is the external part which you can see, and you only need to press down lightly with your cotton wool ball, or ear wipe, at the top of the ear canal to remove any debris being harboured there. Never stick a cotton bud down the ear canal because, being pliable, it could work its way round the bend and puncture the ear drum. After a few attempts, some cats learn to sit quietly on your lap whilst you do this task. However, many will need some form of restraint and often the job is best done with the help of a friend to ensure the cat cannot make a sudden movement and hurt itself.

Regular cleaning should provide some insurance against ear mites, which can usually be identified by dark brown clumps of wax in the folds of the ear. Ear mites are microscopic orthropods and they live off the wax, thereby irritating the skin. If left unchecked this leads to haematomas which can cause permanent damage, resulting in a crumpled ear rather than an upright, pointed ear. The mites cause itching, so another symptom of severe infestation can be seen when the youngster scratches or paws the ears and does a lot of head shaking. It is extremely unpleasant for a cat and needs to be treated swiftly. Ear mites are transmitted from another cat. Kittens can catch them from their mother, if she is infected. If you think your cat has the problem, cleanse the ears daily, but if it is not resolving itself, then you will need to ask your vet to prescribe treatment.

CHECKING EYES
One of the first signs that will tell you if your cat is unwell is the condition of the eyes, which, in a healthy Siamese, are clear, bright and sparkling. Most cats dislike having their eyes touched. There are ways of holding your Siamese securely. Some owners sit their cats on their laps, securing them with their left elbow and holding the front paws with their left hand, while wiping the eyes with a

tissue or cotton wool ball with their right hand. Others kneel on the floor with the cat securely held between their knees, head facing outwards, and, while one hand holds the head, the other hand wipes the eyes. Use the method you find easiest.

Like their human owners, Siamese will occasionally get a little 'sleep' in the corners of the eyes which can be easily removed by a wipe with a tissue or dampened cotton wool ball. Sometimes this sleep will be of a crystalline nature, sometimes it will look as if there is a little mucus there. Providing this is clear, there is little to worry about. It can be caused by many things, such as heavy smoke in the atmosphere, or even allergies. Some Siamese cats' eyes are rather deeply set which can result in mucus collecting. This trait seems to pass down pedigree lines.

If the mucus is a yellowy/green colour flowing out of the corner of the eye down the nose, for instance, this could mean that your Siamese is suffering from an infection or it could be symptomatic of a disease. If the third eyelid (haw) is part way across the eye, you will also need to seek help. If you notice the inside of the eye is reddened at all, go to the vet as soon as possible, as your pet will be very uncomfortable and could be suffering from conjunctivitis. The prescription will probably be an ointment or eye drops and perhaps a course of antibiotics. If any eye infection does occur, make sure you keep your hands as clean as possible, especially if you need to touch other cats in the household. Unless you are very adept at using cotton buds, avoid them. A sudden movement and the bud can go into your pet's eye.

THE NOSE
A few Siamese manage to get food impacted at the side of their nostrils, near the slit (external nares), when they eat. This can form a hard crust, which can easily be removed by holding the cat securely and using either a cotton bud or dampened piece of cotton wool to release it.

THE CHIN AREA
Surprisingly enough, Siamese can be subject to blackheads and acne around their chins. One of the main causes of this is the build-up of oily, dried food flakes from some diets entering into the hair follicles and skin pores which then get clogged, become infected and look just like blackheads, which gives a dirty appearance to your pet. If these areas are not kept clean, they can become inflamed through the growth of bacteria and, in the worst cases, release a pus-like substance. This can be particularly annoying if yours is a show cat, because once the areas become infected, your pet can develop a small bald patch. In most cases the fur will grow back but if you have entered your cat into a show, it will be interpreted as a lesion and you can be rejected at vetting in, losing your show fees.

Your cat will try very hard to keep this area clean by washing but this is not sufficient to remove acne and you will need to help. A mild case will respond to regular washing with a cotton wool ball dampened with warm, soapy water, witch hazel, or Dermisol. Acne can be painful and your cat will not appreciate any hard rubbing in an attempt to remove the pus. In an extreme case the vet will need to shave the area to remove the blackheads. Generally speaking, antibiotics will be prescribed if there is an infection.

THE MOUTH
Cleaning your Siamese's teeth can be a lot of fun for both of you! If teeth are left uncleaned Siamese, like humans, develop an excessive build-up of tartar which can lead to infection. Some pedigree lines are more prone than others to dental decay – some Siamese hardly experience any problems until they are quite old. Providing you start cleaning the teeth when the cat is young, you may save your Siamese from having dental descaling under anaesthetic later on.

Red Point: Ch. Chrisaliz Chillichops. Some Siamese are fair-skinned and are prone to sunburn in the summer months. It is therefore important to provide shade during the daytime.

Photo: Christine Brooks.

For many owners the simplest way of cleaning feline teeth is to brush them with a rubber finger-tip cover that has teeth on its exterior, or to use a small piece of sterile gauze which has been dipped into a home-made salt-and-baking-soda solution. Quantities are half a teaspoon of salt to half a teaspoon of baking soda dissolved in half a cup of boiled water which is then allowed to cool down. Some owners use cotton buds dipped into their home-made cleaning solution, and wipe the bud over the teeth. This method saves fingers being bitten. Most vets sell a specially designed toothpaste that is meat-flavoured and fairly costly. Toothpaste designed for humans is not suitable because some of the ingredients used are poisonous to cats and because it is almost impossible to rinse the paste out of your cat's mouth. Some owners succeed in wiping all their cat's teeth, front and back; some cats will only allow their owners to wipe the front teeth. However, any maintenance in this area is better than no maintenance at all as dental de-scaling is quite expensive and there is always the slight risk of losing your pet under anaesthetic.

Your vet may recommend de-scaling if there are signs of tartar build-up, bad breath, brown teeth and inflamed gums. One of the early signs of dental problems can be seen at home if you notice your cat having trouble holding food in its mouth while chewing. The complete dried cat food that is available nowadays is one of the best ways to reduce dental decay – the crunching of the pieces helps prevent the build-up of tartar.

CLAWS

Claws grow quickly and need to be trimmed regularly. Cat scratching posts are very useful in removing the brittle sheath part of the claw, which usually falls off when your cat is exercising. However, constant exercise results in very sharp claws, which need to be trimmed. Hold your cat in whatever way you find most comfortable and, once secure, all you have to do is lightly squeeze the top of the toe to extend the claw. Make sure you complete this operation in adequate light and, with your clippers, cut off only the white part of the nail. You will also see a pink part of the claw known as the 'quick'. Avoid this area completely. If you do make a mistake and cut into this, your cat will feel a little pain and will bleed – and will also lose confidence in you carrying out this task in the future! Some owners find claw clipping is easier to undertake if another person holds the cat.

There are various implements that can be bought to clip claws, though human nail-clippers can do the job adequately.

DECLAWING
In the UK, it is regarded as unethical to declaw the cat. The GCCF specifically excludes declawed pedigree cats from being shown. However, it is a custom that is still carried out by some veterinarians in the USA, where there is considerable dissension on the merits of this practice. It would appear that the only advantage, if it can be recognised as such, is the limitation to damage within the owner's household. The disadvantages appear to outweigh the cosmetic advantages, namely the physical and mental trauma that can be suffered by the cat having this operation, which is done under anaesthesia and involves cutting across the first joint of the paw and removing the claws. The cat's feet are bandaged for a few days to prevent any chance of haemorrhaging. The cat will also experience pain when attempting to walk after the bandages are removed. A cat allowed out of doors will not be able to scramble up a tree any more or participate in other normal cat play and is totally defenceless. Cat psychologists often have referrals after the operation, because a declawed cat can lose trust in its owner and become insecure and nervous. A few cat fancies in the USA refuse to allow declawed cats to be shown under their rules.

THE TAIL
An entire male Siamese is prone to a condition known as 'stud tail', similar to the acne that some Siamese suffer from on their chin. It is caused by a secretion of oil from the sebaceous glands that are found on the uppermost part of the tail, near the back of the cat. The first symptoms can be identified when the affected part of the tail takes on a very oily appearance. If not treated at this stage, the second phase produces a dark wax that can be seen lying on the skin of the tail under the fur. If you have not noticed the first stage, this dark wax can be very difficult to see on the tail of a Seal or Chocolate Point stud cat, unless you are looking for it. When left untreated, the fur will fall out, leaving the area bare, which will enable infection to set in amongst the blackheads.

Stud tail is very easy to treat; the tail will need washing with a suitable solution and drying off gently with a towel. It is very unlikely that stud tail will affect a neutered male cat. Some Siamese also have trouble washing the tips of their tails. If you look closely at your cat trying to carry out this manoeuvre, you will notice your Siamese has difficulty in keeping it still enough. You can help by holding the end of the tail close to your cat's mouth – who will then lick it furiously. This can become a game between owner and cat.

GROOMING THE COAT
Most Siamese love to be groomed and this is one way of removing any debris or loose hair. Regular brushing will prevent dead hair from being deposited on your furniture, especially during the change from winter to summer coat, and will also prevent your Siamese from developing hair balls. There are various brushes and combs you can buy. Tell the retailer that you have a Siamese, so you do not come home with equipment designed for a long-haired cat. Grooming bars are very useful; they have 'rubber' fingers on one side which tease out the waste hair without you having to brush too vigorously.

If you are preparing your Siamese for a show, a chamois glove or leather, or even a silk scarf, can smooth down the hair and leave a shine on the coat. Some owners use a soft bristle brush which can remove the excess hairs, but not quite as effectively as a grooming bar. Synthetic brush

Grooming equipment needed to keep your Siamese's coat in peak condition.

Photo: Paddy Cutts.

bristles may prove a little too harsh and make the coat stand proud of the body with static. Too much brushing can result in a Siamese with bald spots, which is not desirable, particularly if you are planning to show. If you use a comb to clear the coat of excess loose hairs, then go with the direction of the fur rather than against it. Generally speaking, there is no need to sprinkle any extra preparations, such as unscented baby talc, into your Siamese's coat – this is for their longhaired cousins. There are coat conditioners available to add a sheen and make the coat lie closer to the body. These are usually used after bathing. However, if your Siamese is healthy and regularly groomed, both bathing and conditioners should not be needed.

HAIR BALLS
These can occur if your cat is not groomed regularly. They are caused by a cat licking its own coat or the coat of another cat. Once formed they are usually coughed or vomited out of the cat's body. Excess hair can also be passed out of the cat's body with faeces.

BATHING YOUR SIAMESE
Just occasionally, you may need to bath your Siamese. There is no hard and fast rule which will indicate the best place of all in which to do this, but usually the sink in the kitchen will suffice or the hand-basin in the bathroom, providing your pet is not too big for it. Some owners use the shower tray and shower head, or even the bath. It is more than likely that your Siamese will panic the first time, so it is wise to plan your strategy beforehand and make sure that all you will need is to hand, such as towels and clean face-flannel, plastic jug or cup, a mild cat shampoo (not human shampoo which contains chemicals and scents) or a prescription shampoo if you are sorting out a flea or skin problem, and finally a bathmat.

Bathing will strip your cat's coat of all its own oils, so if you are doing it as preparation for a show, make sure that it is done at least a week in advance. This will allow for the natural oils to return and lubricate the coat again in time for the show. Clip your cat's claws the day beforehand to save yourself from being scratched in places you did not know existed! Also wear a waterproof apron and old clothes. You might find it easier to remove any decorative rings, to save your cat from being scratched. Whatever container you decide to use, there is no point in filling it to the brim, unless you feel you need a bath at the same time! About six inches will be enough for your cat. Test the temperature of the water with your elbow, and if it feels comfortably warm, then you know it is safe for your cat. Make sure that the room is warm enough and that it is cat-proof, so that if your cat slips out of your hands and does a couple of wall circuits, soap, perfume and other bathtime accessories are not going to be dislodged onto your head. All breakables should be removed and any curtains should be hung out of the way. If you have a shower curtain this should be looped over the shower rail. If there is a lavatory in your bathroom, close the lid. Speak gently while closing the door to the room.

Pour a little cat shampoo into the water and gently lower your Siamese into the bath or sink. Be prepared for your cat to struggle out of the water onto your arms or shoulders continuously during the whole process. Pour warm soapy water, using the plastic cup or jug, over back and tail. Try hard to avoid getting any into the cat's eyes. Rub the body gently to lather the soap. If a face wash is needed, use a clean flannel and wipe around gently, avoiding the eyes. Once all areas have been washed, use the shower head to effect a thorough rinsing, or make sure that clean warm water is used for this purpose. Once you are sure that all soap and excess water has been removed, wrap your cat in a towel, and remove to another warm dry area. Most cats love being surrounded by a warm towel, with only their face peeking out, and being rubbed dry. This is the part of the bathing process that can be considered a new game. It is quite likely you may need another towel to finish off the process. A few owners may be able to use a hair dryer but very often the noise upsets the cat.

Once dry, lightly brush the coat back into its close-lying position. It is not a good idea to let your Siamese out into the garden straight after a bath to maybe catch a cold or roll around in the garden dirt. A favourite meal or a new catnip toy will often bring your cat around to thinking that it was not so bad after all.

There is another method of bathing your cat, that is with a dry bran-bath. Get some bran and gently warm it in the oven. Prepare the dry bath area with newspaper or towel and a soft brush to hand. Test the temperature of the warmed cereal with your elbow, making sure it is not too hot. You will need to hold on to your Siamese securely and gently rub the bran into the coat. Some Siamese love the feel of warm bran and sit quietly, allowing you to carry out the procedure; others will attempt to spread a fine layer of it around your room. Gently brush the bran out of the coat. All excessive coat oils and dust particles are removed with it. If you are showing your Siamese after a bran bath, it is best to do this at least a couple of days before the show to give the coat time to settle down and produce a polished sheen. Also make sure that every particle of bran is brushed out, otherwise your exhibit can be disqualified.

FLEAS

Part of the regular maintenance of your Siamese should include checking for fleas. If you run your finger against the lie of the fur on the back of your pet you can check if flea dirt is present. This appears as black specks which will certainly stand out against the cat's pale coat. Research has indicated that fleas appearing on your cat are often due to fleas breeding in your home; they are rarely picked up from outdoors. Warmth is a very relevant factor in the development of the flea, which enables them to breed quickly, and this can now be a year-round problem owing to most homes having central heating.

Unfortunately fleas are also carriers of tapeworms and your cat can become infected whilst licking and ingesting a flea. The life-cycle of the flea is thought to last about two weeks under suitable warm conditions. If the weather is cooler, the life-cycle will last longer. Adult fleas live on the cat. They bite through the skin and feed off blood. After feeding, the female will mate and lay about ten to thirty eggs daily on the cat's skin. These eggs then fall off into the environment and hatch in a timespan of up to ten days. It is at this stage that your home can become contaminated.

The eggs hatch into flea larvae which develop a cocoon before pupation. They can stay in this form for as short a period as two weeks or as long as a few months until the right conditions stimulate the pupa into developing into a flea. Apart from fleas being an irritant to your pet, they can be the cause of a serious skin disease, known as flea-allergy dermatitis, which can be expressed in various ways, the most common being red, hairless skin on the abdomen or hind legs and numerous crusty raised areas over the whole body.

Your vet can help with a number of flea products to enable you to get rid of these parasites, including flea sprays or a drop solution which is applied to the coat with a pipette. This must be placed on the flattest part of the back of the cat to avoid your pet from licking off the contents. Another product available is a packet containing six ampoules of a white-coloured suspension which contains an active ingredient called lufenuron. This is administered by mixing it with your cat's food. The active ingredient works in the cat by being absorbed into the bloodstream and it can last up to one month. It is advised that this product can be given at monthly intervals. If your cat is suffering from flea-allergy dermatitis, your veterinary surgeon can supply you with insecticidal shampoos and flea sprays.

Apart from treating your pet, you will probably need to spray your household furniture, carpets and curtains with a product designed for the purpose. Any used pet bedding will either have to be regularly washed or destroyed, depending on the severity of the infestation. Seek veterinary advice if your pregnant queen succumbs to flea infestation or if you have young kittens.

RINGWORM

This is one of the few fungal infections that can be transmitted across the species barrier, from cat to human and vice versa, as well as other animals. Transmission is very easy and you should consider yourself in quarantine for the course of the infection. It bears no resemblance to tapeworms or roundworms; even though it is called ringworm it is essentially a skin condition. It can be identified by circular inflamed areas which are associated with hair loss. Its passage of infection usually starts with the head, then the neck and front legs, until it covers the whole body. A vet suspecting ringworm will examine your cat under a Woods lamp, which throws an ultra-violet light onto the infection. Diagnosis will also be made from cultures taken off the skin. Development of cultures can take up to fourteen days to provide conclusive evidence and must be repeated at regular intervals until your cat is cleared. Just like ear-mite infestation, a cat with this infection cannot be shown and you will have to supply a clearance certificate from your vet, who will have to state that the whole household is cleared of ringworm.

Ringworm infection is very easy to detect on a short-haired breed such as the Siamese. Unfortunately, it can last for at least a year. Your vet will prescribe tablets or powders which are placed in the cat's food. The fungus basically grows out of the coat. You have to be very careful when handling the cat because of the danger of transmitting the spores from the hairs.

INTERNAL WORM INFESTATION

If you regularly groom your Siamese, you may notice evidence of other worm infestation that will be easy to treat. There are quite a few internal parasites that can live in your cat's digestive tract and occasionally may be expelled through faeces. Intestinal parasites include tapeworms and roundworms. Other worms, which are rarely seen, include feline heartworms, eyeworms, lungworms, ascarids, hookworms, whipworms and flukes. Roundworms are most commonly seen in kittens. There are other sources of infestation but the most common are through the mother's milk or sharing an infected litter tray. The roundworm larvae migrates through internal organs before settling in the intestines. Heavy infestation will manifest itself in external symptoms such as raised third eyelids, very round abdomens looking like 'pot bellies', open staring coat, lack of muscle-tone, coughing, diarrhoea and vomiting. Roundworm can appear like small portions of spaghetti in your cat's faeces or can appear in your cat's vomit. Tapeworms when developed lie in the intestine and attach themselves using one end known as the scolex. All digested food is absorbed by them, so, as they grow, your cat becomes thinner but its appetite will not be diminished. External symptoms can reveal a dull-looking coat and eyes. Tapeworm segments will appear flat and white in the faeces, or segments (looking like rice) can be seen around your cat's. anus. Newly expelled, they are still alive and can move around, carrying embryos which are eaten by fleas, ready to be passed on to another host. If you suspect any internal worm infestation, take your cat, with a fresh sample of faeces, to your vet. Worming preparations can be bought from your local pet shop, but without really knowing the other symptoms that may be present or concurrent with infestation, it is not always wise to take this route.

Could your domesticated Siamese be descended from this fine specimen?

Photo: Steve Franklin.

The aristocratic Siamese is master of all he surveys.

Photo: Paddy Cutts.

A young cat exhibiting the legendary Siamese squint, which makes the eyes appear as though they are permanently looking towards the nose. Photo: Paddy Cutts.

Ch. Killdown Midas, a Tabby Point. Siamese love basking in the sun, and will spend much of the day resting and sleeping. Photo: Paddy Cutts

Siamese enjoy one another's company and will also hunt in pairs. Photo: Paddy Cutts

Busybee kittens: A well-balanced diet is essential in promoting correct growth and development. *Photo: Paddy Cutts.*

Sumfun Soraya, a Seal Point Siamese, with her litter of kittens. **Photo: Paddy Cutts.**

When you are choosing a Siamese kitten, it is helpful to see other members of the family.
Photo: Paddy Cutts.

RIGHT: The Siamese coat will often darken with age.

Photo: Paddy Cutts.

BELOW: An American traditional type Seal Point Siamese, also known as an Apple Head Siamese.

Photo: Diane Dunaway.

ABOVE: A delightful litter of Busybee kittens, ready to go to their new homes.

Photo: Paddy Cutts.

RIGHT: Turevooh Jeu Desprit, pictured at eight weeks, with her litter sister, Turevooh Beaumonde, an Oriental Caramel Tortoiseshell Spotted Tabby.

Photo: Vic Grant.

*Grand Champion
Chaiross Ariel:
The first Chocolate
Point Grand
Champion.*

Photo: Marc Henrie

*Grand
Champion
Chaiross
Androcles.*

*Photo: Marc
Henrie*

Chapter Six

THE BREED STANDARDS

As the breed has developed over the years, so has the system of 'managing' its development. This chapter gives the present registration policy and Breed Standards issued by the Governing Council of the Cat Fancy (GCCF), the main registration and governing body in the UK.

SIAMESE REGISTRATION POLICY

1 FULL REGISTER
Siamese with Full or Provisional recognition which have in their pedigrees within five generations only Siamese (24, 24a, 24b, 24c, 32 1 - 32 6, 32t1-32t4, 32a, 32b1 - 32b4, 32c) shall be registered on the FULL REGISTER.

2 SUPPLEMENTARY REGISTER
Siamese with Full or Provisional recognition which have in their pedigrees within five generations only Siamese (as above, plus 24k, 24n, 24r, 32 7 - 32 9, 32t7 - 32t9, 32b7 - 32b9), Havana (29), Oriental Lilac (29c), Foreign White (35), Oriental Black (37), Oriental Blue (37a), Oriental Red (37d), Oriental Cream (37f), Oriental Tortie (37e, 37g, 37h, 37j, 37m, 37p, 37y), Oriental Cinnamon (37k), Oriental Caramel (37n), Oriental Fawn (37r), Oriental Spotted Tabby (38 to 38y, excluding silvers), Oriental Classic Tabby (41 to 41y, excluding silvers), Oriental Mackerel Tabby (44 to 44y, excluding silvers), Oriental Ticked Tabby (45 to 45y, excluding silvers) shall be registered on the SUPPLEMENTARY REGISTER.

3 EXPERIMENTAL REGISTER
Siamese with Preliminary recognition which have in their pedigrees within five generations only Siamese (as above, plus 24k, 24n, 24r, 32 7 - 32 9, 32t7 - 32t9, 32b7 - 32b9), Havana (29), Oriental Lilac (29c), Foreign White (35), Oriental Black (37), Oriental Blue (37a), Oriental Red (37d), Oriental Cream (37f), Oriental Tortie (37e, 37g, 37h, 37j, 37m, 37p, 37y), Oriental Cinnamon (37k), Oriental Caramel (37n), Oriental Fawn (37r), Oriental Spotted Tabby (38 to 38y, excluding silvers), Oriental Classic Tabby (41 to 41y, excluding silvers), Oriental Mackerel Tabby (44 to 44y, excluding silvers), Oriental Ticked Tabby (45 to 45y, excluding silvers) shall be registered on the EXPERIMENTAL REGISTER.

4 REFERENCE REGISTER
All cats of Siamese appearance (i.e. Siamese type with blue eyes and colour restricted to the points) which have in their pedigrees within five generations any breeds other than the above shall be registered on the REFERENCE REGISTER.

This ruling shall take effect from 20 October 1993 and shall not be retrospective. From 20 October 1993 any cat born from parents of any breed not included in group 2 shall be registered on the Reference Register, and so shall their suitable offspring for the required number of generations.

In the case of breeds of different type or coat quality the number of generations shall be increased to twelve when practicable.

Should any further colours of Siamese be developed as a breed (e.g. Smoke Point, Silver Tabby Point etc.) the appropriate cats may be registered on the Siamese EXPERIMENTAL REGISTER at the request of the Siamese Cat Joint Advisory Committee. Those cats already registered on the Reference Register shall then be treated as if they were registered on the Experimental Register.

Note: All Red Point or Cream Point Siamese with one or more Tabby Point or Oriental Tabby parents must be registered as Red or Cream Tabby Points until proved otherwise.

SIAMESE BREED NUMBERS

THE GCCF STANDARD

Seal Point	24	**TORTIE TABBY POINT**	
Blue Point	24a	Seal Tortie Tabby Point	32t1
Chocolate Point	24b	Blue Tortie Tabby Point	32t2
Lilac Point	24c	Chocolate Tortie Tabby Point	32t3
Cinnamon Point	24k	Lilac Tortie Tabby Point	32t4
Caramel Point	24n	Cinnamon Tortie Tabby Point	32t7
Fawn Point	24r	Caramel Tortie Tabby Point	32t8
Red Point	32a	Fawn Tortie Tabby Point	32t9
Cream Point	32c		
		TORTIE POINT	
		Seal Tortie Point	32b1
TABBY POINT		Blue Tortie Point	32b2
Seal Tabby Point	32 1	Chocolate Tortie Point	32b3
Blue Tabby Point	32 2	Lilac Tortie Point	32b4
Chocolate Tabby Point	32 3	Cinnamon Tortie Point	32b7
Lilac Tabby Point	32 4	Caramel Tortie Point	32b8
Red Tabby Point	32 5	Fawn Tortie Point	32b9
Cream Tabby Point	32 6		
Cinnamon Tabby Point	32 7		
Caramel Tabby Point	32 8		
Fawn Tabby Point	32 9		

GENERAL TYPE STANDARD The Siamese Cat should be a beautifully balanced animal with head, ears and neck carried on a long svelte body, supported on fine legs and feet with a tail in proportion. The head and profile should be wedge-shaped, neither round nor pointed. The mask complete, connected by tracings with the ears (except in kittens), the eyes a clear brilliant blue; expression alert and intelligent.

HEAD – Long and well proportioned, carried upon an elegant neck, with width between the

Sup. Gr. Ch. & UK Gr. Pr. Pannaduloa Blazer: The Siamese is judged by the official Breed Standard, which is a written blueprint for the breed.

Photo: Paddy Cutts

The GCCF Standard General type Standard describes the Siamese at as being: "a beautifully balanced animal, with head, ears and neck carried on a long, svelte body, supported on fine legs, with a tail in proportion."

Brenda Watson.

ears, narrowing in perfectly straight lines to a fine muzzle, with straight profile, strong chin and level bite.

EARS – Rather large and pricked, wide at base.

EYES – Oriental in shape and slanting towards the nose, but with width between.

BODY, LEGS AND FEET – Body medium in size, long and svelte. Legs proportionately slim, hind legs slightly higher than front legs, feet small and oval. The body, legs and feet should all be in proportion, giving the whole a well-balanced appearance.

TAIL – Long and tapering, free from any kink.

POINTS – Mask, ears, feet and tail dense and clearly defined colour, matching in basic colour on all points, showing clear contrast between points and body colour. Mask complete and (except in kittens) connected by tracings with the ears.

COAT – Very short and fine in texture, glossy and close-lying.

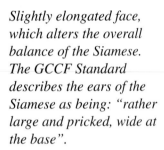

Slightly elongated face, which alters the overall balance of the Siamese. The GCCF Standard describes the ears of the Siamese as being: "rather large and pricked, wide at the base".

Elongated ears making the Siamese appear to have a very long head.

Ears held in the 'bonneted' position.

Drawings: Brenda Watson.

COLOURS – As per individual colour standards, any shading to appear on back and sides. Bib, chest and belly to be pale.

SCALE OF POINTS
TYPE (50)

Head	15
Ears	5
Eye Shape and Setting	5
Body	15
Legs and Feet	5
Tail	5

COLOUR AND COAT (50)

Eye Colour	15
Points Colour	10
Body Colour	15
Coat Texture	10
Total	100

Withhold all Awards for : White toe/s.

Correct jaw position.

Incorrect: Undershot jaw.

Drawings: Brenda Watson.

Withhold Certificates or First Prizes in Kitten Open Classes for:
1. Any abnormality of bite or very weak chin
2. Cast in one or both eyes
3. Eyes tinged with green or green-rimmed
4. Incorrect colour on nose leather or paw pads
5. Any defect as listed in the preface to the GCCF Standards of Points booklet.

Faults:
1. A complete hood, i.e. no contrast on head
2. Lack of contrast between body and points.

SEAL POINT (24)
EYES: Clear, brilliant deep blue.
POINTS: Clearly defined dense Seal brown. Colour to match on all points and showing clear contrast between points and body colour.
BODY: Cream, shading gradually into pale warm fawn on the back. Kittens pale in colour.
NOSE LEATHER AND PAW PADS: Seal brown.

Additional Faults:
1. Any shade of black or grey in body or points colour
2. Heavily marked body (e.g. stripes, spots or bars).

BLUE POINT (24a)
EYES: Clear, bright, vivid blue.
POINTS: Light blue. The mask, ears, legs, paws and tail to be the same colour. The ears should not be darker than the other points.

Small double kink.

TOP LEFT: The GCCF Standard describes the Siamese tail as being " Long, tapering, and free from any kink".

CENTRE: A bobbed tail.

TOP RIGHT: Small kink: The kink that is sometimes seen in Siamese pedigree lines is due to genetic inheritance. It is a trait that is sometimes asked for by pet owners because it is a very definite Siamese trait – a charming reminder of one of the most well-known Siamese legends.

BODY: Glacial white, shading gradually into blue on back, the same cold tone as the points, but of a lighter colour.
NOSE LEATHER AND PAW PAD: Blue.

Additional faults:
1. Cream, fawn or self blue body colours
2. Lack of tracings to the mask.

CHOCOLATE POINT (24b)
EYES: Clear, bright, vivid blue.
POINTS: Milk chocolate; the mask, ears and tail to be the same colour. The ears should not be darker than the other points. Legs paler than the other points should not be too heavily penalised.
BODY: Ivory all over. Shading, if at all, to be colour of points.
NOSE LEATHER AND PAW PADS: Chocolate or pinkish chocolate.

Hooked tail. *Curly tail.* *Long double kink.*

Drawings: Brenda Watson.

Additional Withholding Faults:
Withhold certificates for
1. Cold, dark points colour
2. Heavily shaded bodies.
Withhold First Prizes in Kitten Open Classes for: Cold dark points colour. Pale patchy points in kittens should not be penalised.

LILAC POINT (24c)
EYES: Clear, vivid blue.
POINTS: Pinkish grey.
BODY: Off-white (magnolia) shading, if any, to tone with points.
NOSE LEATHER AND PAW PADS: Pinkish/faded lilac.

Additional Fault: Heavy ringing on tail in adult cats.

TABBY POINT (32)
GENERAL POINTS COLOUR: Same colour essential but varied tones acceptable, i.e. Seal, Blue, Chocolate, Lilac, Red and Cream, accepting that markings on legs will be paler in tone. The standard for Tortie Tabby Points is given below.
GENERAL BODY COLOUR: Pale coat, preferably free from body markings, including back of head and neck, and conforming to recognised Siamese standard for the particular colour of points. Some body shading to be expected, especially in Seal Tabby Points.
EARS – Solid, no stripes. Thumb marks as clear as possible, though these will be less apparent in Blue Tabby Points.
NOSE LEATHER AND PAW PADS: Conforming to recognised Siamese Standard for the particular colour of points or pink.

Tabby Point: Some body shading is to be expected in Seal Tabby Points. However, this amount of shading would be regarded as a withholding fault.

Photo: Paddy Cutts.

MASK: Clearly defined stripes, especially around the eyes and nose. Distinct markings on cheeks, darkly spotted whisker pads.
EYES: Brilliant clear blue. The lids to be dark rimmed or toning with the points.
LEGS: Clearly defined varied sized broken stripes. Solid markings on back of hind legs.
TAIL: Many varied sized clearly defined rings ending in a solid tip.

Additional Fault: Insufficiently ringed tail.

TORTIE TABBY POINT (Breed 32t)
As above with the following exceptions:
EARS: Mottled.
NOSE LEATHER AND PAW PADS: Mottled.
TAIL: As above but mottling permissible.
POINTS: Patched with red and/or cream over Tabby pattern. Distribution of patching on points immaterial. (As in Standards for Tortie Points.)
Note: These cats usually resemble Tabby Points rather than Tortie Points.

RED POINT (32a)
EYES: Bright, intense blue.
POINTS: Mask, ears and tail, bright reddish gold, legs and feet slightly paler in colour. Barring and striping on mask, legs and tail is permissible.
BODY: White, shading to apricot on the back and sides.
NOSE LEATHER AND PAW PADS: Pink.

Note: 'Freckles' may occur on nose, pads, lips, eyelids and ears. Slight freckling in a mature cat should not be penalised.

SEAL TORTIE POINT (32b1)
EYES: Bright, intense blue.
POINTS: Seal brown patched or mingled at random with varying shades of red; any large

areas of red may show some striping. Points need not be evenly broken but each point must show some break in colour no matter how small. Presence or absence of a blaze is immaterial.
BODY: Fawn, shading unevenly to warm brown and apricot on the back and sides.
NOSE LEATHER AND PAW PADS: Seal brown and/or pink.

Additional Fault: Any one point showing complete absence of broken colour.

BLUE TORTIE POINT (32b2)
EYES: Bright, intense blue.
POINTS: Blue patched or mingled at random with varying shades of cream; any large areas of cream may show some striping. Points need not be evenly broken but each point must show some break in colour no matter how small. Presence or absence of a blaze is immaterial.
BODY: White, shading unevenly to pale blue and pale cream on the back and sides.
NOSE LEATHER AND PAW PADS: Blue and/or pink.

Additional Fault: Any one point showing complete absence of broken colour.

CHOCOLATE TORTIE POINT (32b3)
EYES: Bright, intense blue.
POINTS: Milk chocolate patched or mingled at random with varying shades of red; any large areas of red may show some striping. Points need not be evenly broken but each point must show some break in colour no matter how small. Presence or absence of a blaze is immaterial.
BODY: Ivory, shading unevenly to pale chocolate and apricot on the back and sides.
NOSE LEATHER AND PAW PADS: Chocolate and/or pink.

Additional Fault: Any one point showing complete absence of broken colour.

LILAC TORTIE POINT (32b4)
EYES: Bright, intense blue.
POINTS: Lilac patched or mingled at random with varying shades of cream; any large areas of cream may show some striping. Points need not be evenly broken but each point must show some break in colour no matter how small. Presence or absence of a blaze is immaterial.
BODY: Off-white, shading unevenly to pale lilac and pale cream on the back and sides.
NOSE LEATHER AND PAW PADS: Pinkish/faded lilac and/or pink.

Additional Fault: Any one point showing complete absence of broken colour.

CREAM POINT (32c)
EYES: Bright, intense blue.
POINTS: Mask, ears and tail cream. Legs and feet slightly paler in colour. Barring and striping on mask, legs and tail is permissible.
BODY: White, shading to cream on the back and sides.
NOSE LEATHER AND PAW PADS: Pink.

Note: 'Freckles' may occur on nose, pads, lips, eyelids and ears. Slight freckling in a mature cat should not be penalised.

Additional Fault: Points: hot cream.

The introduction of the new colour Siamese has led to the development of a revised Standard of Points for them. While very similar in some areas, there are also some small differences so the whole standard is shown here for reference. At some point in the future, it is likely that the two will be brought in line, as has happened with other breeds.

PRELIMINARY STANDARD OF POINTS FOR:
CINNAMON, CARAMEL & FAWN POINT SIAMESE
AND THEIR ASSOCIATED COLOUR VARIETIES

The Siamese Cat should be a beautifully balanced animal with head, ears and neck carried on a long svelte body, supported on fine legs and feet with a tail in proportion. The head and profile should be wedge-shaped, neither round nor pointed. The eyes should be a clear brilliant blue, the expression alert and intelligent.

HEAD: Long and well proportioned, with width between the ears, narrowing in perfectly straight lines to a fine muzzle, with straight profile, strong chin and level bite, carried upon an elegant neck.

EARS: Rather large and pricked, wide at the base, set so as to follow the lines of the wedge.

EYES: Oriental in shape and slanting towards the nose, but with width between. They should not be deep-set. The haw should not cover more than the corner of the eye.

BODY & LEGS: Medium in size, body long and svelte, legs proportionately slim, hind legs slightly higher than front legs, feet small and oval. The body, legs and feet should all be in proportion, giving the whole a well balanced appearance.

TAIL: Long and tapering, free from any kink.

POINTS: Mask, ears, feet and tail dense and clearly defined colour, matching in basic colour on all points, showing clear contrast between points and body colour. Mask complete and (except in kittens) connected by tracings with the ears.

COAT: Very short and fine in texture, glossy and close-lying. Colours as per individual colour standards, any shading to appear on back and sides. Bib, chest and belly to be pale.

Scale of Points: As original Standard.

GENERAL SIAMESE WITHHOLDING FAULTS
Withhold all Awards for : White markings anywhere.

Withhold Certificates or First Prizes in Kitten Open Classes for:
1. Any abnormality of bite or very weak chin
2. Cast in one or both eyes
3. Eyes tinged with green or green-rimmed
4. Incorrect colour on nose or paw leather
5. A complete hood i.e. no contrast on head.
6. Any defect as listed in the preface to the GCCF Standard of Points booklet.
Faults: Lack of contrast between body and points.

CINNAMON POINT (24k)
EYES: Brilliant intense blue, the deeper the better.
POINTS: Warm cinnamon brown. The legs may be slightly paler than the other points.
BODY: Ivory. Shading, if any, to tone with the points.
NOSE LEATHER AND EYE RIMS: Cinnamon brown.
PAW PADS: Pink to cinnamon brown.

Withhold Merit Certificates for:
1. Pale and/or dull eye colour
2. Cold points or body colour
3. General Siamese withholding faults.

CARAMEL POINT (24n)
EYES: Brilliant intense blue, the deeper the better.
POINTS: Brownish grey, matching on all points although the legs may be slightly paler in tone than the other points.
BODY: Off-white (magnolia). Shading, if any to tone with the points.
NOSE LEATHER, EYE RIMS & PAW PADS: Pinkish grey.

Withhold Merit Certificates for:
1. Pale and/or dull eye colour
2. Points not matching in colour
3. General Siamese withholding faults.

FAWN POINT (24r)
EYES: Brilliant intense blue, the deeper the better.
POINTS: Warm pale rosy mushroom. The legs may be slightly paler than the other points.
BODY: Off-white (magnolia). Shading, if any, to tone with the points.
NOSE LEATHER, EYE RIMS & PAW PADS: Pinkish fawn.

Withhold merit certificates for:
1. Pale and/or dull eye colour
2. Cold points or body colour
3. General Siamese withholding faults.

TABBY POINT (32)
EYES: Brilliant intense blue, the deeper the better.
POINTS: The mask, legs and tail should all show clear tabby markings which should be the same colour on all points, although leg markings may be slighter paler in tone. Paler markings are acceptable in kittens.
MASK: Clearly defined stripes, especially around the eyes and nose, with a clearly defined "M" marking on the forehead, distinct stripes ("ribbons") on the cheeks and darkly spotted whisker pads. The stripes should not extend over the top of the head to form a "hood".
EARS: The edges of the ears should be the same colour as the markings on the mask with a central patch of paler colour resembling a thumb print. These thumb prints may be less apparent in dilute colours and may not be visible in Tortie Tabby Points.
LEGS: Clearly defined varied sized broken stripes. Solid markings on back of hind legs. The

leg markings may be slightly paler in tone than the other points, especially in Red and Cream Tabby Points.

TAIL: Many varied sized, clearly defined rings ending in a solid tip which may show tortie markings in Tortie Tabby Points. The rings should be evident on the top of the tail as well as underneath it and should extend for the entire length of the tail.

BODY: Pale, showing clear contrast with the points as in the equivalent solid-pointed Siamese. Any shading on the body will show the underlying tabby pattern which may be ticked, spotted, mackerel or classic. A Tabby Point should be penalised for shading no more nor less severely than the equivalent solid-pointed Siamese.

Withhold Certificates and First Prizes in Kitten Open Classes for:
1. Pale and/or dull eye colour
2. Lack of clear tabby markings on mask
3. Lack of clear rings on at least half of tail
4. Points not matching in colour
5. General Siamese withholding faults.

CINNAMON TABBY POINT (32 7)
POINTS: clear warm cinnamon brown tabby markings. Nose Leather: cinnamon brown or pink rimmed with cinnamon brown. Eye rims: cinnamon brown. Paw pads: cinnamon brown or pink.
BODY: Ivory. Tabby shading, if any, to tone with the points.

CARAMEL TABBY POINT (32 8)
POINTS: clear brownish-grey tabby markings. Nose Leather: pinkish grey or pink rimmed with pinkish grey. Eye rims: pinkish grey. Paw pads: pinkish grey or pink.
BODY: Off-white (magnolia). Tabby shading, if any to tone with the points.

FAWN TABBY POINT (32 9)
POINTS: clear warm pale rosy mushroom tabby markings. Nose leather: pinkish fawn or pink rimmed with pinkish fawn. Eye rims: pinkish fawn. Paw pads: pinkish fawn or pink.
BODY: Off-white (magnolia). Tabby shading, if any to tone with the points.

CINNAMON TORTIE TABBY POINT (32t7)
POINTS: Clear warm cinnamon brown tabby markings patched and/or mingled at random with shades of red. The ears may be mottled. The distribution and degree of red patching is immaterial.
Nose leather, eye rims and paw pads: cinnamon brown and/or pink.
BODY: Ivory. Tabby shading and tortie patching, if any, to tone with the points.

CARAMEL TORTIE TABBY POINT (32t8)
POINTS: Clear brownish-grey tabby markings patched and/or mingled at random with shades of cream. The ears may be mottled. The distribution and degree of cream patching is immaterial. Nose leather, eye rims and paw pads: pinkish grey and/or pink.
BODY: Off-white (magnolia). Tabby shading and tortie patching, if any, to tone with the points.

FAWN TORTIE TABBY POINT (32t9)
POINTS: Clear warm pale rosy mushroom tabby markings patched and/or mingled at random with shades of cream. The ears may be mottled. The distribution and degree of cream patching is immaterial. Nose leather, eye rims and paw pads: pinkish fawn and/or pink.
BODY: Off-white (magnolia). Tabby shading and tortie patching, if any, to tone with the points.

TORTIE POINT (32b)
EYES: Brilliant intense blue, the deeper the better.
POINTS: The base colour is patched and/or mingled at random with varying shades of red or cream; any large areas of red or cream may show some striping. Points need not be evenly broken but each point must show some break in colour no matter how small; broken pad colour constitutes a break in colour on that leg. Presence or absence of a blaze is immaterial.
BODY: Pale, showing clear contrast with the points as in the equivalent solid-pointed Siamese. Any shading will show patching or mingling and a Tortie Point should be penalised for shading no more nor less severely than the equivalent solid-pointed Siamese.
NOSE LEATHER, EYE RIMS & PAW PADS: In accordance with the base colour and/or pink.

Withhold Certificates and First Prizes in Kitten Open Classes for:
1. Pale and/or dull eye colour
2. Any one point showing complete absence of broken colour
3a. Black in points or body colour in Seal Tortie Points
3b. Dark blue in points or body colour in Blue Tortie Points
3c. Cold dark chocolate in points or body colour in Chocolate Tortie Points
3d. Dark lilac in points or body colour in Lilac Tortie Points
3e. Cold points or body colour in Cinnamon or Fawn Tortie Points
4a. Absence of red in mask, ears and tail in adult Seal, Chocolate or Cinnamon Tortie Points
4b. Hot cream in points or body colour in Blue or Lilac Tortie Points
5. General Siamese withholding faults.

CINNAMON TORTIE POINT (32b7)
POINTS: Warm cinnamon brown with shades of red.
BODY: Ivory. Shading, if any to tone with the points.

CARAMEL TORTIE POINT (32b8)
POINTS: Brownish grey with shades of cream.
BODY: Off-white (magnolia). Shading, if any to tone with the points.

FAWN TORTIE POINT (32b9)
POINTS: Warm pale rosy mushroom with shades of cream.
BODY: Off-white (magnolia). Shading, if any to tone with the points.

Chapter Seven

THE AMERICAN SYSTEM

The interest in breeding and showing Siamese extends around the world. Sometimes British judges are invited to be the guests of American cat clubs, whose shows are sanctioned by one of the many cat associations found within the USA. If more than one cat association is hosting a British judge on a particular trip, it will become evident that the Siamese cat is treated differently by each association.

EARLY AMERICAN CAT SHOWS

The showing of cats has a very long history in the USA, with cat shows being held in the last century for another breed, the Coon cats of Maine. However, in 1895, it is reported that an Englishman by the name of Mr J. T. Hyde, who had visited the Crystal Palace show in England, organised a similar event in New York, in the Madison Square Garden. To this day, there is still an annual show run on the same site. English cats were sent over for some of the early shows in Chicago and New York, and this so much worried the US Government of the day that they imposed a duty equivalent to twenty per cent of the value of the cat. As there were no associations in the late nineteenth century for registering cats, their early registration and that of their American-born progeny became the responsibility of the precursor of what is now known as the US Department of Agriculture. These records were listed on an annual basis by breed and owner.

EARLY AMERICAN SIAMESE

There are varying reports as to the date when Siamese arrived in the USA. It is generally agreed, as listed in the first volume of the Beresford Cat Club stud book and register, issued in July 1900, that two of the earliest arrivals were Lockehaven Siam and Sally Ward. No other details were given:

Volume I   July 1899 - July 1900
138. Seal male: Lockehaven Siam (imp).
139. Chocolate female: Sally Ward (imp).

Both cats belonged to Mrs Clinton Locke of Chicago and she later sold the Chocolate Point Siamese to Mrs Spencer of Ohio.

Volume II 1900 - 1901
308. Chocolate male: Netherlands Tilu (imp), b 1897, breeder Mrs Sutherland.
309. Chocolate female: Netherlands Ma (imp), b 1897, breeder Mrs Sutherland.
These two cats were purchased by Mrs Clinton Locke from Lady Marcus Beresford

Volume III   1901 - 1903
510. Seal male (Neuter): Chone, b 1899, breeder Mrs A.H. Hoag.
532. Seal female: Angora Rowdy (imp), b 1894.
533. Seal male: Angora Sikh, b 1899, breeder Mrs C. Reiss.
708 Seal male: Madison California, b (no date given), breeder Mrs A.H. Hoag

It is recorded that the first Siamese Champions in America were Madison California and Sally Ward.

Louis Wain, who was President and Chairman of the UK National Cat Club, later went to work for the Randolph Hearst Newspaper empire between 1907-1910. At one all-breed show in 1908 he made the Siamese Lockehaven Elsa, Best in Show.

Like the early British Siamese fanciers, the American breeders found it hard to acclimatise the Siamese, but it is recorded there was more success within California. This resulted in more Siamese being bred and shown in this area.

AMERICAN CAT ORGANISATIONS

There are many registration associations in the USA, and all of these have different registration policies and written standards with reference to Siamese and, of course, show rules.

THE AMERICAN CAT ASSOCIATION
The very first registration body to be established became known as the American Cat Association (ACA). It was formed in 1899 to maintain cat registration records, license cat shows and charter cat clubs. It was duly incorporated in 1904. The ACA is still very much in existence today, although it is small by other American registration body standards. Shows run under ACA rules can be found in the southern California area.

The ACA does not allow declawed Siamese to be shown in any of its classes.

THE CAT FANCIERS' ASSOCIATION
The Cat Fanciers' Association (CFA) was formed in 1906 by a breakaway group from the American Cat Association and incorporated in 1919. In these early days of existence, registrations across the few known breeds used to total less than 100 cats annually.

Its proud claim is that it now has the world's largest registry of pedigree cats and registrations in the 1993-1994 show year totalled more than 75,000 cats across 36 different breeds in four continents around the world. With such large numbers of registrations, this association has an equally large number of member clubs which totals nearly 650. The annual number of cat shows held under its rules totals nearly 400.

The CFA does not allow declawed Siamese to be shown in any of its classes.

THE CAT FANCIERS' FEDERATION
The Cat Fanciers' Federation was also formed in the early part of this century, having also commenced existence as a breakaway group. With 90 member clubs, this association sponsors around 30 shows in the New England and Midwest part of the States.

In common with their heritage from the early part of this century, it can be concluded that these older associations share a fairly common hierarchical structure. Cat fanciers are members of clubs which are run in accordance with the rules of their governing associations, who each have an elected board of directors. Each member club elects a delegate who attends either bi-annual or

Sir Chang: An American traditional type Tabby Point, known as an Apple Head.

Photo: Marjorie Griswold.

annual association meetings on its behalf, and who is empowered to vote on policy matters covering the association's constitution and show rules.

The CFF does not allow declawed Siamese to be shown in any of its classes.

THE AMERICAN CAT FANCIERS ASSOCIATION

The American Cat Fanciers Association Inc. was formed in 1955 by a group of Cat Fanciers in the Dallas/Fort Worth area of Texas. This group had several skills to fall back on in the creation of this organisation, such as business management, legal expertise and knowledge of general cat fancy matters.

The aim was to develop "greater flexibility in the development of cats, the activities of cat lovers and greater freedom for growth and harmony with contemporary needs of the individual breeders and the broadening horizons of the Cat Fancy at large".

Once the policies of this democratic organisation became known to cat breeders and fanciers, many decided to become members of this new association, seeing that there was room for "the advancement of the feline".

Two very different features of membership were the requirements to renew membership on an annual basis, and members voting by mail for association officials and changes in association rules. In common with the other three associations, there is an elected board of directors.

What other fancies refer to as The Standard of Points became known as the Standards of Perfection for each breed. It was down to the specific breeders in each region to check, accept or reject these Standards of Perfection. Once agreement had been reached, they could only be changed with the approval of the membership of the Breed Section concerned.

This registration body pioneered some exciting developments in the American showing scene. They introduced the innovative double, triple, quadruple championship and grand championship titles. They also considered the status of the "altered" (neutered) cat, and for the first time in the history of the American Cat Fancy, altered cats were given their own championship classification. Even today, the alters compete in Championship shows under the same rules as entire cats.

What is most interesting is the fact that the ACFA was the first registration body to introduce the "multiple" ring Championship show, which has now been adopted by all the other associations. Until the advent of the four ring show, the usual format of an American show consisted of "one Allbreed Ring and one Specialty Ring".

The ACFA then built on the success of their innovative style of show management and introduced the winning formula of the now popular Back-to-Back show which has 8 to 10 rings held over a weekend. They were also the first body to hold written examinations for trainee judges to achieve their licence. Other firsts included "a training programme for 'trainee' judges and official Judges' Schools", as well as special breed seminars for all interested parties, including judges.

The ACFA allows declawed Siamese to be shown in any of its classes.

THE AMERICAN ASSOCIATION OF CAT ENTHUSIASTS
The American Association of Cat Enthusiasts (AACE) is the newest association of all, being formed in 1993. Membership is rapidly growing and in two years of operation, 15 shows are being held each year across America from west to east, from Arizona to New York.

This association allows both clawed and declawed Siamese to be shown, but actively discourages the declawing of Siamese.

THE TRADITIONAL CAT ASSOCIATION
There is another organisation worth mentioning, which is devoted to the Siamese cat (among other breeds) but which is not a registration body. It is known as The Traditional Cat Association which was founded by cat lover Diana L. Fineran. The motto of this organisation is "To Protect, Preserve, Perpetuate, and Promote the Traditional Cat".

Members who are devoted to preserving the heritage and type of the original Siamese imports breed what is known as "Apple Head" Siamese. Traditional Siamese can be shown in special shows held by the Traditional Cat Society. In one of the more recent shows held in 1992, the National Show, one of their members, Diane Dunaway of San Diego, California achieved Best Seal Point Siamese and Best Chocolate Point Siamese.

THE INTERNATIONAL CAT ASSOCIATION
The second largest registration body in the world was formed initially as a breakaway group from the ACFA in 1976 and it became known as The International Cat Association (TICA), which is based in Harlingen, Texas.

In common with the cat fancier's increasing knowledge in feline husbandry and different breeds, an interest in feline genetics had become especially widespread following the 1971 publication of what is now regarded as the most comprehensive book on the subject, Roy Robinson's *Genetics for Cat Breeders*. So apart from maintaining the ACFA individual membership rules, TICA spearheaded a very novel philosophy with their registration policies being based on well-researched genetic premises.

Essentially, cats are registered according to their genotype, that is their genetic make-up, but TICA's rules allow them to be shown according to their phenotype, that is by how they look.

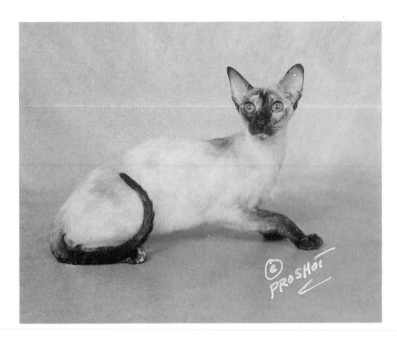

Sup. Gr. Ch. JoRene Rantex: Tortie Point, bred and owned by Irene B. Brounstein.

Photo: Proshot.

Sup. Gr. Ch. JoRene Tearisol: Seal Lynx Point, bred and owned by Irene B. Brounstein.

Photo: Proshot.

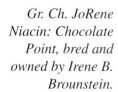
Gr. Ch. JoRene Niacin: Chocolate Point, bred and owned by Irene B. Brounstein.

Gr. Ch. JoRene Prozac: Seal Lynx Point, bred and owned by Irene B. Brounstein.

*(American)
Ch. Gotiers
Gelee
Lavande, a
Lilac Point
Siamese.*

*Photo:
Pelletier and
Goterch.*

Clubs run according to TICA rules number approximately 400 across four continents, with approximately 250 TICA annual cat shows.

TICA allows declawed Siamese to be shown in any of its classes.

THE CLASSIFICATION OF SIAMESE

With each association being formed for different reasons, it is not surprising that the Siamese breed is treated very differently in matters of registration.

These differences extend to the registration of Siamese, which may include other Siamese-type related breeds such as Balinese, Colourpoint Shorthair and Javanese (the long-hair version of the Colorpoint) within their pedigrees. Other Siamese-type related breeds which may appear in pedigrees of Siamese and influence their registration include the Oriental Shorthair and the Oriental Longhair (UK name, Angora). These cats are not pointed in different colours; they are coloured all over and can be found in a wide range of colours and patterns.

The CFA only recognise Siamese in the four basic pointed colours, seal, blue, chocolate and lilac. Siamese showing other colours or pattern conformation such as seal, blue, chocolate and lilac lynx (tabby) points, tortie points, tortie lynx points, red points and cream points are referred to as Colorpoints by the CFA.

The other registration associations, the ACA, CFF and ACFA, differ from the CFA with reference to Siamese that are produced from Siamese type related breeds.

The ACA, CFF and ACFA make no distinction between Colorpoints and Siamese. However, Siamese derived from Oriental breeding or any Siamese with longhaired antecedents are not recommended for use within Siamese breeding programmes.

In TICA Siamese are accepted for Championship status as one of a large number of breed groups, currently numbering 40 different breeds. Siamese/Oriental Shorthair/Balinese/Oriental Longhair hybrids or variants may be shown with the parental breed they resemble and these are considered as one "Breed Group". Their registration numbers will indicate that the Siamese will have other breeds in its pedigree.

The AACE recognise what the CFA terms Colorpoints as part of the Siamese breed. They will also allow a cat that can be defined as a "shorthaired" Balinese (in the UK this would be termed a Balinese Variant), which has one or more long haired ancestors in its pedigree, to be shown as a Siamese. However, Orientals are recognised as being separate, and Siamese produced from Oriental parents are not allowed to be shown as Siamese.

SHOWING IN THE USA

Space does not allow us to record all the information relating to showing and Siamese Breed Standards for every Association – it could easily be subject to a book in its own right. However, to give readers an American flavour, salient points relating to the Siamese breed have been taken from TICA rules together with their Siamese Breed Standard of 1991.

For Championship competition in TICA there are fifteen Divisions, broken down by 'Color' (three Divisions) and 'Pattern' (five Divisions). The three categories of colors are: Traditional, Intermediate and Pointed.

The Siamese breed is classified under the colour 'Pointed' category, for example, seal point, blue point. The term "point" is part of the colour name. The five pattern divisions are: Solid, Tortoiseshell, Tabby, Silver/Smoke and Particolor.

The Siamese breed is, therefore, able to compete in the five pointed competitive divisions: Pointed Solid, Pointed Tortoiseshell, Pointed Tabby, Pointed Silver/Smoke and Pointed Particolor

At shows Siamese cats are judged at a number of different levels, scoring points according to their placing at each level. They can also be judged in an all-breed (AB) ring or a Specialty (SP) ring, and often both types of ring are available at a particular single show. They are judged first on colour, then on breed, then on division, with the best going on to the Finals.

THE TICA BREED STANDARD

HEAD 24 points: Profile 6; Wedge 6; Chin 4; Ears 6; Minimum width between eyes 2.

EYES 12 points: Size and Shape 6; Set (Slant) 6.

BODY 40 points: Size, Structure, Balance 12; Musculature 12; Neck 3; Legs 4; Feet 3; Tail 6.

COAT 10 points: Texture 4; Shortness 3; Closeness 3.

COLOR 16 points: Body 6; Point 6; Eye 4.

RECOGNISED CATEGORY/DIVISIONS/COLORS-: Pointed Category, all Divisions, all Traditional colors.

GENERAL DESCRIPTION The ideal Siamese is a svelte, graceful, refined cat of medium size with long tapering lines. It is in excellent physical condition, very strong, lithe and muscular.
THE HEAD is a long tapering wedge, of medium size, in good proportion to the body. The wedge is created by straight lines extending from the nose to the tips of the ears, forming a triangle, with no break at the whiskers. When whiskers are smoothed back, the underlying bone structure is apparent. There is no less than the width of an eye between the eyes. Allowance must be made for jowls in the stud cat. The desirable profile may be seen as a long flat, straight line extending from the top of the head to the tip of the nose OR, as two

LEFT: Sup. Gr. Ch. JoRene Salivart: Seal Point, bred and owned by Irene B. Brounstein.

Photo: Proshot.

BELOW: Gr. Ch. JoRene Natabec: Seal Lynx Point, bred and owned by Irene B. Brounstein.

Gr. Ch. Jorene Neocurb: Chocolate Tortie Point, bred and owned by Irene B. Brounstein.

flat planes with a very slight change in the angle midway over the eyes. There should be no dip at the nose. A straight line is seen from the tip of the nose to the tip of the chin.

THE EARS are strikingly large, but in proportion to the head. The ears are set so as to be in a continuing line with the wedge, neither too hard not too flared.

THE EYES are almond-shaped, of medium size, set in an Oriental slant toward the nose so that a projection of the line from the inner eye corner through the outer eye corner would extend to the center of the base of the ear.

THE BODY is long, tubular, hard and muscular giving the sensation of solid weight without excessive bulk. The overall body structure is finely boned and well muscled (as a swimmer). Males, in general, are proportionately larger than females.

THE TAIL is long and thin, tapering to a fine point, adding to the overall appearance of length.

THE LEGS are long, slim, and fine-boned in proportion to the overall size of the cat. The hind legs are higher than the front legs. The feet are small and dainty, oval in shape.

While the breed is considered "medium" in size, balance and proportion are to be considered of greater consequence. The cat should "fit together". If it is extreme in one part, all parts should be extreme to retain balance.

WITHHOLD ALL AWARDS-:
See Show Rules, ARTICLE SIXTEEN for rules governing penalties/disqualifications applying to all cats.

With any other registration body, there are rules regarding the withholding of awards, as well as penalties that can be imposed, together with disqualification. If you are unsure about the interpretation of these rules, consult your registration body.

Chapter Eight

SHOWING YOUR SIAMESE

TO SHOW OR NOT TO SHOW?

Some owners buy their pets with the intention of showing them. Many other people start their show career by taking their beloved pet along "just to see what happens". Success at your first show can be very exciting and the pleasure of displaying and discussing your rosettes with friends will provide many hours of happy conversation. However, before you decide to show you should evaluate your pet's chances of winning. Showing is not a cheap hobby, and losing is not as much fun as winning, so you should certainly check some basic points before deciding to enter.

You must also make sure you understand the rules and regulations of the governing bodies responsible for the registration and organisation of such events in your country, and then follow them.

IS YOUR CAT GOOD ENOUGH?

You should find out if your pet has any faults, both obvious and not-so-obvious. Examples include a kinked tail, a squint, "battle-damage", such as scars or torn ears, protruding sternum (breastbone), wrong number of testicles (monorchid or cryptorchid), undershot or overshot jaws, flat skull or flat chest, or being undersized for the age of the cat. If you are in any doubt, you should consult an experienced breeder or your vet.

Basically, if your cat is fit, healthy and has no evident faults, there is no reason not to show. However, to decide if there is a chance of success you need to know whether your cat is a good example of the breed, and this means making a comparison with the Standard of Points. Understanding how it is applied does need some experience. For example, how wide is a 'wide' head? It is better to seek guidance, and the best source of advice is likely to be the breeder of the kitten, who will be interested to know that you are considering showing your pet. If you decide, with consultation, to enter a show, you will find it initially seems very complex. Once you understand how it works, it is actually quite simple, and many people have discovered that their new pet has made them many new friends, and introduced them to an interesting hobby as well.

ENTERING SHOWS

The simplest way to find out which shows are available is to obtain a list from the governing association. You will also find show advertisements in specialist cat publications and you can contact individual clubs directly. If you are a member of a club then you will automatically be sent details of their own show.

When you have decided on one or more possible shows to enter, you need to write to the Show Manager to obtain a copy of the show schedule which contains all the information you will need,

The National Cat Club Show: This annual event, staged in the UK, is a magnet for many foreign cat fanciers. *Photo: Paddy Cutts.*

including an entry form. Usually entries close six to eight weeks before the show, so you should write earlier rather than later, enclosing a large stamped addressed envelope.

Consider the schedule and select the Open class for your cat. There is only one Open Class you can enter (except for Champions and Premiers who can enter the Grand Class), so you only have to find the right one. Firstly, find the Siamese section of the schedule. Then find the right sub-division.

Cats for cats over nine months and not neutered.

Kittens for kittens older than fourteen weeks and under nine months old.

Neuters for cats and kittens that are neutered cats.

Note that age is always "on show day", not when you enter the show.

Within the right section, find the class that describes your cat (e.g. Seal Point) and where appropriate, the sex (e.g. Seal Point male). Record the number of the class (all classes are entered by number) in the "Open Class" part of the show entry form.

If your cat is in the Assessment Class, you must also include a copy of the Standard of Points with your entry form.

Then choose other classes. Most shows include three classes in the entry fee in addition to the Open, and in some cases you can pay extra if you want to enter more than three. Different shows vary, so you must read the schedule carefully.

The main extra classes are called 'Miscellaneous' and you need to ensure you choose from the Section that is for Siamese. The definition of each class is given in the front of the schedule and you will probably find that there are several you can enter. Which you choose is purely personal, but the choice of Judge is most often used as a major factor by experienced exhibitors.

As well as Miscellaneous classes, there are also Club Classes – these are listed separately from Miscellaneous – and sometimes other classes such as 'Signs of the Zodiac' or Charity classes. All of them count towards the total classes you enter unless the schedule states otherwise. The numbers of these extra classes must be put in the appropriate box on the entry form.

The rest of the cat's details must be filled in following exactly the details on the registration slip. Be careful to note spaces and spellings correctly – some apparent mis-spellings are actually correct, as breeders use very strange names for some of their cats. If you make an error, you could receive a letter from GCCF or even be disqualified – more information on this is given in the schedule.

SHOW PREPARATION

Between entering for a show and the show day itself there are two areas of preparation. The first is to ensure your Siamese looks its best for the show and the second is to make sure that you have all the equipment that you will need on the day itself.

Generally speaking, the Siamese is an easy breed to prepare. Provided you have been following the advice on health and grooming, you should have no major additional tasks. However, you should monitor your Siamese carefully in the run-up to show day, always watching for problems – has the cat been in a fight and received scratches, for example, or are there signs of any eye infection?

About a week before the show you should check the condition of the coat. If it is greasy, or there are signs of stud tail in an entire male, then you should consider bathing the cat. You may want to do daily brushing, particularly in hot weather, to remove excess fur, and the use of a chamois leather or silk scarf will help to keep a good, glossy shine to the coat.

A day before the show, check inside the ears and clean them if necessary. Be careful not to overdo this, or you could make them appear red which could lead to possible rejection of your cat at vetting-in.

Show equipment is quite simple to obtain, and most people get the basics in advance, so that they are not panicking on show day. The basic items you will need are: litter tray and litter; water and food bowls; blankets for your cat to sit on; ribbon or white elastic (to hold a tally round your cat's neck if required).

In the UK at all GCCF shows (except the Supreme Show) all these items must be white. This is because the Judge actually goes to the pen to judge the cat, and to preserve anonymity each pen should look the same. At shows where ring judging is operated, they can be of any colour you choose and it is usual to decorate the pen as well.

You will want to take a cat-safe disinfectant to clean the pen before putting your cat into it, for extra safety, although the pens are cleaned between shows. You will also want grooming items for putting a final polish on the coat and a current vaccination certificate as required in the show rules. Don't forget a litter scoop in case you need it!

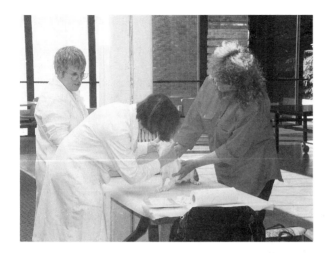

"Vetting-in" at the Siamese Cat Association Show – a nerve-wracking experience for the cat's owner.

Photo: Sally Franklin.

Judge John Shewbridge with his steward, Di Brown, assessing Shades Monsieur Jacques, a Chocolate Point.

Photo: Sally Franklin.

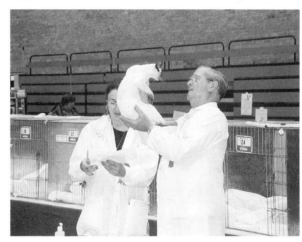

Rosie Meekings gives Gr. Pr. Rantipole Vandal, a Seal Tabby Point, a congratulatory hug.

Photo: Sally Franklin.

For Assessment classes you should take a copy of the Standard of Points to place at the top of your pen, if there is not one already in place. A Judge will not judge an Assessment stage Siamese without this.

ENTRY TO THE SHOW HALL

Make sure you leave in time on the day, allowing time to find a strange venue. Sometimes there is a long walk from the car park and there can be a queue to get into the show hall past "vetting-in". The show schedule will tell you the times to arrive.

On the way in you will be given an envelope containing such items as entry pass and tally with pen number. Your cat will be examined by a Veterinary Surgeon. This can be quite detailed, covering ears, eyes, nose, mouth, coat and general condition as a minimum, with checks to see if a queen is pregnant, if a male has the testicles descended correctly or if there are any defects or abnormalities.

Hopefully, your cat will be allowed in – rejections at vetting-in are not common. If rejected, you will have to take the cat away or, in some cases, the cat could go to an 'isolation' pen during the day. You will receive an official form stating the reason for rejection and confirming what action you must take. This could mean that your whole household of cats has to be examined by your own vet, who will need to certify them as clear and healthy.

At most shows a vet will remain on duty during the whole day and can reject, at any point, a cat that looks unwell. Whilst this may seem very "heavy-handed", it is for the welfare of all the cats. Even with this support there are exhibitors who will testify that their cat picked up an illness at a show hall, and this is a risk you take when you show.

After vetting-in, you can take your cat and equipment into the show hall. Go to the pen number shown in the details you received on arrival. Read them carefully, because often the class numbers are also given and some novice exhibitors have put their cat in the pen number of their Open class! At the pen, clean it, put in the blankets, litter tray and water bowl and lastly your cat. Take time to reassure your cat, who may burrow under the blankets to hide. This is quite normal and although many cats will relax and end up on top of the blankets later in the day, some will always prefer to avoid the hustle and bustle of the show hall by staying out of sight.

If a 'tally' is supplied, you should tie this to the pen or around your cat's neck, as required by the show. Leave your cat's carrier under the pen. If you are at a show where it is allowed, you should, of course, decorate your pen before putting the cat into it. At all shows, you should check to see it is secure. Because they are dismantled for transportation and re-erected each time, pens can sometimes become loose. If you have any concerns, talk to the show management; don't wait to see if your cat can escape. Sadly many owners today try to put food and water bowls at the back of the pen, to avoid any possible poisoning or tampering by other exhibitors. Whilst not common, there are definitely recorded cases of poisoning at cat shows. Also, you should keep an eye on your cat during the day and as a good neighbour watch for any suspicious behaviour or evident tampering with other cats. If you see anything, report it to the Show Manager immediately. Hopefully, none of this will apply to you and you can settle back and enjoy the day's showing.

AT THE SHOW

During judging of the Open Classes, exhibitors are asked to leave the hall and you should ensure that only blankets, filled litter tray and filled water bowl (no food or food bowl) remains in the pen during this time. You can buy a catalogue, which will show you who your cat is competing against, and you should check that your cat's details are correct in it. The catalogue is an "official" document, used for checking the show as well as for informing exhibitors, and you should inform the Show Manager of any errors or mispellings etc. Judges write the results of the classes on slips of paper which are posted for exhibitors to see. These start appearing during the closed period and are displayed progressively during the day as each class is judged. You go back into the show hall at lunchtime and spend the rest of the day doing one of several things: watching your cat, checking the results board, chatting to friends and to members of the public who want to admire your cat.

As the results are announced, you will receive cards and/or rosettes on the pen confirming the results. At some shows you will have to collect your rosettes yourself (sometimes there is a prize money alternative), using the cards supplied and your vetting-in slip for identification purposes.

If you have been awarded a Certificate this will be placed on the pen towards the end of the day, as the Judges sign the Certificates after they have finished judging. If you entered an Assessment class you will also receive a copy of the Judges' comments about your cat. Some shows have a 'Best In Show' judging at the end, often split into Adult, Kitten and Neuter and then Best Overall Exhibit. These are sometimes judged by a panel sitting at a table and cats are compared with each other to decide the best. This is a very nerve-racking time if your cat is one of the lucky ones chosen and a BIS award is one you will treasure for a very long time.

Many judges will walk round the hall at the end of their judging engagement, talking to exhibitors about their cats. You should never talk to a judge before they finish judging: this could lead to disqualification of your exhibit, as the judge could know it was your cat.

Once the Show Manager announces the show is finished you can remove your cat and equipment from the pen, return to your car and join the queue to leave the car park!

RING JUDGING

The main principle of ring judging is that a cat is taken to the judge who remains in a specific judging area – the 'ring'. Cats are collected by stewards from their pen and moved to pens around the ring from where they are actually judged. As you can imagine, stewards have to be careful not to confuse which cat is which, so it is important to remember to tie your tally round the cat's neck and to label the carrying basket clearly with the pen number

There are two main advantages to ring judging from an exhibitor's point of view. Firstly, you can decorate the pen in any way you like. A minimum level of decoration is probably just your coloured drapes, but many people take time to prepare complex and innovative designs themed around their cat. Also you can display your cats' rosettes and certificates.

The second advantage is that you can watch your cat being judged openly. Of course, you must not identify yourself to the judge at any stage, but you can watch as part of the general audience.

Chapter Nine

SEAL POINT SIAMESE

THE EARLY DAYS

Harrison Weir's Siamese Standard of 1892 for the Royal Cat of Siam described what is now known as the Seal Point Siamese, the first variety of Siamese to gain recognition.

The Rabbit Keeper and Show Reporter was a magazine published in the North of England and the forerunner to the well-known *Fur and Feather*. On November 1st 1888 it reported on the Twentieth Annual Cat Show at the Crystal Palace in London. It said this was the largest cat show ever held up to that time, and had attracted five hundred and twenty-four entries. The comments about the Siamese cats indicated their popularity. The judges were Mr Harrison Weir, Mr Jenner Weir and Mr G. Billett.

The details of the awards in the Any Other Variety Class are interesting: the first prize went to Mrs Lee for her "magnificent Siamese 'Meo', who also won the quaint Wedgwood tea service mounted in silver, presented by the Crystal Palace Company for the best short-haired cat, the National Cat Club's gold medal for the best short-haired cat belonging to a member, the silver medal and the extra prize for the best cat in classes 10 to 19." The second prize went to Mrs Vyvyan: "fine Siamese, colour dull."

From 1890 onwards a few more Siamese were imported into England and subsequently bred with. Details were recorded in the Registers of the National Cat Club, which was formed in 1887 with Harrison Weir as its first President. Some re-appeared later in Volume One of the Registers of the Governing Council of the Cat Fancy, which was started in 1910. Among the early importers and breeders were Lilian Veley, whose brother Mr E. B. Gould had been the Consul in Bangkok and ran a cattery there; Miss Forestier-Walker, daughter of a General and recipient of four cats from the King of Siam; Mrs Vyvyan, who bred one of the earliest Siamese Champions; and Lady Dorothy Nevill, the owner of the first Siamese Harrison Weir ever saw.

Two imports direct from Siam were recorded in the first volume of the Siamese Cat Register:

164 Dick. m., particulars unknown, imported from the King's Palace, Bangkok, b. July 1891. Owner, Mrs Blackwood. Prizes: 3rd C.P. 1895.

211 George of Siam. m., pedigree unknown, br. H.M. The King of Siam. Owner, Mrs Alfred Loder.

In this manner did the hobby of the King of Siam become known!

The first Siamese to win the title of Champion was Wankee, owned by a Mrs Robinson. He was born in Hong Kong on September 28th 1895 and, as already mentioned, possessed a kinked tail. His breeder, Mrs Hastings, recorded his sire's name as Robert and his dam as Mons. In the National Cat Club Stud Book and Register No. Six, his show wins are recorded as 1st Botanic 1900, 2nd Crystal Palace 1900, and 2nd Botanic 1902.

According to the first volume of the Siamese Cat Register, issued by the Siamese Cat Club which was formed in the UK in 1901, he also received a First at the National Cat Club Show in 1898 and two other Firsts with the Westminster Shows of 1899 and 1900. So he certainly became a Champion in 1900.

THE TURN OF THE CENTURY

The frontispiece of the Sixth and Seventh Volumes of the *National Cat Club Stud Book and Register*, which were printed as one volume, claimed that details of Siamese cats had been included from 1900 to 1905, but in reality others born before the turn of the century were also recorded – in Isobel North's handwritten copy of the registers a total of thirteen male Siamese were entered in Volume Six, with fourteen Siamese females including Mrs Vyvyan's own-bred Eve, who became a Champion in 1901. Champion Eve had been born in February 1899 and her owner's name was recorded as Mrs Backhouse. Volume Seven included six male Siamese and only two female Siamese!

In her foreword to Volume Two of the Siamese Cat Register, Mrs Veley referred to different types of Siamese, one having a 'marten-face' type of head. This meant the Siamese had a pointed head accompanied by a slimline fawn-coloured body. She stated that males tended to have the slimline body shape. The other type of Siamese had a much rounder head sitting on a light cream and seal coat covering a more heavy-boned body. This type was more associated with female Siamese.

Already some form of artificial selection was taking place with these newcomers on the scene: it was recorded that there was a distinct preference for the cream-bodied Siamese with dark points. This type of cat was called the Royal Siamese Cat. Breeders were advised not to mate this type with Siamese showing the chocolate coat, as it was thought that this would cause shading on the coats of the resultant kittens.

At the turn of the century a young cat was born who was given the lovely name of Ah Choo. She was bred by Lady Vyvyan, her sire being Tiam O'Shian III and her dam was Polyphema. She was registered as No. 2 in the first volume of the Siamese Cat Register. There were several generations of Tiam O'Shian and they had numbers appended to their names in delightful American fashion.

The first GCCF Stud Book gave details of only three males, Ming, Pukit and Champion Sancho, whilst the first volume of the Siamese Cat Register recorded details of several Siamese who were born between 1900 and 1910.

1911–1920

In the next decade covering the years of the First World War it is all the more remarkable that the variety survived. The first Siamese Cat Register reveals details of several Siamese who were owned by Mr A. M. Shakespear and it appeared they were all registered with the Burnham prefix, followed by their name. Mr Shakespear also showed the results of some of his breeding, as the records of Burnham Tah and Burnham Tree illustrate.

92   Burnham Tah. f, s. Ch. Sancho, d. Carnac Lady, br. Owner, b. June 1st, 1911. Owner, Mr. A. M. Shakespear. Prizes: 1st N.C.C. 1912.

93   Burnham Tree. m, 499 G.C.C. II., s. Burnham Trice, d. Burnham Tah, br. Owner, b. April 15th, 1919. Owner Mr. A. M. Shakespear. Prizes: 2nd S.C.C.C., 3rd Croydon 1920.

Two very well known Siamese cats were Bobolinko and Genifer, who were both owned by Mrs Robinson. These were the parents of the famous litter brothers, Bigabois and Litabois, who were born on September 14th 1918. Looking back it becomes evident that both boys carried the genes for chocolate and blue, for most Chocolate Point and Blue Point lines go back to them.

*Ch. Prestwick
Perak.*

THE TWENTIES

Another famous Champion, known as Bonzo, was born the year of the first Siamese Cat Club
Show in 1924. He appears behind many Siamese lines and the breeder Mrs Greta Hindley, owner
of the famous Prestwick prefix, recorded using him at stud with her queen Kechil. The resultant
kittens were born on June 19th 1925. One of them was given the name of Bonchibois. He was sold
to Miss Busteed for three guineas in July 1925 but sadly he did not live long, dying in August
1925. Greta Hindley recorded that Bonchibois and his litter sister had long tails, light coats and
deep blue eyes. Their mother had a bob-tail.

Greta Hindley used Champion Bonzo again in 1925 and took her queen Prestwick Perak (whom
she described as having the perfect marten head) to him on March 27th 1925. The litter of kittens
was born on May 31st 1925. Out of this litter she kept Prestwick Para who was described as
having "Mask, ears, paws, tail all very dark. Eyes – Good intense blue. Head – Typical wedge-
shaped. Coat – Light and silky. Body – Long and lithe like Perak's. Disposition – Gentle and
affectionate, but independent."

Obviously there were other outstanding Siamese during the era of the 1920s, one of the most
famous being Champion Simzo (Ch. Bonzo's son) who was born on April 3rd 1926. He became a
Champion in record time, obtaining his title at the Siamese Cat Club's Third Championship Show
in 1927. He was used frequently for stud purposes by Greta Hindley and he had a bob-tail. He also
managed to pass on this trait to his kittens, and his second litter of four kittens with Kechil
produced three bob-tails and one long tail. Nevertheless Greta managed to sell her bob-tail kittens
for two guineas each!

Out of this mating appeared Prestwick Mata-Biru who became a Champion and was a lovely
kitten with a long tail. When he became adult his eye colour was recorded as "Very good, deep

Prestwick Penglima Pertama: This Seal Point proved to be very influential in the breeding of Chocolate Points.

bright blue" and his tail was described as "long with slight kink".

Another famous cat of the 1920s was Champion Morgan le Fay. It is recorded that she "swept the board" for prizes at the Siamese Cat Club Show in 1930.

THE THIRTIES

Miss Florence Dixon, who was Ch. Simzo's breeder, bred some other champions including Ch. Bonzette, Ch. Simzo's litter sister, Ch. Simzette and Ch. Pita. She also owned Ch. Simple, whom she bought from Mrs Ellaby, and another famous stud cat of the day, Hoveton Emperor, who had been bred by Mrs Blofeld.

Ch. Simzette was born on April 13th 1927. Her dam was Ch. Simple and her father was Ch. Bonzo. She started her show career at the Siamese Cat Club Show in 1927 when she achieved a 2nd in the 3-6 months female class. Later in the year, at the Croydon show, she won a 1st in her own class, a 1st in pairs with her litter brother, Sibo, and a 1st in teams with Sibo and their mother, Ch. Simple.

Unfortunately Sibo brought back infectious enteritis from that show and it spread right throughout the cattery, killing his mother Ch. Simple. Apparently Simzette confined herself to the airing cupboard whilst the infection raged its course. Sibo also survived, and it was from these two that Miss Dixon's line survived.

Famous progeny from Ch. Simzette were Aouda, Chote, who was born on April 13th 1929, Matapa and Sy Tuan. In 1934, Ch. Simzette had a very bad time during kittening and, according to the January 1937 account in *Cats and Kittens* magazine from Mrs Phyl Wade, "she had one very large kitten which had to be taken from her with instruments (it was born dead), and another which was born later, also dead, and since then she has never bred."

Apparently Miss Dixon regarded thirteen as her lucky number. It was the date of her birthday and strangely enough all her winners were also born on the thirteenth of the month. Ch. Pita was

Ch. Prestwick Pertana.

born on June 13th 1933. His dam was Ch. Simzette's daughter, Aouda, and his sire was Southampton Jupiter.

He started his show career as a kitten, winning at the Crystal Palace show in 1933 and later in the year at Cheltenham, where he became Best Siamese exhibit. Like his grandmother, he won his title at three consecutive shows, with Certificates from Mrs Basnett at Cheltenham, Phyl Wade at the Southern Counties show, and Mrs Yeates at Exeter.

Ch. Pita became known for siring large litters in which, apparently, male kittens predominated. Some of his prize-winning progeny included Wivenhoe Tityania, Blarney of Bedale, Wivenhoe Perzi, Dimps of Bedale, Ayo of Bedale and Tinka and Tora of Abingdon. He was recorded as having a "most lovely head and eyes" and a gentle nature. He also kept his pale coat throughout his life.

In October 1937 Phyl Wade published an article in *Cats and Kittens* magazine on Greta Hindley, starting with the observation: "Have you ever noticed how well Siamese cats go with old houses – those old houses that have the walls oak-panelled and are furnished with old oak furniture? That sort of house and Siamese cats make a really lovely combination for a perfect colour scheme. If you don't believe me go and visit Mrs Hindley and see for yourself.

"Mr and Mrs Hindley were out in Malaya for some years. There they first made the acquaintance of Siamese cats and, like everyone of discrimination, they fell victims to their charms. Although they acquired Siamese out in Malaya they did not breed them there – only keeping them as pets. But when the time came for them to return permanently to England they decided to bring home with them a Siamese lady by the name of Puteh, which means white.

"And so to Puteh goes the honour of founding the world-famous Prestwick catteries. She was mated to Ch. Mon Dek, owned by Captain Paget. From this strain, Mrs Hindley got two very famous cats – Kechil, a female which appears in very many of the best Siamese pedigrees today, and her son Ch. Prestwick Mata Biru – seven times champion and winner of innumerable prizes and specials.

"By this time Mrs Hindley was infected with the Siamese fever. She got the germ so badly that we hope most sincerely that she will never be cured. She is also an artist above the average and her miniatures have several times been hung in Burlington House for the Royal Academy. Perhaps this accounts for her love of that most marvellous colour scheme, the Siamese cat. But she determined early in her career to improve the eye colour of these cats. It is with this object in view that she has been breeding for the last sixteen years. It is given to very few of us to realise our ambition to the extent which she has hers. Often now you hear breeders say about a kitten with glorious eye colour: 'It has the Prestwick eye colour.' To obtain that 'Prestwick' eye colour is the ambition of every good Siamese breeder today. It must be seen to be believed, and every cat at Prestwick has it, and she has fixed it in her stock to such a degree that I think she could never lose it and, thanks to her, many of us will get it in our humble catteries.

"There are so very many Prestwick cats which we all remember because we admired them so much, and because they swept the board at various shows. Who does not remember beautiful little Pit-a-Pat, the mother of Ch. Prestwick Perling, probably the most lovely Siamese female we have ever had in this country. She died after a show, having previously won a championship and brought back infection to all her litter except Perling, who had luckily been sold previously. We all remember Pra who went to Mrs Shimmin as a stud, and his brother Punya. Prestwick Parma, who was Best in Show at Croydon some years ago, Pippit the mother of Mrs Hindley's present Pugi. Para who won at the Siamese show in 1925 and was lost just before his first adult show: probably he was run over by a car but no one is certain of his end. Puteh Punyo, with his lovely head and eyes; he was neutered when he was about four years old because he threw light front legs to his stock. We all remember that grand old queen, Ch. Perak, who won at the age of ten and a half years."

Greta Hindley's reputation spread far and wide and in her later years she was accepted as the doyenne of the cat fancy and the fount of all knowledge about the Siamese breed. She even self-published her own book on *Siamese Cats, Past and Present* in 1967, acknowledging the help of her special friend Mrs Mary Dunnill, who was also a prestigious breeder and one time Honorary Secretary of the Siamese Cat Club.

The thirties era would not be complete without mentioning the Oriental prefix of Miss M. C. Gold. She owned Angus Silky who was bred by Mrs Siddons Budgen. In the fifth volume of the Siamese Cat Register he is listed:–.

2977 Angus Silky. m, Miss M. C. Gold; by Southampton Darboy ex Zaroui, b. Oct. 6th 1932; br. Mrs Siddons Budgen. Wins, 1st and Ch. C.C.C., 3rd N.C.C., 1st and Ch. S.C.C.C., 1933/4.

He was noted for the set of his ears and was the sire of Oriental Silky Boy, from whom many well-known lines descend. At the Siamese Cat Club Show held in 1935 Angus Silky achieved the award of 'Best Stud Cat'. He also sired many other cats for Miss Gold, such as Oriental Silkoe and Oriental Thai Num.

The Oriental line really came into its own with the importation of Oriental Nai Tabhi. A copy of an original pedigree shows him as having been imported with Tabhi spelt as Tabbi. It is recorded in an article on Miss M. C. Gold in *Cats and Kittens,* December 1937, that: "In another double house lives the imported stud, Oriental Nai Tabhi, known as Toby to his many friends. He has the loudest voice of any cat in this cattery, and the sweetest disposition imaginable. The texture of his coat is quite ideal, and although he is seven and a half years old his colour remains a beautiful pale fawn."

He sired many Siamese for Miss Gold and the sixth volume of the Siamese Cat Register lists nine of his progeny out of a total of twenty-six Orientals. All the registrations for these twenty-six Oriental Siamese recorded their year of birth as being in the 1930s.

Miss Gold also incorporated the Pen-y-Bryn line of Mrs James Robertson of Caernarfon. One of her stud boys was known as Pen-y-Bryn John and *Cats and Kittens* magazine of December 1937 records: "His dam is Longham Kaguya, and his sire comes from one of the most famous strains in the country – Mrs Blofeld's Hoveton cats. He is Hoveton Sinbad, bred by Mrs Blofeld and owned by Mr Sadler Stockton. John has inherited his sire's glorious eye colour, and this he hands down to his progeny. He is the sire of that most perfect kitten shown by Mrs Duncan Hindley this year, Prestwick Apollo."

Mrs Allen-Maturin, who advertised regularly in the various volumes of the Siamese Cat Register, bred Siamese under the Southampton prefix. The last three mentioned in her advertisement were Southampton Mr Wu, Southampton Minky Nama and Southampton Romeo. Stud fees were advertised from twenty-five shillings.

An advertisement used to illustrate the Siamese Cat Club's catalogue for the Sixtieth Championship Show revealed that Mrs French, who had imported quite a few cats, had one at stud who had one white toe. This was a fault that had come down in some lines and it is interesting to remember that there had been the report and picture of a Siamese at the Crystal Palace show in 1871 with the same fault. The thirties were very much the golden era of the Seal Point Siamese.

THE FORTIES

The Siamese breed, like many others, suffered with the advent of the Second World War. The July 1946 issue of *Cats and Kittens* featured a photograph of Chinka, who was a Siamese neuter owned by Mrs P. Humber of Jersey. This Siamese was said to have existed on a diet of potatoes and limpets during the years of the German occupation there.

Mrs Thompson, a well-known judge and breeder, commented on the deprivation of the war years with the following remarks in the *Cats and Kittens Year Book* of 1948: "To breed pedigree cats at all during and after such a devastating war has entailed in many cases hours spent in queues for food, and various negotiations with fellow fanciers to procure horse flesh when it has been unobtainable in one's own district."

Many breeders disposed of their stock to country homes and others decided not to mate their queens as they were not prepared to rear kittens under war-time conditions. Finding suitable stud boys caused an additional problem as "severe paper restrictions curtailed the space allotted to stud advertisements in various journals."

During the war years there were reportedly only two Siamese stud boys in the whole of the London area. The older one of the two was Wansfell Ajax who had been born in 1938 and was known for his strong eye colour, and the other was Prestwick Prithie Pal who had been born in 1941. He was owned by Mrs Lucy Price. These two boys were not short of work and the many Siamese lines that mushroomed in the late 1940s, after the war years, had these two cats as common ancestors.

Mystic Dreamer, who was born on July 14th 1944, also came from a very interesting breeding line that had been kept going during the war years. His sire was Ch. Jacques of Abingdon and his dam was Petite Pasht. The dam of Ch. Jacques of Abingdon was Rachel of Abingdon who had been mated to the famous Ch. Hoveton Emperor of Mrs Blofeld's breeding.

Mystic Dreamer became the sire of one of the most famous of all, Lindale Simon Pie, who was owned by Mrs Linda Parker. He was born on February 9th 1948 and his dam was Beaumanor Bricky, a great grand-daughter of Wansfell Ajax. Mystic Dreamer was also the grand-sire of the outstanding Ch. Killdown Sultan.

A lovely story was printed in the Derby Evening Telegraph of September 23rd 1949, about one of Ch. Lindale Simon Pie's litters: "Nina is a slinky black cat of seventeen years and she just loves kittens. To-day she is lapping up her milk with a new elegance for she is a heroine in her own right. It all started two months ago when a temperamental Siamese cat called Chinki Moon Goddess, owned by Miss Nancy Follows, of The Knoll, Duffield, presented her mistress with five lovely cream kittens. But instead of mothering her offspring as a well-bred cat should do, Chinki Moon Goddess took one look at the bundles of fur and just spat and hissed at them. Within five hours of being born the kittens had been taken from their angry mother and put in the care of Nina, a common black cat.

"As regularly as clockwork Nina has presented her owner, Mrs E. M. Mather, of Rose Cottage, Duffield, with two litters of kittens a year so that one more family to care for meant nothing to her – but little did she realise that the father of the kittens was Siamese Champion Lindale Simon Pie.

"Nina took the kittens into her wicker basket and washed and fed them with as much care and attention as she would have devoted to her own children, and when the kittens became too obstreperous, Nina's four-year-old Judy was there to lend a hand and restore the peace.

"Then two weeks later Miss Follows' other Siamese cat, Chinki Poppy, produced a litter of six kittens, and although she was rather more affectionate towards her family than Chinki Moon Goddess had been, she could not feed them all. So Nina was called upon again. Three more Siamese kittens were transferred from The Knoll to Rose Cottage and Nina took the new members of the family into the fold without even a switch of her sleek black tail.

"She purred over her family day in and day out and the only time she showed signs of being ruffled was when Mrs Mather's Alsatian became curious and poked his nose into the basket to take a look at the kittens.

"Today the eleven kittens are all as perky as can be, with pink ribbons tied round their handsome necks – and although Chinki Moon Goddess is still too proud to acknowledge her family the kittens are not really bothered.

"Their father, Lindale Simon Pie, has already won seventeen first prizes, six silver cups and a number of other awards, while at last year's Kensington Show he was elected champion Siamese cat. He is said to be worth at least several hundred guineas.

"Each one of the kittens is worth at least four guineas, and with championship blood running through their veins there is every chance that in a few years time they will be following in father's footsteps and become champions.

"And now Nina, her job completed, is back in her basket at Rose Cottage, awaiting the arrival of her next family of kittens."

The Hillcross line of Elsie Towe came into their own with Champion Hillcross Song, Champion Hillcross Melody, Hillcross Picot and Mrs Towe's stud boy, Hillcross Cymbal. The Hillcross line in many cases was descended from Greta Hindley's Prestwick Prithie Pal and Miss M. C. Gold's Oriental Silky Boy.

Other lines descended from Prestwick Prithie Pal included Mrs France's stud boy Sco-Ruston

Galadima, Ch. Inwood Shadow, Ch. Holmesdale Chocolate Soldier, and Helen Martin's stud boy Lancy Palladin. Mrs Elsie Hart, who remarried and became known by the name of Kent, produced a prize winning line from Sealsleeve Shah-Pashah. She was the mother of Sealsleeve Shah Danseur, who was born on October 9th 1946 and later mated to Miss Gold's Oriental Silky Boy. The subsequent litter produced one of the progenitors of the Killdown line, Ch. Killdown Jupiter, who was born on June 10th 1949.

Helen Dadd's Sabukia line started in post-war years and her foundation queen Saphire Sally was behind most of the Sabukia prize-winning strain.

THE FIFTIES

Life by this time had begun to settle down to normal and even though people still carried identity cards and there was still some form of rationing, the Seal Point lines began to recover after the forties.

It was reported that Champion Clonlost Yo-Yo received his sixth Challenge Certificate at the Siamese Cat Club Show in 1952. Mrs Lilian France stated that: "I really cannot see any point in collecting them after the third, which makes a cat a full Champion. Mr Warner and I discussed the subject and he does not agree with me at all."

Linda Parker also won 1st and Challenge Certificate with her Ch. Sabukia Sweet William at the Midland Counties Golden Jubilee Championship Show. He was bred by Mrs Helen Dadd.

THE SIXTIES

Another famous Seal Point Siamese, by the name of Ch. Sabukia Sirocco, was also bred by Helen Dadd and owned by Isobel Keene. He was born on July 12th 1962. Ch. Sabukia Sirocco was sired by Ch. Killdown Kerry and his dam was Ch. Sabukia Saina. To judge from his photograph he had the most wonderful ear-set for his time.

Grace Denny bred Ch. Pi-Den Capricorn in 1967 and he includes both the Starshine and Doneraile lines in his pedigree. Marjorie Hudson's prefix was also well-known throughout the 1960s. She bred Supra Cassandra, and at the Scottish Cat Club Show, in 1965, he became Best Siamese Adult.

THE LAST TWENTY-FIVE YEARS

In the last twenty-five years many breeders have specialised in Seal Point Siamese that have brought great credit to their owners. Many of the breeders during this period have gone on to become full judges but sadly others are no longer with us. It is impossible to mention all the Seal Point Siamese over this period

A star by the name of Gr. Ch. Pennyraut Picasso was born on March 4th 1974, bred by Mr V. Athavale and owned by Mrs Tatjana Folkes. Her prefix of Cymbeline is still very well known today. Gr. Ch. Pennyraut Picasso lived a long and happy life and he was last exhibited at the West of England Cat Club Show when he was fifteen years old. Even at that wonderful age he had a lovely pale coat and still showed off the beautiful typy head and ear set he had inherited from the Killdown line.

His dam was Cymbeline Katishe who had been sired by Ch. Killdown Vanguard, and his sire was another Killdown cat by the name of Gr. Ch. Killdown Beauregard.

Another famous Seal Point Siamese was sired by Gr. Ch. Pennyraut Picasso and he was known as Gr. Ch. Amberseal Electo.This lad simply oozed style and type and it is now very hard to find a Seal Point Siamese who does not have Gr. Ch. Amberseal Electo in its heritage. He was owned by Mrs Joan Grabham and bred by Mrs J. Walker.

Gotier Little Lord Gannymede: Imported from the USA.

Photo: Karen Holder.

Breeders became interested in the Siamese lines bred to stamp in Gr. Ch. Amberseal Electo's type, with the result that some pedigrees now have more than four lines going back to this one boy. Most of these lines are behind the show winners of the 1990s.

The Beaumaris line of Brian and Anne Gregory featured prominently and their success in breeding was very much personified in Ch. Beaumaris Unknown Ajax who became the Supreme Exhibit of the Siamese Cat Association show in 1974.

The Killdown line featured another Killdown Seal Point Siamese by the name of Ch. Killdown Madonna who became Best Female Kitten at the Northern Siamese show in 1975 and was later nominated three times for Best in Show.

By 1974, Ch. Kaloke Fingal, bred by Mary Key, had obtained five Challenge Certificates and one Grand Challenge Certificate, highlighting a very prominent and successful line that is still in existence today. The Kaloke line commenced with Cymbeline Chemeli who was mated to Sabukia Sirocco. Out of this mating came Gr. Ch. Kaloke Pharoah who was the father of Ch. Kaloke Fingal.

Some interesting prefixes have come to the fore with the breeding of Seal Point Siamese in this decade, building on the successes of the 1970s.

Ch. Lovinamist Cavalier was behind some very successful Seal Point Siamese in the 1980s. His descendants include Gr. Ch. and Pr. Lovinamist Jillyann, Gr. Ch. Lovinamist Limelight and Gr. Ch. Lovinamist Talisman.

One of the most well-known lines in the 1980s is that of Mrs Jean Murchison, who owns the Fistra prefix and who bred both Fistra Marcus and Fistra Stringobeads. These two cats are in the pedigree of her currently advertised stud boy, Gr. Ch. Fistra Marco Polo, who has sired some lovely Seal Point Siamese.

Other well-known Seal Point Siamese born in the 1980s include Ch. Ikumfurst Yamuchi, Gr. Ch. Subairn Excalibur, Ch. Tabbra Isabella and Ch. Penthouse Modesty Blaize. Gr. Ch. Swanky Sonofagun, was bred by Mr and Mrs Turner on July 6th 1991. His sire is Swanky Schubert and his dam is from the outstanding prize-winning Shermese line of Mrs Celia Simpson, Shermese Candy Stripes.

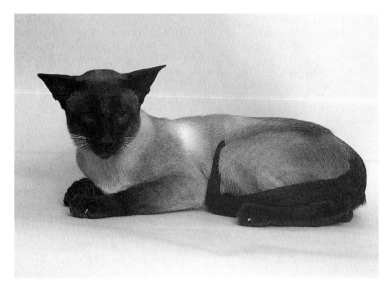

Gr. Ch. Pebblebeach
Lysander.

Photo: Paddy Cutts.

The Sharue prefix is very well known and it has provided some beautiful examples of Seal Point Siamese on the show bench in recent years. Gr. Ch. Sharue Sun Prince has brought his owner and breeder, Mrs S. Hauser, great credit.

No record of Seal Point Siamese would be complete without a mention of UK Grand Champion Shermese Stringalong, who has been the only twenty-four series Siamese to be awarded this title in his lifetime. He was another prize-winning Shermese Siamese and was proudly owned by Peter and Sheila Oldroyd. The November 1994 Supreme Cat Show saw Miss Sue Walls' Loluya Kissmekate obtain her UK Grand Premier title. This Seal Point was bred by Geraldine Sidnell.

In the last few years an example of what can be regarded by some breeders as the more traditional type of Siamese was imported by Karen Holder from the state of Florida in the USA. This Seal Point Siamese was registered by his breeders, Henri Pelletier and John Goterch, as Gotier Little Lord Gannymede and he was born on February 26th 1990.

His Cat Fanciers Association certified pedigree is most interesting in that it reveals both of his parents being descended from the English breeding line of Cymbeline, Mrs Tatjana Folkes, including Gr. Ch. Pennyrallt Picasso and Gr. Ch. Killdown Beauregard. His father's line goes back to the Sumfun line through Mary Dunnill's export, Sumfun Banhari.

It will be interesting to see how Seal Point Siamese breeding will feature in the next century with such a rich heritage to fall back on.

Chapter Ten

BLUE POINT SIAMESE

The Blue Pointed Siamese was the next variety of the Siamese breed after the Seal Point to gain recognition in the UK from the Governing Council of the Cat Fancy.

THE FIRST EXAMPLES

Like all new varieties, there had been examples in existence well before the date of recognition, the earliest known being attributed to Mr Spearman, a young Englishman recently returned to England from Siam.

At the Holland House Show held in 1896, Mr Spearman exhibited his Blue Point Siamese. Apparently Mr Louis Wain, one of the officials, refused to judge the cat, let alone recognise it as a Siamese. An argument ensued, whereupon Mr Spearman informed him that there were several other cats in Siam like the one he had brought home with him. It is not clear if this cat was Lady Blue Blue of Pegu, who was registered as being owned by Mrs Spearman.

Apparently this cat was blue instead of biscuit-coloured. It is not known whether the coat was all blue or whether the colour was restricted to its points. Some sources indicate that this cat may have been a Korat – which, if correct, was the first to be seen outside Siam.

One of the earliest references of all to the existence of the Blue Point Siamese was made by Frances Simpson who in 1902, in her book *The Cat*, stated she had heard of Blue Siamese but fanciers did not appear to like them. Apart from the theory that a few Seal Point Siamese carried the gene with them when they were imported into Britain, it was also suggested that the blue colour was introduced by an accidental mating with a Russian Blue at the turn of the century.

However, a perusal of the first Volume of the Siamese Cat Register reveals nine Blue Pointed Siamese being recorded, the oldest known cat registered being:–

531 Rhoda. f., s. Jacob I., d. Zoe, br. Owner, b. June 21st, 1894. Owner, Mr W. J. Evelyn. Col., blue points.

This Mr W. J. Evelyn may have been the Mr W. T. Evelyn later mentioned as owning other Blue Pointed Siamese.

Some of the others recorded in this volume were:–

108 Caruso. m., particulars unknown, br. R. M. Clark. Owner, Miss Ruby Clark. Col., blue points.

166 Donatina of Cornwall. f., s. Billson, d. Susan, br. Mrs Scott Russell, b. May 8th, 1923. Owner, Miss C. Fisher. Col., blue points.

This young cat was eventually exported to the USA with another Blue Point Siamese by the name of Eve of Woodrooffe.

167 Donato. m., 501 G.C.C. II, s. Errol, d. Siki, br. Mrs Mott, b. March 22nd, 1921.

Owner, Mr. A. Percival. Col., blue points. (In the copy referred to, Mrs Mary Dunnill had written in, over the dam's name, Si-Hi.)

      320 Lady Blue Blue of Pegu. f., particulars unknown, imported. Owner, Mrs Spearman. Colour blue points.

      367 Menam. f, 201 C.C. i., s. Jacob II, d. Rhoda, br. Mr C. J. Evelyn, b. July 17th, 1898. Owner, Mrs Johnston. Prizes: 3rd Westminster 1900. Col. Blue points.

Rhoda was mated to her half-brother, Jacob II (whose mother is recorded as Rose) to produce more Blue Pointed Siamese. They shared the same father, Jacob I, whose details in the Siamese Cat Register are recorded as unknown. He was also owned by Mr W. J. Evelyn.

Further Blue Pointed Siamese appeared in this country and Volume Two of the Siamese Cat Register recorded another seven Blue Pointed Siamese. The stated parentage of these cats evolved from pedigree lines out of Seal Pointed Siamese different from those mentioned in Volume One of the Siamese Cat Register.

CHAMPIONS AND OPPONENTS

Phyl Wade had very little to report on Blue-Pointed Siamese in her book *The Siamese Cat* 1934. She did admit that they could be regarded as lovely, with one of the best being Chinky Blue, who became one of the two Blue Point Siamese stud boys of the breeder Grace Cox-Ife. However, it was obvious that her real love was for the Seal Point Siamese variety and she felt that it would not be worthwhile trying to breed the Blue Point variety. At least she acknowledged that the variety appeared unsolicited from certain known Siamese lines, with nothing in their pedigree to indicate that there would be a change in colour. In June 1936 *Cats and Kittens* magazine published an article by Grace Cox-Ife, who was one of the 'champions of the cause' of Blue Pointed Siamese. She described the colour points of the Blue Pointed Siamese as being "silvery blue" with the body colour being of the palest possible cream. Others described the points as stone grey or even a lavender blue colour; perhaps the latter category could have been some of the early Lilac Point Siamese.

Grace Cox-Ife mentioned that it should be the aim of breeders to obtain this type of coat without any form of shading at all. Shading was recognised as being part of the ageing process, although some lines had a natural tendency to a paler body. She felt that selective breeding would sort out any tendency to shading. In all other respects the Blue Pointed Siamese would resemble the Seal Pointed Siamese in type.

She also pointed out that breeding experiments had revealed that Blue Pointed Siamese mated together bred true to colour. It had been previously suggested that the Seal Point Siamese who had produced Blue Pointed Siamese were badly-pigmented Seal Pointed Siamese.

She therefore advised breeders to aim to develop this variety independently of the Seal Point Siamese variety, although she stated that the early stage of development would probably involve using selected Seal Pointed Siamese to improve on type. She referred to keeping a register that would confirm her advice and breeding policy, especially as she was determined to seek official recognition for them.

As to the origin of these "freaks" or "sports", as they were known – and continued to be known for some time, especially after Phyl Wade's book had been published – it was conjectured that they had been born blue as a result of matings that would have occurred originally in Siam between the Siamese and Korat breeds. Some Siamese would, therefore, have carried the gene for blue, and Grace Cox-Ife was certain that Blue Pointed Siamese had existed in Siam for some time, with some of the original Seal Pointed Siamese imports carrying the gene for blue.

Grace Cox-Ife also referred to the possibilites of a chance mating with a Russian Blue in her article but such a cross mating had only resulted in the birth of Seal Pointed Siamese, Blacks or self-blue hybrids. There had been no published information on any possible F2 matings between F1 progeny.

Apparently the first Blue Point Siamese kittens were exhibited at the Siamese Cat Club Show in 1926 and interest slowly developed, so that by the 1930s the variety had quite a following of interested breeders. Some cat shows allowed Blue Point Siamese entries into the hall but they were limited in the classes which they could enter.

ACHIEVING RECOGNITION

The variety was recognised by the GCCF on February 19th 1936 and given the separate breed number of 24a and championship status. From this date onwards, official recognition meant that Blue Point Siamese could compete for awards at cat shows in their own classes.

One of the very first shows that Phyllis Lauder visited in the late 1930s had a Blue Point Siamese entry. She remembered standing enraptured looking at this different colour of Siamese and overheard the following remark: "I think they're wishy-washy looking things!" Even as late as 1937, Phyl Wade wrote that few people knew of the variety. Perhaps she meant the general public; breeders of Siamese were well aquainted with it. However, justice had a strange sense of humour. Ironically one of the first two Blue Point Siamese to become a Champion in 1936 was Sayo of Bedale, who was actually bred by Mrs Phyl Wade, owned by Mrs Greta Hindley, and eventually sold to a New York fancier.

Following hot on his heels was another Blue Point Siamese, Miss Busteed's Grisnez. She was given a fifth prize at Newbury Show in 1930 and her third Challenge Certificate at the Southern Counties Show in 1937 at the age of seven years. One of her ancestors was the famous Champion Carlisle Lad who was born in 1910.

Phyl Wade gave an account in the *Cats and Kittens* magazine, dated August 1937, of her visit to a cattery earlier in the year, belonging to Mr and Mrs Cox-Ife at Linden, near Oxted. She reported on their activities in trying to "fix a breed of Blue Pointed Siamese" and recorded that, back in 1934, Grace Cox-Ife started to breed Siamese with this object in view and in 1935 she was organising meetings for interested breeders of the variety. At the time of the visit, Grace Cox-Ife had two Blue Pointed studs, Reekie and Muski, and three Blue Pointed queens, Blue Angel of Fleet, Loraine and Wantele Scheherazade. Blue Angel of Fleet was reported to have "really glorious eye colour" and she had recently given birth to a litter of three kittens by Reekie.

Also in 1937 it was reported that the fourteenth Annual Siamese Cat Club Show had put on two additional classes for Blue Pointed Siamese, male and female contenders for Championship were divided, and there was also a Debutante Class for adult cats making their first appearance.

In 1938 Zy-Azuree, owned by Mrs Towgood who had shared Grace Cox-Ife's early interest in the variety, became another Blue Point Siamese Champion and Mrs Godfrey's Blue Point Siamese Tang-Sheng-Chin won her first Championship card. Luckily for her she obtained the other two necessary Championship certificates needed for her title just before cat shows ceased in 1939, the year the Second World War broke out.

These pre-war years had witnessed the development of the variety with light clear coats and contrasting blue points. The writer Sidney France reported that for some years before the advent of World War Two, interest was beginning to be shown in the variety. In fact this interest had been channelled into the birth of the Blue Pointed Siamese Cat Club in 1944, founded by Greta Hindley, whose members were determined to let interested parties know that the variety would indeed breed true. This club became the first specialist Siamese Cat Club covering a Siamese variety. Grace Cox-Ife became the Club's GCCF delegate.

The early members met a great deal of opposition from the Siamese Fancy, including that of the influential Chairman of the Siamese Cat Club – who was none other than Phyl Wade. The Blue Point Siamese Cat Club offered special classes and trophies in an attempt to publicise the variety.

POST-WAR PROBLEMS

However, there was a set-back when the Siamese Cat Club held its first Show after the War in 1946 in London. By all accounts there were nine exhibits, and it became apparent in most cases that the Blue Point coat had lost its clarity. This was attributed to the travelling difficulties experienced in the war years, together with the lack of Blue Point Siamese stud boys. It inevitably led to Blue Point Siamese cats being mated to Seal Point Siamese cats to keep the breed going through these difficult times.

Devotees of the Blue Point Siamese spoke out against mating two varieties together. It was felt that this type of mating was responsible for losing the glacial white coat as laid down in the Standard of Points of the Blue Pointed variety. The clear white coats had given way to shaded coats and, in some cases, a fawn tint. At least there was one advantage: the Seal Point Siamese did appear to develop lighter coats as a result.

However, some breeders still produced show-winning stock and, on January 28th 1948, there was visible proof that the variety had achieved popularity by the appearance on television of Blue Point Siamese cats. This occurred after the Southern Counties Cat Club Show, when Mrs K. Williams invited some of the winners to go with her to the television studios at Alexandra Palace. Included in the party was Mrs Macdonald with her winning Blue Pointed Siamese male, Raard Blue Sacchi and her two winning kittens, Raard Blue Pamela and Raard Blue Wynne.

Later in the same year, Ch. Pincop Azure Kym, another Blue Point Siamese, won the coveted award of Best In Show at the Siamese Cat Club's Championship Show. He was owned by Mrs Lamb of Little Browndreys, Carhampton in Somerset. Even at the age of eleven years in 1956, he still lived very happily in his 'own little wooden house in a big grass pen'. He still retained his character at this advanced age and became known as a grand old man.

He sired many beautiful Blue-Point Siamese Champions including Ch. Tailand Oberon, Ch. Pincop Azure Zelda, Ch. Pincop Azure Tingasha and Ch. Konowana Kym.

In 1949, the Siamese Cat Club defined the following classes for either Seal Point or Blue Point Siamese for that year's annual show. At least by this time the two varieties were recognised on equal terms.

"The entries in the brace, pair and team classes had to be of one colour, either all seal pointed or blue pointed."

COLOUR CONCERNS

In the late 1950s the problem of shaded coats and incorrect colour of points became a burning issue with some breeders. Apparently the cats' type could not be faulted. As always, part of the blame for these faults was attributed to the stud cats of the day, but some attached to the breeders, who were proving resistant to the idea of selective breeding for a glacial white coat and cold tone blue points. A cat who had blue points 'running' into the coat should not be used for breeding at all. It was also thought that the 'fawn-shaded' coats were due to a seasonal factor or even the condition of the cat.

Thetis Randall suggested that the glacial coat could appear again in Blue Point Siamese by mating the very few pale-coated stud boys to pale-coated queens. The product of this type of mating should then be mated to a similarly endowed cat for colour of coat. He then explained that after four generations of such breeding, the desired result would be apparent when the kitten was only a few months old. The quality of the coat colour at this age would enable the breeder to make an informed judgement as to the quality of the kitten's coat in adult life.

Other breeders had suggested that the best way of producing a glacial white coat was to mate a Blue Point Siamese to a Lilac Point Siamese cat in an attempt to lighten the body colour. The counter-argument to this proposal suggested that this type of mating would result in a very dark coat with little contrast between points and body colour.

It was also felt that judges could play their part in improving the colour scheme of the variety. All they had to do was to withhold Challenge Certificates from cats who did not conform to the Standard of Points for Blue Point Siamese!

WORTHY CHAMPIONS

By the early 1960s some outstanding examples of the Blue Point Siamese variety made their appearance, one of the most notable being Ch. Linton Ajax, who was bred and owned by Mrs Elizabeth Biggie. He became a Champion at the South Western Counties Cat Club Show, held in Exeter in September 1962. He was also voted the Best Shorthair Exhibit at the Herts and Middlesex Show and was the father of the Best Short Haired Kitten at the Croydon Cat Club Show held in November 1962.

The 1961-1962 list of Champions also contained another well-known prefix, Arboreal Blue Pandora, owned by Mrs S. Wallington and bred by Mrs Dyte.

The Misselfore prefix produced some lovely prize-winning progeny – Daltrees Blue Adito sired by Misselfore Tempest and Shikaree Mahcoboy and Bitchet Wedgewood sired by Ch. Misselfore Ryken.

Even the judge, Elsie Hart, admitted that Blue Point Siamese had improved enormously and referred to several beautiful specimens on the show bench. One of these was Mrs Ireland's kitten, Gaytail Wendy, who became Best Exhibit at the Siamese Cat Club Show.

Breeders acknowledged that the crossing of the two colours, Seal and Blue Pointed Siamese, was a mistake and they began to mate Blue Point Siamese to Blue Point Siamese with the result that the later decades of this century have seen some very good examples of this variety.

THE SEVENTIES

In the 1970s, John Shewbridge's Ch. Tamruat Blue Lancer gained his title in record time. Mrs Guthrie's Ch. Roseangle Khavirondo won her Grand Challenge at the Northern Siamese Cat Society Show. Other cats who won Grand Challenge Certificates included Mrs Gamble's Ch. Zyclon Jacinth who was bred by Mrs Stallard, and Ch. Chalmi Tzuthai, whose breeder was Mrs Imlach.

One of the most well-known Blue Point Siamese around in this decade was Ch. Coromandel Blue Beau who was born on April 25th 1975, bred by Jean Gamble. Beau was born in Jean Gamble's first Siamese litter, which comprised three kittens, all Blue Point Siamese. The previous year Jean Gamble had bought Beau's mother, Zyclon Jacinth, for breeding and showing. Following advice to take her to an experienced stud boy, Beau's sire, Cantarra Blue Byou, owned by Suzanne Smith, was chosen.

Beau developed into a quiet, gentle cat with balanced type and excellent colouring. He was booked in to be neutered, but at this time his father, Byou, died and so Beau went to live with Suzanne Smith. He sired many Champions and Premiers for his owner. After she gave up breeding, Beau went to live with Mrs Venita Cook who later had him neutered. He died at ten years of age, having to be put to sleep with kidney failure.

Ch. Tyemead Gentleman Jim.

Photo: Paddy Cutts.

THE EIGHTIES

The interest in the Blue Pointed Siamese variety continued through the 1980s with Gillian Mason's Gr. Ch. Eirrem Smart Alec and neuter Gr. Pr. Falcon Blue Ophas who was bred by Mrs Hall. His owner was Mrs Hazel Turnbull. Rosemary Bennett also bred Blue Point Siamese under her Thairano prefix. Mrs Dot Bailey bred and owned Gr. Ch. Zenobia Fast Mover, whose name appears in many Siamese pedigrees of today.

One of the most interesting and recent Blue Point Siamese lines started with Mrs Elizabeth Biggie's Blue Point Siamese, Ch. Craigiehilloch Blue Bryony, who was bred by Mrs Dora Clarke. Bryony was the mother of Linton Blue Selene who was owned by Mrs Jane Wyatt. Jane Wyatt went on to breed from Selene and produced Ch. Moonswift Madame Butterfly who was owned by Mrs Margaret Tyce. This Blue Point Siamese became the mother of Ch. Tyemead Gentleman Jim who became Best Blue Point Siamese at the Supreme Cat Show in 1986.

THE NINETIES

The 1990s have continued with some lovely examples of the variety being shown, and in 1994 the Siamese Cat Association, at their annual show, held an exhibition under the banner of "Pride of Siamese Cats". Four Blue Point Siamese were exhibited. One was Ch. Amberwych Moody Blue, who is owned by Mrs G Churchill and bred by Mrs J Jobson. Another Moonswift Blue Point Siamese bred by Mrs Jane Wyatt, Moonswift Samarkand, took his pride of place accompanied by his owner, Miss L. Dinsdale. The Eirrem prefix made an appearance with Ch. Eirrem Lordsnooty, who is bred and owned by Miss Gillian Mason. This prefix has a wonderful history of beautiful, strongly bred Siamese cats. One of the earlier cats mentioned in the Eirrem pedigree is Merrie Christmas and the prefix is Merrie spelt backwards. The last Blue Point Siamese on exhibition was Gr. Ch. Roysterer Oberon who was bred by Mrs Dawn Williams together with Mrs J. Hirst. His owner is Mrs Hazel Turnbull.

Many articles refer to the Blue Point Siamese character, stating it was and is very different from that of the Seal Pointed variety. Owners had observed that Blue Point Siamese appeared to be more affectionate and more easy-going – they were more able to adapt to new situations in life.

There was also another difference noted – that out of all the Siamese varieties, Blue Point Siamese produced bigger litters of kittens!

THE BLUE POINT IN THE USA

In the USA, the Blue Point Siamese variety fared a little better in the 1920s. They were allowed to compete with Seal Pointed Siamese in the non-specific Siamese classes in North American shows. It is recorded that in the early 1930s, the Boston Cat Club had allocated the variety a class of their own as they had been recognised by the C.F.A. in 1932 and given Championship status.

In 1947 the Siamese Cat Society of America published The Official Siamese Standard. The booklet it appeared in, together with many photographs of Seal Point Siamese and Blue Point Siamese, was dedicated to the memory of Louise Selden Frith. The American Cat Association and The Cat Fanciers Federation had authenticated the booklet by stating that this published Standard was the one used in their Siamese Speciality Shows.

The standard laid down for the Seal Pointed Siamese was to be used for the Blue variety in every way except for colour: "the coat is to be of a silvery blue, slightly darker across the shoulders, changing gradually to an oyster white on the stomach and chest. Points to be of a much darker blue, but of the same tone as the coat. There must be no warm tone of fawn in the coat. Allowance made for older cats. Kittens lighter in color."

Zenobia Baboushka.   *Photo: Paddy Cutts.*

In the 1950s, it was recorded that the coats of the Blue Point Siamese in the USA had developed a pale, cold body tone with the points being a grayish blue in colour.

Nowadays the variety has two shades of blue colour points that are both acceptable in the North American show ring; one is a deep slate blue and the other is a lighter "silvery" blue. The body should be a pale grey blue as opposed to a fawn colour. Like Seal Point Siamese, they darken with age.

Chapter Eleven

CHOCOLATE POINT SIAMESE

FIRST REFERENCES

One of the earliest references to the Chocolate Point Siamese variety, the third variety to gain recognition, must be the cat whose recorded name was Fatima. She was born in either 1885 or 1886. At the age of two and a half years she won the first prize at the Pulborough show which was held on Whit Monday and Tuesday in 1888. The report dated June 7th 1888 on the 'Any Other Class, females' in *The Rabbit-Keeper and Show Reporter* said "A very bonny Siamese took the coveted card in the females."

The show report of the Bawtry show held on September 4th 1889 included details of Mrs H. Young's "Chocolate Siamese, very good in colour and coat." This cat had been entered in the Persian or other Foreign Cat class, which had five entries.

Again, as with the other varieties, it is difficult to establish whether any of the imported Siamese cats were actually Chocolate Point Siamese or whether the gene for the colour was carried by Seal Point Siamese imports.

In some of the prominent Chocolate Point Siamese lines the passage of the colour can be traced back to the matings that occurred between an import by the name of Kew Prince of Siam and Musidore.

Their entries in Volume One of the Siamese Cat Register give very little information about them:–

> 265 Kew Prince of Siam. m., particulars unknown, imported. Owner, Mrs Norris.
> 413 Musidore. f., particulars unknown. Owner, Mrs Sutherland.

There is no date attached to either of these entries but, when reviewing the dates of birth of their progeny, it can be assumed that the sire and dam's date of birth would have been around late 1895 or early 1896.

DEBATE ABOUT COLOUR

What is most interesting about the following entries is that the Siamese cats are not described as Chocolate Points in the way that similar entries were described as Blue Points. This has led early researchers to think that perhaps these cats had an overall brown body colour without the Siamese restriction pattern for colour points. Maybe these early cats were examples of the Burmese breed type with yellow eyes. Nobody knows for certain, but Major Woodiwiss certainly included these entries in the first Volume of the Siamese Cat Register. Perhaps other entries in this volume were actually Chocolate Pointed Siamese but thought to be Seal Pointed Siamese – and poorly coloured ones at that.

In the late 1890s a few Chocolates were born and they were recorded in Volume One of the

Siamese Cat Register. A few of them are reproduced here:

345 Ma. f., s. Prince of Siam, d. Musidora, br. Mrs Sutherland, b. Aug 1st, 1897. Owner, Miss Hester Cochran; second owner, Lady Marcus Beresford. Col. chocolate

387 Missis. f., s. Prince of Siam, d. Kinck, br. Miss Sutherland, b. Aug 1st, 1897. Owner, Miss J Derby Hyde. Col. chocolate

629 Sood. f., s. Prince of Siam, d. Musidora br. Mrs Sutherland, b. March 10th, 1897. Owner, Miss Sutherland. Colour, chocolate.

There is a further entry of another Siamese import by the name of Prince of Siam.

468 Prince of Siam. m., s. imported, d. Keo Fah, br. Mrs McNaught, b. March 6th, 1910. Owner, Mrs M. Finigan.

But, of course, he was born too late to be the father of the aforementioned Chocolates. It was, therefore, assumed that Kew Prince of Siam was the father. The Siamese Cat Register recorded that at least one of these entries was taken to the Westminster Cat Show in 1900 and won a second prize. In reviewing the National Cat Club Registers Numbers Five and Six, it is interesting to note that there is not one reference to a chocolate-coloured cat. However, there is a record of a cat named Nisthamee, no. 290a, owned by Mrs Nield, bred by Mrs Sutherland, who had the same parentage, of Prince of Siam and Musidora, but a later date of birth – April 28th 1899 – than that of the other chocolates recorded in Volume One of the Siamese Cat Register. Perhaps this cat was Chocolate or a 'poorly coloured' Seal Point Siamese.

In the early 1920s, as mentioned in the Seal Point section, Mrs and Mrs Duncan Hindley returned from Malaya accompanied by a Seal Point Siamese by the name of Puteh. The speculation is that Puteh may have carried the Chocolate gene, but Greta Hindley has not recorded this fact in her own personal records.

Puteh, born on May 16th 1919 and described by Greta Hindley as having a bob-tail and narrow face, appeared as an ancestor in later pedigrees behind Chocolate Point Siamese.

Evidence of light points in the Prestwick line were described by Greta Hindley when she wrote that Prestwick Puteh, who was born on April 20th 1925 had a very light cream coat, rather pale but good china blue colour eyes, a fairly dark mask, and her tail and paws were much too light. She had a very affectionate disposition. Her mother was Puteh and her father was Miss Busteed's Litabois! Sadly she died on February 5th 1926 of enteritis, having been mated to Chepping Giles on January 26th 1926. Puteh's daughter, Kechil, by Lieutenant Paget's Ch. Mon Dek, who was born on April 16th 1923, was mated by Ch. Simzo and produced Prestwick Mata Biru on July 9th 1928. He was described by Greta Hindley as a lovely kitten with a long tail. He was mated to Ch. Morgan le Fay and together they produced Sir Morganore de Listinoise, born March 26th 1932, which linked the Prestwick and de Listinoise lines together.

Later it became obvious that Litabois and his litter brother Bigabois carried both chocolate and blue genes and it is interesting that they were also the descendants of Kew, Prince of Siam. Many Chocolate Point Siamese can trace their colour back to these lines in conjunction with many of the Prestwick Siamese cats. Many other breeders registered their Chocolate Point Siamese progeny as Seal Point Siamese with the GCCF because they could not be registered as Chocolate Point Siamese. Generally they were looked on as the 'poor relations' of the Seal Point Siamese and many were not allowed to live. The luckier ones who did survive found homes as pets, because many of those owners expressed a preference for the lighter coats.

THE STRUGGLE FOR RECOGNITION
However, the Siamese Cat Club courageously included a Chocolate class in its show on September 24th 1925 and an imported cat by the name of Adastra won first prize. As the variety had still not

been recognised, the Chocolate Point Siamese were not able to compete for Challenge Certificates.

Mary Dunnill, one time Secretary of the Siamese Cat Club, spoke often of a cat called Granny Grumps, imported by Mrs French – it is possible she was fascinated by the name. In 1927 she was mated to Ch. Bonzo and produced a litter of kittens that included Timkey Brown.

Although the register does not record his coat colour it was reported that he was brown all over, the colour of 'cafe au lait' – which has, half a century later, been used to describe another colour in Siamese points and Orientals, Caramel! (This should not be taken to mean that these Siamese lines carried the dilute modifier gene.)

If the very early records in Volume One on chocolates were actually describing cats whose coats were chocolate all over, then perhaps Timkey Brown corresponded to these earlier descriptions. He also had greenish-yellowy eyes. Mary Dunnill's records showed that he won a special award for the 'best chocolate body' at the Siamese Cat Club Show held in 1928. Also at this show were some kittens he had sired, and it was generally held that their coat was similar to the brown colour of a Havana cigar, with even darker points. The question of this greenish-yellowy eye colour was raised by Phyl Wade, and Major Woodiwiss's reply – that the Club only supported the breeding of blue-eyed Siamese – became quite famous!

THE GERMAN CONNECTION

There was another reference to 'an all-over' Chocolate Siamese in Berlin, Germany, bought by Frau Koch in Lausanne in 1929. Details and a photograph appeared in a much later edition of *Fur and Feather*, December 1935.

"The mother was a most lovely Siamese, self brown with eyes the colour of turquoise, neither blue nor green and with the mask much darker than the rest of the body. When I mated her to an ordinary Seal-pointed with very good eye colour, the whole litter was Seal-pointed. When mated to a Seal-pointed with a very dark coat, she had either all chocolate kittens or one ordinary and all the rest chocolate. In the photograph she is seen with one pale kitten and two like herself."

Later evidence of possible Prestwick chocolates can be found in Mrs Greta Hindley's records of Tondelayo, who was born on March 15th 1929, sired by Ch. Bonzo x Boobette. She was later mated to Prestwick Puteh Punya on January 9th 1930 and two kittens were born with light points, very pale coats and bright china blue eyes.

However the first Siamese cat to be registered as a Chocolate Point Siamese with the GCCF was known as Eryx, who was born on July 4th 1931. His breeder and owner was Mrs M. Watson. In checking back on his pedigree it can be seen he is a great-great-grandson of Kew Prince of Siam, the possible sire of Mrs Sutherland's chocolates recorded in Volume One of the Siamese Cat Register. In the USA there was one outstanding breeder by the name of Mrs Mary Purdue Klein of the Purr-Du prefix, who specialised in Chocolate Point Siamese from 1938.

DEVELOPMENTS IN THE THIRTIES AND FORTIES

The decades of the 1930s and 1940s saw further interest in the variety and some prefixes and suffixes became associated with producing Chocolate Point Siamese. One of the most famous suffixes was de Listinoise, which belonged to Miss Wentworth Fitzwilliam. She also owned the Slingsby prefix, which she used for registering her Seal Point Siamese. One of her most well known Chocolate Point Siamese queens was Mira de Listinoise, who was born in April 1926 out of Sir Brian de Listinois and Semiramis. In her turn she produced mixed litters of Seal Point and Chocolate Point Siamese. She was also a grand-daughter of Litabois.

An example of such a mixed litter occurred when Mira de Listinoise, from a mating with Jimbois, a Seal Point Siamese, produced the famous Ch. Morgan le Fay who has already been mentioned. She had two Chocolate Point Siamese litter sisters by the names of Mirage de Listinoise and Mirabelle de Listinoise. Mirabelle was mated to Mrs French's Somme det Tjao, an imported Seal Point Siamese, and out of this came Slingsby Sea Maiden and Slingsby Sea Mist. Although both were recorded as being Seal Pointed Siamese, Slingsby Sea Maiden carried the Chocolate gene and, when she was mated to Skitsey, Seafoam de Listinoise was born on April 30th 1944. Sadly Mirabelle de Listiniose died in 1936 whilst giving birth to another litter of kittens.

Seafoam de Listinoise was mated to a very well known Seal Point Siamese who carried Chocolate by the name of Penybryn Mont who had been born in 1938. One of the progeny was Seashell de Listinoise, a female born in 1947, who became one of the earliest Chocolate Point Siamese Champions when shown by her owner, Mrs K. F. Williams, after the variety received recognition. However, when she was first registered with the GCCF she was recorded as a Seal Point Siamese. Penybryn Mont also sired another famous Chocolate Point Siamese from a mating with Mrs Peerybingle. The kitten was registered as Henham Chloe on July 3rd 1946, and she became the most famous of all, being the first Chocolate Point Siamese to receive the title of Champion in 1951 after the variety received recognition.

The description of 'a rich cafe au lait' was applied to the Chocolate Point Siamese lines in the 1940s by Miss Wentworth Fitzwilliam who had made the cause of the Chocolate Point Siamese her own. Chocolate Point Siamese lines also received a tremendous boost with the birth of Prestwick Penglima Pertama in 1946 who could trace his lines back to Greta Hindley's Puteh.

In his turn he sired the first male Chocolate Point Siamese Champion, Ch. Holmesdale Chocolate Soldier who was born on October 17th 1950, and other Chocolate Point Siamese Champions by the names of Ch. Shushard, born 1950, and Ch. Sayam Zar Prak who was born in 1952. To these three Chocolate Point Siamese can be attributed the Chocolate Point Siamese lines of today, together with Ch. Henham Chloe and Ch. Seashell de Listinoise.

Ch. Prestwick Penglima Pertama's father was Prestwick Person who was born in 1942. He also sired another well known cat by the name of Southwood Kuching, who was the progenitor of the Craigiehilloch Chocolate Point Siamese line, bred by Dora Clarke.

DEFINING THE CHOCOLATE POINT LINE

In 1948 a meeting was called to link all the parties interested in the breeding of the Chocolate Point. One of the objectives was to study pedigrees to see if there was a particular line that could be identified as contributing towards the progression and recognition of this variety. There were Chocolate Point Siamese existing in France. Sidney France, who was invited to judge at a French cat show held in January 1948, thought that they were of very good quality but that their owners appeared to have no knowledge of the origin of the colour, let alone their lines. This opinion was echoed by Miss Yorke who was invited to judge at another French cat show a few months later.

Kit Wilson recorded that Mr Brian Stirling-Webb, who was the Hon. Treasurer of the Siamese Cat Club, thought that the Chocolate Point Siamese variety in France would have similar roots to those in England. A further meeting was held in 1949 by Miss Wentworth Fitzwilliam's group to discuss and draw up a Standard of Points for the variety. A thirteen-year-old Chocolate Point Siamese by the name of Georgiana was used as the model for this.

GAINING RECOGNITION

The case for recognition and the proposed Standard of Points was discussed at the October 1949 meeting of the Siamese Cat Club and it was agreed that the Club's delegates should request the GCCF to recognise the variety and agree a breed number. Recognition was granted in 1950 and the breed number of 24b was allocated. It could be said that recognition opened the 'flood-gates' for the re-registration of poor Seal Point Siamese as Chocolate Point Siamese. Figures given in both Volume Ten and Volume Eleven of the Stud Books bear witness to the increase in the number of registrations. The early show reports indicated that there was no problem with the colour of the points in the Chocolate Point Siamese variety. Mary Dunnill remembered that the colour could be described as a 'good milk chocolate' which had obviously been obtained and passed down the lines from their Seal Point Siamese relatives.

DECLINE IN COLOUR

Elsie Hart reported that Mrs K. F. Williams' Doneraile Brun Boy, in 1950, "was not a bad seal but a real chocolate at last." His mother was Ch. Seashell de Listinoise. He had been originally registered as a Seal Point Siamese and was re-registered as a Chocolate Point Siamese in 1950. At the Southern Counties Show in that year Elsie Hart obviously remembered Doneraile Brun Boy as a kitten in her write-up but she reported that his points were a "little brindled as an adult". A later report on the same cat in 1951 indicated that Mrs Holroyd, his judge, had written him up as having a "brindled tail". A 1954 report from the Notts & Derby Cat Club show by Mrs Frame on Sayam Zar Prak referred to lovely body colour and points of good chocolate even though they were not fully developed on the front legs and tail. He was owned by Miss Wells, whose prefix was Carson. As he became older his colour developed into a most stunning shade of milk chocolate and he sired a litter in 1953 for Dora Clarke containing the first Craigiehilloch champions – Chozara who was male and Chojula who was a female.

By 1957 it looked as if some of the earlier promise regarding the type and colour of the points of the Chocolate Point Siamese variety had been lost, and Kit Wilson wrote of her disappointment over this fact in the 1957 seasonal review. It was also recorded that the variety was prone to points that were too seal, or lacked colour, and to incomplete masks.

However, there were one or two surprises in store. Ch. Craigiehilloch Chozaro sired two promising kittens by the names of Sunland Sirius and Sunland Sijui for Miss Bennett. Sunland Sirius went on to get his title of Champion and it was reported by Miss Yorke in 1959 that his points were of the correct colour and that his coat colour was very good.

Ch. Craigiehilloch Chozaro had also sired Camley Fudge, who was born in 1956. Elsie Hart had reported that he had good head and type and was "rather big still". After gaining his title he sired five Chocolate Point Champions, who were Ch. Bradgate Yippee, Ch. Misselfore Chocolate Whey, Ch. Jaddyx Quoff Deander, Ch. Bradgate Nina, who was renowned for the colour of her points and Ch. Bradgate Folly. The same situation regarding the quality of the colour of Chocolate Point Siamese carried on to the mid 1960s, with only three Chocolate Point Siamese gaining their titles between the period of 1964 and 1968. One of these was Ch. Bradgate Yippee and the other two were Ch. Samsara Dante and Ch. Kirash Curry, who was bred by Sally Beeley.

From 1968 to 1973 the situation turned around and within a period of five years a large number of Chocolate Point Siamese achieved their titles. Some newer prefixes achieved prominence – Flume, Physalis, Druries and Grace Denny's Pi-Den. The Kirash line became renowned for producing excellent quality Chocolate Point Siamese both for colour and type. Ch. Kirash Curry sired Elizabeth Wildon's own-bred Ch. Sunjade Chocolate Domino and Ch. Boidheach MacGille. Pat Turner's Ch. Scintilla Apollo (Lilac Point) sired an outstanding champion, by the name of Ch. Roundway Osmanthus, and his litter brother, Roundway Ourisia, who was owned by Mrs Isobel Keene.

GRAND CHAMPIONS

Inevitably with time, interest in the variety attracted further breeders who cared just as much about

Gr. Ch. Pentangle Beauman.

Photo: Paddy Cutts.

the type of their Siamese and the correct colour of the points. One of these was Ross Mort-Williams who bred the first Chocolate Point Siamese Grand Champion, Chaiross Ariel. He could trace his descent back to Ch. Boidheach MacGille and so on back to the old lines famous for their development of the variety. In his turn Gr. Ch. Chaiross Ariel sired another Gr. Ch. winner, Chaiross Androcles and to this day the Chaiross line is still going strong.

Grace Denny undertook a brother/sister mating between Ch. Pi-Den Cupid and Ch. Pi-Den Chianti, who had been sired by Roundway Ourisia, which stamped in the colour of the pedigree line which was passed down to their descendants. A close mating such as this is a very good way of testing the pedigree line for inherent faults. The two Pi-Dens became the grandparents of Ch. Kimoki Dagmar who was owned by Sally Beeley. He sired many Chocolate Point Siamese with milky chocolate points and it has been recorded that he lightened "a whole generation of 24b Siamese". Included in his record are his two sons, Gr. Ch. Pentangle Beauman and Gr. Ch. Kaprico Rhinegold.

COLOUR CONCERNS

By the end of the late 1970s the situation that had faced Chocolate Point Siamese breeders in the middle 1960s had come about again full cycle. This was confirmed by one judge who, having bred some outstanding Chocolate Point Siamese, wrote of the poor quality that had crept into the adult classes. She tried to reinforce the point that selective breeding was needed, together with a knowledge of pedigree lines, to produce the overall correct colour of ivory coats and milk chocolate points and, of course, type for this variety.

It appeared in the 1980s that there were only a few breeders specialising in the variety, but they had good results. One of these was Elizabeth Wildon who carried on producing some lovely Chocolate Point Siamese cats under her Sunjade prefix. Ross Mort-Williams has also kept interest going with his well-known Chaiross line personified in Gr. Ch. Chaiross Androcles.

Other lovely Chocolate Points include Mr and Mrs A. Single's Gr. Ch. Sinope Super Nova, Mrs Anna Hill's Gr. Ch. Anorwa Deltoid, Sally Beeley's Ch. Kirash Joss, Pr. Sunsylph Daniel, who was bred by Gillian Murray, and Ross Mort-Williams' Gr. Ch. Sinope Athene, the first female Grand Champion Chocolate Point Siamese. The 1990s have seen Margaret and Peter Hardy with their own-bred Ch. Ginnistam Mad Carew who was born on October 14th 1990 and is renowned for his milk-chocolate points and coat colour. The Chocolate Point Siamese is now a variety looking for fresh impetus, and hopefully some breeders will embrace it within the next few years.

Chapter Twelve

LILAC POINT SIAMESE

CONTROVERSIAL BEGINNINGS

The next colour to gain recognition was Lilac and when one examines the history of its development within the Siamese breed, it can be seen that there are two distinct genetic routes, one of which caused a great deal of controversy in the early 1960s.

Kittens had been born with colour points that were recognised as being different from a normal Blue Point Siamese. In the early days there were many attempts to describe this colour in order to distinguish it from the normal Blue Point. Adjectives were used such as 'lighter', more 'silvery', 'lavender blue' and with a 'pinkish undertone'. Others regarded Siamese sporting this colour as

Lilac Point: This colour is obtained through the simple inheritance of recessive blue and chocolate genes.

Photo: Paddy Cutts.

'freaks' or 'sports' but their beauty was appreciated because it was often remarked that they had the palest of cream coats with this unusual colouring of points long before the Laurentide hybrids made their appearance.

Some breeders had placed their progeny on the show bench and these specimens were judged against the standard for Blue Point Siamese. Few prizes were won by these cats, because they were reported to have 'poor colouring', before the cat fancy finally appreciated that the colour being shown was distinct in its own right.

USA RECOGNITION
An example of failing to meet the Standard occurred in California, USA in 1949. A Siamese which would now be described by some American Cat Fancies as a Frost Point was entered into the Blue Point Siamese class but did not get placed. However, much to the owner's surprise, this cat did win a 'first' in an all-breed class and this was put down to its 'novel beauty'.

The frost colour of this cat attracted breeders in the USA. The CFF and ACA accepted this colour in 1954 to allow the cats to compete for titles. Recognition from the other North American bodies followed in 1955.

The early standard for Lilac Point Siamese of the Siamese Cat Society of American Inc. and the American Cat Association read, under "Points Colour: Very light, silvery Blue. There is a slight rosiness to the points, especially the ears, as a result of the blood showing through the very light pigment"!

UK RECOGNITION
Five years after USA recognition the colour was recognised in Britain, in 1960, and allocated the breed number of 24c. It was decided that the use of the descriptive Lilac was preferable to Frost as it described an actual pastel colour. The formation in 1961 of The Lilac Point Siamese Cat Society followed on quickly after recognition and, with the requisite numbers in membership, soon became affiliated to the GCCF.

THE SOURCE OF THE COLOUR
The naturally occurring Lilac Point Siamese obtains its colour through the simple inheritance of the recessive blue and chocolate genes. These genes have to be carried by both parents to result in the Lilac pointed colour of Siamese kittens; these genes are not sex-linked in order to be expressed. The lilac gene is a double recessive, in other words it is the result of double blue and chocolate genes from sire and dam. A Lilac Point Siamese male mated to a Lilac Point Siamese female will only produce Lilac Point Siamese kittens.

Phyllis Lauder held strong views on the 'natural' occurrence and development of the Lilac Point Siamese and her views were shared by the late geneticist A. C. Jude. In her book *The Siamese Cat* she recorded that she had received a letter from him suggesting that someone should try to breed a Lilac Point Siamese.

It gradually became known that some of the original Seal Point Siamese imported lines carried the blue gene whilst other pedigree lines carried the chocolate gene. Therefore, the necessary genotype already existed for the natural evolution of the Lilac Point Siamese, and it is claimed that the "first kitten born from Siamese lineage was from Phyllis Lauder's breeding."

An example of this natural occurrence manifested itself with the birth of the Lilac Point Siamese, Belhaven Apple Blossom, who was known as 'Pommie'. His sire was the Seal Point Siamese Sloppy Joe, who carried the blue and chocolate genes, and his dam was the Chocolate Point Siamese Carson Truffle, who carried blue. His heritage was pure Siamese and therefore he was registered on the Ordinary Register. Phyllis Lauder wrote in the first issue of the *Siamese Cat Association Journal*: "A small number of Lilac Pointeds have been shown in the 1959-1960 season, and they are all, I believe, related to the Laurentides. This makes me into a maker-of-maddening-mistakes, for I bred a nice male who bore no relationship at all to Mrs Hargreaves' strain and, finding him more loving than most, I neutered him. Mea culpa – but he lives comfortably, and what has been done once can be done again."

In this paragraph she is referring to her cat, Belhaven Apple Blossom. She then mentions that although Sloppy Joe was now dead there were other descendants and a similar mating could be carried out to prove her point. According to Phyllis Lauder, there would be a one in sixteen chance of obtaining a Lilac Point Siamese by mating together two Seal Point Siamese both carrying blue and chocolate, and the odds would definitely be shortened to one in four by mating a Blue Point Siamese carrying Chocolate and a Chocolate Point Siamese carrying Blue.

"Of course, two 'Blues' known to carry Chocolate, or two 'Chocolates' known to carry Blue, can also 'do the trick'; it is an important 'trick', for the Fancy will need more than one strain of 'Lilacs', in order to avoid in-breeding. It may, of course, be that Apple Blossom is not the only 'Lilac' unrelated to the Laurentides ...."

Other claims do exist to the first naturally born Lilac Point Siamese, and the Denhams in *The Siamese Cat* refer to a good one being shown in 1953. Colin Campbell informed the Denhams that he thought he had produced a Lilac Point Siamese way back in the 1930s, but not knowing any different then, he thought it was simply a poor-coloured Blue Point Siamese.

A BREEDING PROGRAMME

In another issue of the *Siamese Cat Association Journal*, Mrs A. Hargreaves had written an article entitled *This is my story* , and her reasoning for breeding the hybrid Lilac Point Siamese was based on advice from a Dutch geneticist by the name of Dr Hagedoorn. He had written that: "Siamese would greatly benefit by 'out-crossing' to increase their hardiness."

Mrs Hargreaves stated what she felt to be common belief, that many potential buyers would not buy Siamese on account of the breed lacking stamina, which is not really surprising when, as I have mentioned, there were only two known active stud cats working in the whole of the London area during the Second World War.

She therefore wrote to Dr Hagedoorn for advice and, based on his reply, she formulated her breeding plans. This involved mating a Seal Point Siamese queen by the name of Laurentide Ludo, who was born in 1946, to the Russian Blue, Ch. Silvershoen Blue Peter, 16a. It was felt that this would be a suitable outcross on the following grounds: "There was little chance of inheriting wrong type, markings or length of coat; and if the kittens which followed did lose some of the Siamese voice no doubt there would be purchasers who would not grumble!"

The pedigree for Laurentide Mercury shows what actually happened in Mrs Hargreaves' breeding programme. The first generation (F1) reveals that the female cat by the name of Laurentide Ephone Ebony, breed number 15, was black all over, as indeed were all her siblings. Uncertified records show she was born in August 1948. Her overall black coat pattern occurred because when one parent is Siamese and the other parent is a complete out-cross, the resultant litter will not express the characteristic Siamese points pattern.

Mrs Hargreaves carried out some experimental breeding with these black cats who were mated together, but she also mated some of the females to other Siamese stud cats. Laurentide Ephone Ebony was mated to the Seal Point Siamese male, Inwood Ching, 24, and Laurentide Ephtoo Sapin (F2) was the result of this mating. He was born on May 18th 1950 and registered as a Seal Point Siamese. Another mating took place between Laurentide Ephone Jet registered as breed number 15 (litter sister to Laurentide Ephone Ebony), and a delightfully named Seal Point Siamese male by the name of Morris Sirdar, who was born on July 27th 1948, produced Laurentide Ephtoo Jade (F2), registered as a Seal Point Siamese and born on May 1st 1950.

This part of the breeding was neatly summarised by Mrs Hargreaves as: "It was very interesting to watch the Mendelian laws at work, the Siamese handing down their pattern to every kitten, while the self-coloured half-Siamese could only pass this on to about half. So that the second generation were mostly Blacks and Siamese."

The third part of the breeding programme resulted in the birth June 6th 1951 of Laurentide Ephree Amethyst (F3 generation), registered as a Blue Point Siamese.

You are probably wondering where in all this is the Lilac Point Siamese result of these matings. It came in the next generation, and was later subject to great controversy.

Laurentide Ephree Amethyst was mated to another Blue Point Siamese by the name of Ch. Chatwyn Tamarack, who himself had been born on November 19th 1953.

His lineage was also interesting; his mother was known as Mistery Maid, a Seal Point Siamese queen who was born on April 24th 1952. Her pedigree shows she was the daughter of Laurentide Ephtoo Sapin who can trace his pedigree line to the original Siamese/Russian mating. Out of the mating of Laurentide Ephree Amethyst to Ch. Chatwyn Tamarack two male kittens, Laurentide Mercury and Laurentide Quicksilver (who were eventually determined to be Lilac Point Siamese), and two female kittens, Laurentide Heliotrope and Laurentide Olivine were produced.

This background breeding led to Mrs Hargreaves exhibiting Lilac Pointed Siamese at the Siamese Cat Club Show of 1955. She summarised her breeding programme with this statement: "The kittens I was now breeding were very hardy, and some were exceptionally friendly. They were almost bi-lingual, using Russian for conversation and Siamese for matrimonial purposes or giving orders!"

THE VARIETY DEVELOPS

Interestingly enough, Mrs Phyllis Lauder's comments on hybrid breeding in another article entitled Lilac Logic in the *Siamese Cat Association Journal* were: "As to the tales of Lilac-pointeds which are said not to be 'pure' because it is thought that they have Self Lilac or Self Blue ancestry, these are of no great importance. Apple Blossom has, as far as a long pedigree goes, none but Siamese ancestry, but in a cat to be used for breeding it would not matter if he had; the points colour, and the restriction-of-colour-to-points of a Lilac pointed Siamese are both recessives, and they will breed true; mate two Lilac-pointed and, no matter if their grandsires were alley-cats, they will produce none but Lilac-pointed kittens – and these may well gain in the matter of stamina, though perhaps not much could be expected in way of 'type'."

The first recorded all Lilac Point Siamese litter was bred by Mrs K. Williams in 1959, sired by Kyrine Lilac Khan, 24c, dam Dodbrook Czarina, 24c.

According to the May 1961 issue of *Our Cats*, the first Lilac Point Siamese in the UK to receive the title of Champion was Mrs Brenda Thompson's, Ch. Devonmoor Salamega, who was bred by Mrs Gregory. The sire of the first Champion was Dodbrook Dandy, 24c, whose own father was Laurentide Mercury, and whose mother was Phen Khae Mai. The dam of Devonmoor Salamega was Laurentide Adularia, who was bred by Mrs Hargreaves.

In December 1960 Phyllis Lauder, still championing the cause of the Lilac Pointed Siamese variety, wrote: "But though they have made their debut and have become established, there are still some worlds for them to conquer." She referred to the Chocolate Pointed and the Blue Pointed varieties who went through the same difficulties, namely the combination of type with colour. She felt this was hardly surprising in view of the odds in finding cats of 'good' type with the desirable recessives to produce Lilac Pointed Siamese. Her advice to breeders was to aim first for colour, for a Siamese without the correct colour would not be a good example of the Lilac Pointed Siamese variety.

She summed up the quality of the Lilac Point Siamese being shown in the 1960-1961 show season as having too much blue in their points, referring to advice given to her by the late A. C. Jude: "You can have a Blue Chocolate, or a Chocolate Blue. Lilac is a delicate, fugitive colour, and the importance of seeing the rosy tinge of the Chocolate-combined-with-Blue cannot be over-stressed...we need to get rid of those shocking Tabby rings which might suit the tail of a racoon, but not that of a Siamese cat!"

The variety gained in popularity and further titles were awarded. In the November 1961 issue of *Our Cats* another new Champion is mentioned – Angela Sayers' Lilac Pointed Siamese female, Ch. Doneraile Lilac Laretta, who was out of Kyrine Lilac Khan and bred by Mrs K. R. Williams.

PROBLEMS ARISE

However, after recognition had been granted, the registrations of the hybrid Lilac Point Siamese descendants suffered a setback. A letter, received by the late Mary Dunnill from a breeder raised the question as to why breeders of Lilac Point Siamese who had Laurentide Mercury in their pedigrees were having their kittens registered on the Supplementary Register, even though the parents had been registered on the Ordinary Register.

The breeder's argument was that GCCF rules stated that three generations after a hybrid mating, the kittens could be registered on the Ordinary Register. To her knowledge at the time of writing there had been no amendment to these rules.

Phyllis Lauder informed Mary Dunnill that she was not interested in the genetics or politics of the matter, she only wanted to find out why the rule did not appear to have been adhered to. Elsie Towe, who specialised in breeding only Seal Point Siamese, commented that she did not see why people with experimentally bred cats should have the same privileges as those who kept to true breeding, but she was anxious that the right thing should be done in the circumstances.

The situation gathered momentum from March 1962 onwards, with other breeders writing letters as to the Supplementary Registration of their Lilac Point Siamese kittens.

A further letter from Phyllis Lauder then asked for clarification on the matter, quoting the heritage of her Belhaven Apple Blossom in her letter dated April 7th 1962. Although her pet's ancestors were from pure Siamese lines, she argued that because he was of the Lilac Point variety of Siamese, he should probably have been registered on the Supplementary Register.

A further problem showed itself with the registration of related kittens with three generations of Siamese breeding behind them but also with Laurentide Mercury in their pedigrees, with one being registered on the Ordinary Register whilst the other was placed on the Supplementary Register.

The controversy seemed to turn around the interpretation of the word "variety" and Phyllis Lauder maintained that, independent of the politics of the situation, there should have been consistency in the registration of the kittens concerned.

Further questions were raised by another Lilac Point Siamese breeder who felt that the pedigrees of her Lilac Point cats must include some inaccuracies as all generations indicated pure Siamese breeding. There was no sign at all of the earlier Siamese/Russian Blue cross mating. A correct version of Laurentide Mercury's pedigree reassured her that, as her Lilac Point Siamese line at that time was five generations away from the original cross, her progeny should not be registered on the Supplementary Register.

The newly formed Lilac Point Siamese Cat Society offered to help the Siamese Cat Club with the matter of the Lilac Point Siamese registration in May 1962. At the end of May 1962 Elsie

Towe informed Mary Dunnill that the hybrid litter brothers Laurentide Mercury and Laurentide Quicksilver were originally registered as Blue Point Siamese on the Supplementary Register, but these had been subsequently changed to Chocolate Point Siamese.

According to the handwritten copy of a transfer certificate by the then Registrar, Mr A. A. Towe, Laurentide Mercury was mated to the Blue Point Siamese Phen Khae Mai, and out of this mating had come Dodbrook Dandy. All Dodbrook cats, according to Mrs Elsie Towe, were registered as either 24 or 24a. The Blue Point Siamese Dodbrook cats derived from Laurentide Mercury and Laurentide Quicksilver were registered on the Supplementary Register, whilst the Seal Point Siamese Dodbrook progeny were placed on the Ordinary Register.

Mrs Hargreaves was far from happy with some of her cats being placed on the Supplementary Register and so the issue of Laurentide Mercury's registration was raised. Mary Dunnill recorded that the debate at the next GCCF meeting was rather lively, to say the least, and questions were asked about the actual colour of Laurentide Mercury: was he a Blue Point Siamese, a Chocolate Point Siamese or was he, as Mrs Hargreaves maintained, a Lilac Point Siamese? He had originally been registered as a Blue Point Siamese, 24a. It was decided that two judges should see Laurentide Mercury and report on their findings to the Secretary of the GCCF, Mr S. E. Barnes. Mr and Mrs Lamb agreed to undertake this duty.

As a result of their visit and of considerable discussion at the next Council meeting, Laurentide Mercury was registered as a Lilac Point Siamese and placed on the Supplementary Register. It was decided that any progeny of Laurentide Mercury would be placed on the full register according to GCCF rule 4(f), providing the mother of the kittens also had three generations of the same variety in her immediate ancestry.

A further ruling was approved regarding Lilac Point Siamese; it was decided that any cat or kitten of this variety which also had three generations, irrespective of colour, in its pedigree line, would be entitled to be registered in the Ordinary Register as Lilac Pointed Siamese.

BREEDING RECOMMENDATIONS

Mary Dunnill always felt that the early Lilac Pointed Siamese looked rather heavy with small ears and too short a wedge shaped head: perhaps this was due to the Russian influence in their genetic make-up. It was also recorded that the colour of the early Lilac Point Siamese's points varied from being too blue or too "yellowy", which was attributed to the lack of intensity of the chocolate pigment in the cat's genetic make-up. Many Lilac Pointed Siamese were mated with Seal Pointed Siamese and these matings were held responsible for producing shady coats and dark "brownish" tails.

It was, therefore, recommended that to produce a good-quality Lilac Pointed Siamese for colour, it was necessary to mate Lilac to Lilac then, if this was not possible, to use a Blue Point Siamese "without the Seal factor". The colour to avoid completely was the Chocolate Pointed Siamese. Any evidence of stripes and/or ringed tails was considered detrimental to the development of Lilac Point Siamese.

It was also felt that Lilac Pointed Siamese required more show preparation than the other varieties because their coat could appear very "dingy". However, apart from the initial problem relating to the registration of the Laurentide hybrids, it can be concluded that the Lilac Pointed variety of Siamese has made rapid progress over the decades, with many securing titles of Champion and Grand Champion.

Elsie Towe thought that Mrs Carol Stafford's Gr. Ch. Kaprico Iceberg was the most beautiful Lilac Point Siamese ever shown. On checking back in pedigrees he was certainly used by a number of other Siamese breeders and he features in many Siamese and, now, Oriental lines.

AMERICAN VIEWPOINTS

During the same period of the 1960s in the USA the Frost – Lilac – Pointed Siamese became equally popular and registrations revealed that they were being born in considerable numbers, with the Western section of the country having a greater density of this variety than the Eastern section.

The editors of *The Siamese Cat Association Journal*, Elsie Towe and Mrs H. Martin, published an extract from a letter received by an American member: "I handled a very nice Lilac Point male which I made 'Best Kitten', excellent fine-boned type, long but not extreme head, very good eye shape and colour, delicate near-lilac points coming in against perfectly white close coat. I can see why these could become popular, but the trouble is that every gradation between Chocolate Point and Blue Point seems to be appearing so that although they breed 'true', in that one does not get any Chocolate Points or Blue Points again, they are a very mixed lot. This gives rise to the Frost Point Description, for the ones with lighter, more bluish points and very white body. All very confusing and American."

LILAC POINT CHAMPIONS

There were some very well-known Lilac Point Siamese born in the 1970s: these include Gr. Ch. Kaprico Iceberg and Gr. Ch. Kirash Tamsin. These cats were mated together and produced one of the most well known of all, Ch. Maytime Landucci who was the father of Ch. Sunsylph Allegro, born on February 11th 1978. Ch. Sunsylph Allegro was owned by Melva Lingard, and sired many kittens before he died in December 1994.

Gr. Ch. Daunus Pascali was born on November 11th 1979, while the 1980s saw the birth of Gr. Ch. Simone Spooks. Gr. Ch. Shonalanga Moonraker was sired by Gr. Ch. Cachet Tabbeoca Tiptoes. Gr. Ch. Popplebee Tigi Wigi was born in 1986.

Other notable Lilac Point Siamese appeared in the 1990s, including Ch. Eirrem Lordship, Gr. Pr. Roysterer Iced Flutterby, Gr. Ch. Roysterer Lord Catmando, Gr. Ch. Roysterer Lady Freyja and Gr. Ch. Roysterer Shermesian. Gr. Ch. Willowbreeze Going Solo was sired by Ch. Nikana Blue Max.

Chapter Thirteen

TABBY POINT SIAMESE

The Tabby Point Siamese variety is one of the more recent additions to the Siamese breed and once again there are records of earlier examples existing before recognition. These were described by many names – Shadow-Point, Silver Point, Tiger Point and Attaby. One of the most popular was Lynx-Point, which appealed to most people's imagination with a hint of the wild cat. In the USA they are still called Lynx-Points by some Associations.

References go back to the early 1900s. Frances Simpson mentioned them as "Any Other Colour Siamese Tabby" in her *Book of the Cat* in 1902 – but for her there was no other Siamese but a Royal Siamese (Seal Point). There were further examples born to Mrs Hood in Scotland in the 1940s. Mrs Mary Dunnill had photographs of some of these early cats dated between 1944 and 1949 and records to show that Mrs Hood's progeny were referred to originally as Silver Point Siamese.

In 1952 there was a record of the existence of the Kutjing Lynx Points. This prefix was owned by Mrs Hood. She brought a Seal Point Siamese female into England who managed to get herself mis-mated by a moggie. The phenotype of the resultant kittens was described as having mackerel-striped coats on a Siamese body shape. One of the kittens was kept; she had inherited the Siamese gene for restriction of colour to the points and, in due course she was mated to other Seal Point Siamese stud boys, which resulted in the birth of several Tabby Point Siamese "lookalikes".

After Mrs Hood's death, her experimental breeding was carried on by Mr Vernon Green. Two kittens from his breeding, a female, Teenyweenyone and a male, Tambu of Gwent, went to live with Kirstie Buckland, who bred further generations successfully.

It was known that there were other lines of Lynx Point breeding but there appear to be no further records detailing what happened to the progeny.

It is strange to think that the books published on Siamese in the late 1960s and early 1970s referred to Tabby Pointed Siamese as a new variety: nowadays they are very much part of the Siamese scene and accepted by most for what they are, an aesthetically charming variety with a Siamese coat pattern. The variety was certainly popular in its early days, with Kit Wilson predicting in 1962 "a great future for this new colour!"

ORIGIN OF THE VARIETY

Inevitably the story behind these kittens was typical of most mis-matings – Miss Eileen Alexander's Seal Point Siamese queen by the name of Lady Me disappeared from the house. But the brazen queen was caught and taken over to Mrs Buttery's Seal Point Siamese stud boy, Druid to be suitably mated. Nine weeks later Miss Alexander did have her expected litter which comprised five kittens including one "cuckoo in the nest" who had a Siamese coat with tabby points, suggesting that Lady Me had been dual-mated.

Looking back it became clear that the father, like numerous others in the free-ranging cat population who can be the result of mixed matings between pedigree Siamese and non-pedigree moggies, carried the Siamese coat pattern for restriction of points. Whenever a kitten is born sporting a difference, whether it be of colour or coat pattern, it usually manages to find its own home by staying with its owner, and this Tabby Pointed kitten, who had been given the name of Patti, was no exception.

When Patti came of mating age, she was taken by Miss Alexander to Mrs Buttery's other Seal Point Siamese stud boy, Samsara Saracen. This mating produced four more Patti lookalikes out of a litter of six kittens.

In 1961 Miss Alexander (who eventually became the Vice-President of the Tabby Pointed Cat Society), took her Tabby Point Siamese kittens, who had seal tabby striped points and Siamese type, to the Croydon Cat Club Championship Show to be placed in the Any Other Variety classes. Mary Dunnill remembered this particular show very clearly, with crowds gathered around the show pen all day asking questions. One of the most interested was her friend Greta Hindley, who bought a female kitten by the name of Tansy.

Tansy and her litter mates were regarded as being of very good Siamese type with lovely blue eye colour. Greta Hindley was most respected in the "world of the Siamese" and this unexpected purchase gave the Tabby Point Siamese an instant boost in popularity; she had given the variety her seal of approval.

Another friend of the two women, Mrs Marjorie Hudson, also bought one of the litter mates, a male Tabby Pointed Siamese by the name of Faux Pas, who had a pale coat and densely striped points. After the show she wrote one of the most descriptive accounts of this litter: "I could not take my eyes off them, such exquisite little creatures with cobweb-brushed faces, upstanding striped tails and the most glorious sapphire eyes."

After he came to live with her she had no definite plans for him but just felt that he could not be neutered. She later decided to keep him at stud and this fact was only mentioned to her two close friends, Mary Dunnill and Greta Hindley. So she was most surprised to find that another friend of hers, by the name of Phyllida Warner, had taken in a female Tabby Point Siamese queen to her stud boy Ch. Spotlight Troubadour. This queen had a totally different pedigree line that could be traced back to the breeding lines of Muriel Bennett of Reigate.

Mrs Bennett owned a Siamese queen by the name of Macji dom Dija who also had a penchant for a non-pedigree partner, but I have not been able to find this reference from any other source. The resultant litter of kittens took after their father, with coat pattern which was reported to be fawny-grey with mackerel striped markings. The moggie father had a round head and was described as Abyssinian type. Mary Dunnill did wonder if there had been any Burmese blood in this moggie's ancestry which may have passed along the dilute modifier gene to his Tabby Point Siamese offspring. This can be read about in the last chapter under the Caramel and Apricot heading.

Mrs Bennett kept one of these hybrid kittens for herself, giving her the name of Tiggi (sometimes spelt Tiggie). When older, she was mated to a Seal Point Siamese called Chancasta. The result was some more beautiful Tabby Point kittens.

One of the female kittens was known as Miss Tee Kat, nicknamed Misstee, and she went to live with Mr and Mrs Pears in Surrey. She was the first Tabby Point of this line and, when older, was taken to Mr Richard Warner's Champion Spotlight Troubadour to be mated.

The litter of kittens was born in January 1962. Phyllida Warner bought a female named Praline, who became the progenitor of the Spotlight Tabby Points. Miss Eileen Alexander, who had kept

Patti out of the other Tabby Point Siamese line, bought Mister Buttons as an unrelated mate for her cat and Mrs Hudson bought Lady Lynx (sometimes spelt Links), known as Shadow, whom she intended to be mated to Faux Pas later on.

It was most interesting that Eileen Alexander and Marjorie Hudson intended using the same blood lines to found their own Tabby Point Siamese lines. When fully grown, Lady Lynx's coat was described as: "sleek and pale, her ringed tail long and slender, whilst her head, deeply traced, is triangular and arresting. Her ears have the same sooty thumb marks on the back and her long body and lithe legs are daintily marked. Both Faux Pas and Lady Lynx have almost identical markings – strong and clearly defined." Unfortunately Lady Lynx was killed at a very young age by a motor car. Faux Pas became the first registered Tabby Point Siamese to be at stud and his picture showed him to be of a heavier type than that of Lady Lynx. Even more remarkable was the fact that the early Tabby Point Siamese had retained a white coat free of Tabby markings except for the shading down the dorsal part of the back. The description of "cobweb faces" stuck to them and the quality of their type placed the Tabby Point Siamese on a par with the best that could be found in the four recognised colours.

NAMING THE VARIETY

In 1962 there was much discussion about allocating the variety its breed name. Phyllida Warner pointed out in correspondence in *Fur and Feather* that, in being known as Lynx, they could be likened to the Asian Lynx, as the markings on both cats were similar. Breeders who liked the name of Lynx argued that the use of the word imparted an aura of mountain heritage and large black-tipped ears. Others used a weak argument saying that the use of the word implied that the variety would be perceived as being related to the wild Lynx cat.

Purists in the Siamese section argued for not including Tabby Point Siamese as part of the Siamese breed – they should be classified as a totally new breed. Roy Silson entered the debate by explaining the variety's genetic heritage. To all intents and purposes the variety was initially Siamese with the exception of one gene.

Considering accidental matings had precipitated the development of this variety, the breeding programme that produced each successive generation could not be improved upon. Examination of Spotlight Pendy Lynx's pedigree in 1963 revealed fifteen great great grandparents whose blood lines were Siamese, the sixteenth line going back to the illicit matings which had provided the means to a new variety.

Breeders realised that the introduction of a new blood line had created a Siamese that was recognised to be strong and healthy. One lovely example was Nancy Hardy's Prestwick Pervenche who was bred by Greta Hindley out of Spotlight Polar Mynx and Tansy. Greta Hindley maintained her interest in Tabby Point Siamese to the extent of playing an active part, in 1964, in the formation of a new Siamese club which became known as the Shadowpoint and Progressive Breeders Cat Club. (Nowadays, this club is known as the Tabby Point Siamese and Progressive Breeders Cat Club.) Another specialist cat club was formed in 1964, that of the Lynx-Pointed Cat Club which, in July 1969, became the Tabby-Pointed Cat Society.

RECOGNITION

In 1966 the Siamese Cat Club accepted the variety to be known as Tabby Point Siamese and requested the GCCF to allocate a breed number and championship status. The Club asked that the variety should not be part of the already known and accepted 24 series, but that it should be allocated the separate breed number of 32, which would distinguish the variety from its solid-pointed cousins.

Chocolate Tabby Point: Gr. Ch. Simone Strawberries.

Photo: Paddy Cutts.

Chocolate Tabby Point: Sup. Gr. Ch. Zachary Apollo.

Photo: Paddy Cutts.

Chocolate Tabby Point: Milestone Chotacrystal, aged twelve, enjoying a happy retirement.

Photo: Christine Brooks.

FIRST CHAMPIONS

The first Tabby Point Siamese to gain the title of Champion was Spotlight Penny Lynx. Her mother was Praline who had been mated to Whiteoaks Malahide. The show where Spotlight Penny Lynx gained her Challenge Certificate was the Siamese Cat Society of the British Empire, where she also picked up the award of Best in Show. Her other two Certificates were awarded at the Siamese Cat Club Show and the Wessex show. It was reputed that she was in all probability the first Tabby Point Champion in the world. She was described as a cat with "silver grey ears overbalancing her". Her owners were besieged with requests for a kitten to look just like Penny.

Penny produced Ch. Spotlight Rouble and his sister Ch. Spotlight Kopeika in 1969. However, occasionally a year can bring nothing but bad luck and this occurred for the Warners with the birth of Kopeika by Caesarian and the death of Spotlight Penny Lynx at the age of seven. The shining cloud on the horizon was the fact that Spotlight Kopeika was regarded by many as the ultimate Tabby Point Siamese of all. At the age of five months she was awarded the accolade of Best Exhibit at the Siamese Cat Association show which was held in Hastings. This award was felt to be even more remarkable when it became known that she had to be kept alive by oxygen after her birth. May Eustace also fell under her spell. She wrote in *Fur and Feather:* "Spotlight Kopeika, to my mind the Tabby Point of the year, is an exquisite fine boned kitten with the best whipped tail I have ever seen. She has gorgeous eye colour and a very long head, ending in a fine muzzle, tail beautifully ringed, in fact simply oozing type ..." By the time this little girl was one year old, she had obtained her title and, as the Warners did not believe in overshowing, she was retired from the show bench. She produced some outstanding kittens but she alone could be regarded as true to the Tabby Point Siamese standard of the day. Other breeders took to Tabby Point Siamese, including Mrs A. Aslin who bred Seremban Liger. He became the first Siamese cat to gain the title of Grand Champion. He was renowned for his excellent type; a photograph shows him as having well-set eyes and ears and typical tabby spotting on his whisker pads. He had been sired by Spotlight Siegfried.

THE LAST 25 YEARS

The mid 1970s show season saw Tabby Pointed Siamese having the least number of Challenge

Certificates withheld out of all the Siamese varieties. Pam Wilding brought Ch. Dandycat Mischief Maker out of semi-retirement to win a Grand Challenge Certificate. Two other Tabby Pointed Siamese gained their titles of Champion – Mrs Choules' Shirotae Kruger and Miss Leach's Elbaraka Obed.

Another outstanding young man gained two titles in 1974-75 show season, Mrs Daniel's Lymekilns Som Chai, who was bred by Mr and Mrs A. Saunders. He gained the title of Champion and followed this with the title of Premier after he was neutered. This was not all – he also obtained a Grand Premier Certificate at the Northern Siamese Cat Society Show.

A well-respected prefix was advertised with Sislinki Tanchai, who gained his title of Premier. He was owned by Mrs Dear and bred by Mrs Pat Neale.

The popularity of the breed was enhanced when Ch. Moondance Jocasta, bred and owned by Mrs J. P. Brain, achieved the award of Supreme Adult Exhibit in 1976.

Another Supreme Award in the 1980-1981 Show Year followed for Ch. Zachary Bat Girl, a Lilac Tabby Point Siamese who was bred by Mrs J. Lynn. She received the title of Best Kitten at this show.

This achievement was followed in 1982 with Zachary Apollo, a Chocolate Tabby Point Siamese, who was bred by Mrs J. Lynn and owned by Mrs Doreen Sillis, being awarded the accolade of Supreme Grand Champion. His owner was absolutely stunned yet delighted. His name now appears in many Siamese (and Oriental) pedigree lines. He was Ch. Zachary Bat Girl's half-brother. In 1984 the Tabby Point Siamese variety gained even greater popularity with a young male Red Tabby Point, by the name of Soria Sanjo Panza, being awarded the title of Supreme Grand Champion. He was bred and owned by Mrs M. E. Hunt, and his father was Supreme Grand Champion, Zachary Apollo.

Gr. Ch. Simone Strawberries features in many pedigrees today; he is registered as a Chocolate Tabby Point Siamese and was bred and owned by Mrs Wendy Summerfield.

The decade of the 1990s has seen some outstanding examples of the Tabby Point Series, some of whom appeared in the "Pride of Siamese Cats" exhibition at the Siamese Cat Association Show held in 1994. This exhibition showed quite a colour range amongst this variety.

The Tabby Point Siamese cats listed in the catalogue included some of the most well-known prefixes in the Siamese fancy. There was Gr. Pr. Bluecroft Sunsationallad, 32/6, a Cream Tabby Point Siamese. He was bred by Mrs P. Mapes and is owned by Margaret Brazier. A few pens down the row saw Gr. Ch. Ginnistam Culprit, 32/1, a Seal Tabby Point who was bred and is owned by Mrs Margaret Hardy. Also in competition were Gr. Ch. Midamyst Handfulapromises, a Red Tabby Point bred and owned by Mrs J. Bright, and Gr. Pr. Ootha Miss Tiddles, a Chocolate Tortie Tabby Point bred and owned by Miss M. Davidson-Smith. Both these cats added variety of colour to the show.

The on-going quality of the Tabby Point Siamese variety was demonstrated at the Supreme Cat Show, November 1994, when Paul Taylor's Seal Tabby Point, Gr. Ch. Kwai Ashburnipal, gained his first UK Grand Challenge Certificate.

In the CFA in North America, Tabby Pointed Siamese are known as Colourpoint Shorthairs. This description covers all the colours produced in the Lynx Tabby Point series. Other registration bodies in North America combine Lynx Point Siamese under the description of Siamese.

Chapter Fourteen

THE SEX-LINKED SERIES OF COLOURS

The issue of *The Rabbit Keeper and Show Reporter* dated September 19th 1888 included an item about a very interesting Siamese seen at the Bawtry show which had been held on September 4th: 'Kittens, 2nd (Mrs H. Young), salmon Siamese, a very beautiful one'. The use of the word 'salmon' is most interesting: was the reader to interpret the kitten as being 'Salmon Red' in colour and, if so, was this kitten's phenotype that of a Red Point Siamese? The answer to this question will never be known.

There is, however, another early record of two Red Point Siamese cats being exhibited, this time at the Siamese Cat Club Show in 1934. *Fur and Feather* referred to 'ginger' pointed Siamese. They were also described as 'orange' points. The cats had white bodies, red points and blue eyes; they looked Siamese and they certainly aroused a great deal of interest. Correspondence in *Fur and Feather* stated that the parents were two Seal Pointed Siamese – which left people wondering where the ginger came from.

However the owner of the sire, Mrs Basnett, corrected this and confirmed the sire was a 'densely pointed Siamese' and that the dam actually had tortoiseshell points. In all other ways she looked like a typical Siamese. When mated, it was confirmed that some of the male kittens produced by this "Tortoiseshell Point Siamese" had red points, whilst some of the female progeny had tortoiseshell points.

The dam's pedigree was most interesting; she was the result of a Siamese male mating with a shorthaired half-Siamese tortoiseshell female. Her maternal grandfather was reputed to be Ch. Bonzo, the well-known Seal Point Siamese, born in 1924.

THE SEX-LINKED GENE INHERITANCE
The breeding behind the Red Point Siamese exhibited in 1934 revealed the sex-linked inheritance of the gene for orange. This gene expresses itself in cats in the colours of red, ginger and marmalade. However, the early Tortoiseshell Pointed Siamese were recorded as lacking Siamese type and they had very round heads. Their tortoiseshell colour markings tended not to be restricted to the points – they 'bled' into the white part of the coats.

There are always genetic exceptions to the rules, but tortoiseshell cats are usually female. Very occasionally a male tortoiseshell will appear, but such cats are usually sterile.

INVESTIGATIONS INTO BREEDING
The present-day Red and Tortie Point Siamese lines are the result of breeding investigations carried out in Britain in 1948 by the New Zealander, Dr Norah Archer

A similar breeding investigation, by the English-born Mrs Alyce de Filippo started in the USA in 1947, using a Seal Point Siamese female and a Red Tabby long-haired male. In 1951 she took Red Point Siamese to the Beresford Cat Show in Chicago. The variety was recognised in the USA as early as 1956, classed as Red Colour Point Short-hairs. Some American registration bodies still class this variety as Colourpoint Short-hairs whilst others recognise them under the classification of Siamese. Dr Norah Archer wrote a synopsis of her breeding programme in an Australian magazine *The Cat World*, which was the official journal of the Governing Council of the Cat Fancy. It was reprinted by *Our Cats* magazine in the UK.

"In breeding Red Points we are deliberately combining genetic factors which have not until recently been studied in association. The officially recognised breeds of Siamese cat, Seal, Blue and Chocolate, all have the same basic pigment, melanin. It is modified in the Blue and Chocolate breeds by a dilution factor specific to each breed. Red colour in cats is produced by an entirely different basic pigment. Whether this pigment would behave differently from the black pigment when combined with the Siamese restriction factor could only be discovered by experimental breeding and observation.

"So far as I have had the opportunity of watching colour development in Red Points, the story is precisely the same as in Seal Points. The kittens are born white, and within a few days begin to show colour in the ears and tail. Later the mask, forelegs and hind feet gradually become pigmented, and when growth is nearly complete, a shading of gold appears on the back.

"To plan successfully the production of a Red Pointed Siamese strain *de novo*, it must be clearly appreciated that the pigment genes in cats are sex-linked. That is, they are carried in special chromosomes, called the X chromosomes. The female possesses a pair of these chromosomes, while the male has only one X chromosome, his pair being completed by the Y chromosome which makes him a male. It follows from this that a Red male can be bred from a Tortie or a Red female, irrespective of the colour of his sire, whereas a Red female can only be bred from a mating in which red pigment is present in both parents."

HISTORY OF A RED POINT SIAMESE
For the British breeding investigation, Dr Archer had been given a Red Point Siamese kitten, born in 1948, by Lucy Price, who eventually became the President of the Red Point and Tortie Point

Red Point: Sup. Gr. Ch. & UK Gr. Pr. Pannaduloa Blazer.

Photo: Paddy Cutts.

Siamese Cat Club. He was registered as Somerville Scarlet Pimpernel. His antecedents were most interesting. His father was a Seal Point Siamese by the name of Yewtree Yaanta, owned by Mrs Gordon Wilson, and his mother was known as Amanda. She was a tortoiseshell of Siamese type and her mother was Devoran Sally Girl (Ming), born in 1945 and bred by Lucy Price out of Little Miss Moffet, sired by Prestwick Prithie Pal. Ming's owner, Mrs Matthews, accidentally let her out and she was mated by a red Tabby moggie who must have carried the Siamese coat pattern.

Somerville Scarlet Pimpernel, known as Robber, had inherited the Siamese gene for restriction of colour to points and he was described by a past committee member of the Siamese Cat Association, Miss Dukes, as having dark colour points. However, his type was definitely Siamese and he had almond-shaped eyes which were described as "forget-me-not" blue. His colour was deep gold, with his mask being described as a lighter gold in colour. Apparently when young the gold socks on Robber's feet took some time to come through. His nose and pads were pink in colour. One of the features expressed in the sex-linked colours is that of tabby markings and, in the case of Robber, the colour on his tail showed through in typical tabby rings.

When older, Robber was mated to Doneraile Dew who had been born on April 21st 1947. One of the reasons for choosing a Seal Pointed Siamese female was to maintain the Siamese type in the line. Out of this mating came a Tortie Point Siamese by the name of Somerville Harlequinna. She, in turn, was mated back to her father, Robber, and a daughter of the resultant litter was kept by Dr Archer.

BREED REGISTRATIONS UNDER AOV

This female was registered as Somerville Golden Seal, who was the first Red Point Siamese female. Somerville Harlequinna was given to Mrs Dunks. In time she was mated to Gracedieu Luan and this resulted in the birth of two females who were registered as Cheyne Harlequin Mies and Cheyne Gem. The male kitten in the litter was registered as Cheyne Red Robin. The GCCF registered them with the 'blanket' breed number of 26, under the description of Any Other Variety.

These matings were followed by others, one of which resulted in the birth of Cheyne Harlequin Sari, bred by Mrs Dunks, who was a Tortie Point Siamese, also registered under the AOV 26 breed number. However, her type was perceived to be so good that she won a First Prize at a cat show held in Kings Lynn for her owner, Mrs Statham. Unusually for a Tortie Point Siamese she had one solid seal leg but all other points showed densely marked tortoiseshell colours. At the same time Mrs Statham also showed a Red Point Siamese by the name of Martial Red Monkey.

THE PENARWYN PREFIX

Miss A. Ray of the Penarwyn prefix started her breeding line in the early 1950s with a Somerville Tortie Point Siamese from Dr Norah Archer, which ultimately led to her producing a Red Point Siamese female in three stages. The Tortie Point Siamese was mated to a Seal Point Siamese stud boy. Out of this mating came a Red Point Siamese male and a subsequent mating, back to his mother, produced a Red Point Siamese female. Miss Ray then proceeded to comply with Rule 4(f) of the GCCF Registration Rules (as mentioned in the Lilac Point section) by carrying out a breeding programme designed to produce Red and Tortie Point Siamese over five generations.

APPLYING FOR RECOGNITION

The next stage was to apply for recognition, but the GCCF felt they could not allocate a breed number as a Siamese variety at this stage of development. They counter-proposed a registration policy together with a breed number under the classification of 'Foreign Shorthair'.

This was not accepted by Miss Ray, because her breeding line, after ten generations of breeding, looked Siamese in type, and a further attempt for recognition was made in 1958. The GCCF sought the services of the Siamese Cat Club who debated the matter and, in their reply, brought up the argument of tabby markings which appeared in conjunction with the sex-linked colours.

It would appear that at that time there were no cats around with solid red points to indicate otherwise. The Siamese Cat Club's final conclusion on this attempt for recognition was that there were not enough breeders who were interested enough to justify the proposal.

FORMATION OF A NEW CAT CLUB

By 1965 interest in the red and tortie varieties had increased so much, with many cats being registered under the AOV breed number of 26, that a new Siamese Cat Club, The Red Point and Tortie Point Club, was formed by Mrs Lingard and Mrs Cahill. One of the first tasks to be undertaken by the members was to prepare material on Red Point Siamese for an application for recognition.

At the committee meeting of the Siamese Cat Club held on July 7th 1966, a decision was taken to recommend to the GCCF that recognition should be granted to cats 'of Siamese pattern and type' currently registered as AOV 26. The separate breed number of 32 was suggested, using the subsidiary letters of 'a' and 'b' to indicate different varieties. These two varieties were to be given the breed names of Red Point Siamese and Seal Tortie Point Siamese respectively. These recommendations were put before the GCCF on July 13th 1966 and the two varieties were granted Championship Status. In the following year, May 1967, the Red Point and Tortie Point Siamese Cat Club became affiliated to the GCCF.

Sadly, Miss Ray did not live long enough to see her interest in the variety rewarded in this way.

EARLY LINES AND CHAMPIONS

The first Red Point Siamese to become a Champion was Pitapat Zeno Belili, whose red colour was derived from Mrs Maureen Silson's Southview line behind Southview Belili. He was bred by Mrs Holt. Mrs Angela Sayer of the Solitaire prefix was also interested in breeding the variety.

One of the most famous prefixes of all time was that of 'Darling', owned by Irene George. When she started breeding Red Point Siamese she lived in the North of England. She bred show winner Gr. Ch. Darling Red Shadow, who was owned by Mrs Deakin. Darling Red Hawk was born on May 8th 1974 out of Ch. Taurus Kountry Boy and Syming Neapoliton. He was owned by Mrs S. Chapman. He later achieved his title of Champion. Double Grand Champion Darling Red Rufus became well known in West Germany, and another Darling became very well known in the USA, Ch. Darling Red Shade of Tintadel. Ch. Shiva Red Admiral was very well known in his time, and he obtained his colouring through his mother, Darling April Showers.

Other Red Point Siamese of that decade included Moonfleet Sandpiper who was bred by Mrs B Greenland and owned by Mr and Mrs McGinty. He was shown at the Siamese Cat Association Show on June 7th 1975, having been born on July 30th 1974.

The most famous Red Point Siamese of all was Mr John Hansson's Pannaduloa Blazer. He obtained the title of Supreme Grand Champion in 1986. As the Judges were deciding which cat would be awarded this prestigious title, a group of interested onlookers had gathered around the podium. The atmosphere was almost electric as Blazer's win was announced. Cheers and clapping filled the hall for a most popular cat and his breeder.

Another outstanding Red Point Siamese is UK Grand Champion Bluecroft Birthday Boy, bred by Mrs P. Mapes, and he has been very influential in siring many show winners. His progeny include Gr. Ch. Littlefeat Cajun Girl, 32a, Gr. Pr. Littlefeat Red Streamliner, 32a, Gr. Ch. Tikoon Antares Leo, 32a, and Gr. Ch. Serenata Serengeti Sun, 32a. He has also sired many other Siamese

*Seal Tortie Point: Ch.
Cobweb Mist.*

Photo: Paddy Cutts.

*Seal Tortie Point:
Crisaliz Ladyeleanor.*

Photo: Christine Brooks.

show winners in other varieties, including Gr. Pr. Helsbels Hocus Pocus, 32c, Gr. Ch. Summerdown Gold Medal, 32c, and Gr. Ch. Rantipole Entropy, 32bl.

In the 1990s Ch. Crisaliz Chillichops, a Red Point Siamese who was bred by Ms C. Brooks and Mrs E. M. Brooks and owned by Mrs Rosie Meekings, obtained his title of Champion. Averil Moon's own-bred Gr. Ch. Stravanganza Scarlet Lady was acknowledged to be the best Red Point Siamese at the Supreme Cat Show in November 1994.

THE EARLY TORTIE POINTS
It was recorded that the early Tortie Point Siamese were not very typy; they had rather round heads and their markings 'bled' into their coats. These failings were soon remedied when breeders recognised that this variety, which are nearly always female, were most useful in their breeding programmes in producing a wide range of other coloured point Siamese.

As type improved the variety picked up their Challenge Certificates and Daphne Deakin's Rivendell Apache became the first Tortie Point Siamese Champion. Another Tortie Point Champion received her title in 1969, Mrs McLean Inglis' Ceedee-Em Seraphina. Mr and Mrs Rimmer's Ch. Asuni Ki Sin became very well known for her type and tortie colouring.

PROMINENT PREFIXES

The Palantir prefix of Miss Julia May was seen behind a few Tortie Point Siamese – Palantir Galadriel, Palantir Laurelin and Palantir Lorien, who was owned by Miss J. Hutchison. Another famous prefix was that of Mrs S. Humphris, who bred this series of Siamese under the Patrician prefix. Patrician Tiffany was born on June 25th 1974, having been sired by Whiterose Merlin. On June 14th 1980 one of the most unusual Tortie Point Siamese of all was born, Ch. Marilane Harlequin, whose breed number was 32b1. He was bred by Mrs Glenda Ford and was the only male Tortie Point Siamese on the show bench. He was found to be fertile as well and bred as a Seal Point Siamese. His genetic make-up was investigated at Bristol and he was found to be XXYY. He died on July 28th, 1994 at the grand age of fourteen and a half years. An up and coming Seal Tortie Point Siamese youngster who achieved the Best in Show Kitten award at the 1994 Siamese Cat Association Show is Rantipole Pandemonium (now a champion), born in 1993. Her sire was Ch. Crisaliz Chillichops and dam was Ch. Rantipole Entropy. She is bred and owned by Rosie Meekings. At the 1994 Supreme Cat Show the title of UK Gr. Champion was awarded to Patrician Mistral, bred bnny Mrs Humphries, owned by Averil Moon.

Red Point: Chrisaliz Solarflare. 'Solar' was originally registered as a Red Tabby Point Siamese because he had a Tabby Point Siamese father. However, his progeny have proved that he breeds as a Red Point, and so his registration has been changed.

OTHER SEX-LINKED VARIETIES

Looking at the history of the other varieties covered by the heading of the Sex-Linked series, another decision was taken at that committee meeting of the Siamese Cat Club held on July 7th 1966. This recommended to the GCCF that recognition should be granted to all other Siamese varieties under the heading of 'Any Other Dilutions' (AOD), breed number 32c.

This was agreed by the GCCF on July 13th 1966 and for a few short months it appeared that Siamese cats under this classification enjoyed Championship status. However, in September 1966, the GCCF decided to postpone the granting of Championship status to this group until more investigative work in breeding and the clarification of breed standards had been carried out.

This 'AOD' group included the many variations arising from the combination of matings that could occur with the Red series. This series included Cream and its accompanying combination of matings, Cream being the dilute shade of Red. Another 'sub-variety' included the Tabby-Tortie Point Siamese.

THE COLOURPOINT, REX COATED AND AOV CLUB

Then another cat club arrived on the scene, The Colourpoint, Rex Coated and AOV Club. Their first Newsletter, produced in September 1967, described them as being affiliated to the GCCF and catering for the interests of Colourpoints, Rex coated cats, Long Haired, Bi-colours and all varieties not recognised for breed classification or Championship status by the GCCF

In October 1967 this particular club requested the Midland Cat Club to put on a Club Class for Red Point, Tortie Point, Cream Point, Blue-Cream Point, Chocolate-Cream Point and Lilac-Cream Point Siamese. This caused some concern because the varieties listed already had a cat club which had been specifically formed to look after their interests. The Colourpoint Rex-Coated and AOV Club eventually advertised themselves as "Catering for the interests of all unrecognised breeds".

NEW CLASSIFICATION

On February 14th 1968 it was suggested to Mary Dunnill, in her capacity as Honorary Secretary of the Siamese Cat Club, that an attempt should be made to create a logical classification and registration system for all varieties of Siamese cats to include the new colours. She sent out a letter to members of the Siamese Cat Club dated April 19th 1968 announcing the conference on new colours and patterns of Siamese to be held at the Meeting Rooms of the Zoological Society of London on Saturday April 27th 1968. It was announced that there would be a representative exhibition of cats to include a "Red Point, Cream Point, Seal Tortie Point, Blue Tortie Point (also known as Blue/Cream), Chocolate Tortie Point (also known as Chocolate/Cream), Lilac Tortie Point (also known as Lilac/Cream), Seal Tabby Point, Blue Tabby Point, Chocolate Tabby Point, Tabby Tortie Point etc."

The proposal for the reclassification of these Siamese varieties was enclosed with the letter for the purpose of discussion. Some of the experimental breeders of the day, including Mrs Pam Evely, Kernow prefix, and Mrs Maureen Silson, Southview prefix, brought along cats for the conference.

But by 1969 Elsie Hart was sadly reporting in *Fur and Feather* that the litter class of that year's Kensington show was "an eye-opener of what was happening to Siamese breeding". Most of the litters of kittens on exhibition were mixed in colour and a Siamese breeder would be fortunate "to find a sire and dam guaranteed to throw all of one colour".

The established breeders thought that the early 1970s saw some strange-looking Siamese! By February 1971, the Siamese varieties of Blue, Lilac and Chocolate Tortie Point Siamese, which had been identified under the classification of AOD, Any Other Dilutions, 32c, were moved to

Red Point: Patrician Papoose.

Photo: Paddy Cutts.

share the breed number of 32b with the Seal Tortie Point Siamese and they became eligible to compete for Championship status.

The rest of the Siamese left under the breed group of 32c included Cream Point Siamese, Red, Cream and Tortie Tabby Point Siamese and any other unclassified colour combination bred with a Siamese pattern.

However, it was not long before some of these other varieties obtained a breed number and Championship status. In October 1973, Red, Cream and Tortie Tabby Points were included under the breed number of 32, which had been originally allocated in 1966 to the Tabby Point variety of Siamese.

CREAM POINT SIAMESE

The number of Siamese varieties being registered under the breed number of 32c was rapidly being reduced. By this stage it only included Cream Point Siamese with a few other Siamese 'oddities' resulting from other breeding programmes of the Havana, Foreign and Oriental Breed Group, now known as the Oriental Cat Association.

The Cream Point Siamese had another mountain to climb before eventually achieving recognition. In 1974, the Red Point and Tortie Point Siamese Cat Club requested Championship status for Cream Point Siamese, which was refused. But the variety were half-way towards achieving this, because their Standard of Points was approved and they were given sole use of the breed number of 32c.

Two well-known prefixes showed Cream Point Siamese at the Siamese Cat Association Show on June 7th 1975; these included Ch. Nikkys Red Enka who was born on January 18th 1974 and Mrs

B. Greenland's Moonfleet Masquerade who was owned by Mrs J. Yerbury.

On 1st June 1977, the Cream Pointed Siamese finally obtained Championship status. Their cause had been championed by Mrs Margaret Baxter who described them as having soft pinky-beigy points with white bodies "flushed" with this colour. In the USA, there had been a reference to them as Ivory Point Siamese.

One of the early Cream Point Champions and Premiers was Ch. and Pr. Palantir Tom Bombadil, born on May 31st 1979, bred by Miss Julia May. He was sired by Ch. Coromandel Blue Beau and his dam was Ch. Palantir Nenya.

An outstanding Cream Point Siamese male epitomising the 1990s decade for style is Gr. Pr. Dazzling Jen Tsun, who was born on March 10th 1991 and bred by Nick Gourley and Andy Leonard. Other 'Dazzling' Cream Point Siamese progeny who are winning well on the Show Bench include Dazzling Princeofspirits and Ch. Dazzling Dreamside, both owned by Mrs Mee. These two Cream Point Siamese were sired by Gr. Ch. Dazzling Devilindisguise, who is owned by Mrs J. Lynn. Another son sired by Gr. Ch. Devilindisguise is Pr. Dazzling Krishna, owned by Mr and Mrs Steve Pullen.

OTHER VARIETIES

The reclassification of the Cream Points left the other unrecognised varieties of Siamese without a breed number for registration purposes and so they were classified under 32x. It was decided to implement a new registration policy to clarify matters.

A breeder's advertisement in The Nottinghamshire and Derbyshire Cat Club catalogue of the Thirtieth Championship Show held on January 3rd 1976 made interesting reading. Mrs Sheila Hocken advertised her kittens that were available from Sharlroi Tudor Rose who was registered as a Red Tabby Point. In brackets was the comment 'two Challenge Certificates, one as a red point, one as a tabby point'! This comment was due to a change in registration policy that apparently Red Point Siamese with a Tabby parent should be registered as Red Tabby Point Siamese.

In 1977 a new scheme involving the use of an Experimental Register was introduced so that Siamese cats and kittens who came under this category could be registered without a breed number. It was also decided that they could no longer enter competitive classes at Cat Shows held under GCCF rules. At the same time the registration of the AOV, Breed 26 and Any other Colour Siamese, 32x, ceased.

Further sub-classification of the Tortie Point variety of Siamese occurred in February 1979 when the GCCF sanctioned the use of numbers to make the registration of Tortie Point clearer: Seal Tortie Point became 32bi, Blue Tortie Point, 32bii, Chocolate Tortie Point, 32biii and Lilac Tortie Point, 32biv.

Finally, in February 1980, revised Standards of Points came into operation for all Siamese varieties including Red Point Siamese, Tortie Point Siamese and Cream Point Siamese.

Many other prefixes specialised in breeding these varieties well into the 1980s and some have carried on into the early 1990s. Well-known names include Edna Cahill's 'Warah', Julie M. Dray's 'Bickyroo', Mrs Davie's 'Marrondon', John Hansson's 'Pannaduloa', Sandra Soper's 'Leolee', June Hutchison's 'Syntax', Glenda Ford's 'Marilane' and Margaret Brazier's Sunsational prefixes.

The Sex-linked series of Siamese in all its amazing colour variations is still very popular today, even though the problem of identifying between the Red and Cream colours in Siamese still exists. In the last two years an experienced breeder has noticed that at least five Red Point Siamese have been shown as Cream Point Siamese and one Cream Point Siamese has been shown as a Red Point Siamese!

Chapter Fifteen

GENETICS OF THE SIAMESE

by Roy Robinson, F.I. Biol.

The Siamese cat originated in the region of Thailand several centuries ago as a mutant form of one of the basic genes for production of hair pigment, namely, the full colour gene C which all cats must possess if they are to be fully coloured (tabby, black, etc.). Cats with the Siamese mutant have characteristic seal or sepia coloured coats. The Burmese is another mutant of the same basic gene and the coloration is similar, although with a generally darker coat.

The pigment granules which are responsible for colouring the hairs are normally an intense blackish-brown mediated biochemically by the C gene. However, in the hairs of the coat in the Burmese and Siamese, the granules are a lighter brown due to reduction of the amount of pigment within them. The effect of the modification is to produce a sepia brown to the human eye. The modification is not uniform throughout the coat, for it is typical of cats with these mutants to have "points" (nose, ears, feet and tail) darker than the general body colouring. This is shown by both the Burmese and Siamese, very noticeably for the latter. The eyes of the Siamese have less pigment than normal, with the result that the irises appear blue.

The Siamese mutant gene is inherited in a straightforward, simple manner. That is to say, if a black cat is mated to a Siamese, the offspring (known as the F1) will be black in colour. If the F1 blacks are mated together, the offspring (known as the F2) will be expected to consist of three black and one Siamese. If the F1 are mated to Siamese, the expectation for the offspring (known as the BC, meaning back-cross) is one black and one Siamese. This pattern of heredity represents typical dominance/recessive heredity of the genes.

Anyone with an inquiring mind should ask the questions: how can the above ratios be explained? How is it that these particular ratios are to be expected? The reason resides in the physical basis of heredity, the chromosomes. Each body cell contains a constant number of matched pairs of chromosomes. In effect, there are two of each chromosome. Now, the genes are carried by the chromosomes, one after another, like "beads on a string". It follows that each gene is present twice. On the other hand, the reproductive or germ cells contain only one of the matched pairs of chromosomes and, ipso facto, one of each gene. The germ cells are the sperm of the male and the ova of the female.

To facilitate the discussion of the inheritance and genetic constitution of the various colour varieties of Siamese, the genes are denoted by symbols, not merely as a convenient shorthand but to convey information: capital letters for dominant genes and small letters for recessive genes. The full colour gene is represented by a capital C. The Siamese is represented by c^s, small c to indicate that the gene is a recessive mutant gene of C and the superscript s to indicate precisely that the gene is the Siamese. A black cat will possess two full colour genes CC while a Siamese will have two Siamese genes $c^S c^S$. When the germ cells are formed, the number of chromosomes are halved and each germ cell will have one gene. Gene C in the case of the black cat and c^S for the Siamese. If the two cats are mated, the union of the germ cell will have the constitution Cc^S. Practical breeding experiments have shown these F1 cats are black in colour. Note that genes carried by the F1 are dissimilar. This means that the germ cells will be of two kinds, some carrying C and others carrying c^S. Furthermore, these will be produced in equal numbers.

The F2 offspring of mating the F1 to each other will be the outcome of the random union of the C and c^S bearing germ cells. Gene C from one parent has an equal chance of meeting up with either C or c^S from the other parent to give offspring of constitution CC and Cc^S; while gene c^S has an equal chance of meeting up with either C or c^S to give offspring of constitution C^S and $c^S c^S$. Summing these chances gives a total of 1 CC, 2 Cc^S and 1 $c^S c^S$. Since CC and Cc^S are both black cats, the F2 will be comprised of an expected ratio of 3 black and 1 Siamese kittens.

The random union of the C and c^S germ cells is shown diagrammatically by Fig. 1.

	C	c^S
C	CC Black	Cc^S Black
c^S	Cc^S Black	$c^S c^S$ Siamese

Fig. 1 The expectations in the F2 generation from breeding inter se the black F1 from an initial mating between a black and a seal Siamese.

The BC generation of the F1 mated to Siamese will produce the expected 1:1 ratio of black and Siamese kittens because, while the F1 will be producing two sorts of germ cells (C and c^S), the Siamese will be producing only one (c^S). The random union of the germ cells will result in kittens of constitutions Cc^S and $c^S c^S$.

These expectation are shown diagrammatically by Fig. 2.

	C	c^S
c^S	Cc^S Black	$c^S c^S$ Siamese

Fig. 2. The expectation in the backcross generation from mating the black F1 of an initial mating between a black and seal Siamese to seal Siamese.

The backcross may be made to the black parent but there is little point in doing so because all the offspring will be black. The F1 will be producing germ cells C and c^S but, now, the black parent will be producing only C. The random union of these will give CC and Cc^S kittens in equal numbers but both will be black.

The Siamese bred in the F2 and BC generation to the Siamese will breed true for the colour. This follows because these have the constitution c^Sc^S and can only produce c^S germ cells. It should perhaps be cautioned that this will only apply to colour; other features contributed by the initial black grandparent may be very un-Siamese-like.

THE FOUR BASIC COLOURS

For many decades, the only recognized colour varieties of Siamese were seal, blue, chocolate and lilac. Seal is the combination of black with the Siamese pattern. The points are seal brown instead of black, and the body fur is sepia shaded, because of the effect of the Siamese gene on the pigment granules. If Siamese is combined with blue, the points are blue and the body blue-shaded; similarly for the chocolate and the lilac. In each case, the points are typical of the colour, but paler, while the body is appropriately shaded tending to pastel. The eyes are consistently blue for each variety.

These colours may be regarded as the basic colours of cats for they recur in many breeds in addition to the Siamese. The genes which produce the colours are well known. These are d (blue) and b (chocolate), being mutant forms of gene D for intense coloration and gene B for black pigment respectively. When combined with each other, the genotypes are BBDDCC (black), BBddCC (blue), bbDDCC (chocolate) and bbddCC (lilac).

The genetic constitution of the black or seal Siamese is $BBDDc^Sc^S$. In other words, a pair of Siamese genes (c^Sc^S) have replaced the full colour genes (CC) which are normally present. Similarly, the blue Siamese will be $BBddc^Sc^S$, the chocolate, $bbDDc^Sc^S$, and the lilac, $bbddc^Sc^S$. This is because the c^S gene is a mutant of C and is inherited as an alternative to it, effectively displacing the C gene in the genotype.

At this time, few people will be contemplating crossing Siamese with other breeds except for the express purpose of creating new varieties. On the other hand, crossing between varieties of Siamese is common and for a number of reasons, such as increasing the numbers of the rarer colours, improvement of mediocre stock or to avoid too much inbreeding.

GENETIC INHERITANCE

A fundamental property of heredity is that the genes are inherited independently and recombine at random. The above four colours will illustrate the point. Suppose it is desired to produce the lilac point and no cats of the colour are available; however, the "raw material" of blue point and chocolate point is available. How would one proceed? The answer is to mate these two colours together. The F1 will be seal point and mating these together will produce a F2 of 9 seal point, 3 blue point, 3 chocolate point and 1 lilac point. The lilac point emerged due to the recombination of the genes for blue point and chocolate point.

The two gene pairs involved are B versus b and D versus d. The genetic constitution of the blue is BBdd and that for the chocolate is bbDD. We are now dealing with the simultaneous inheritance of two genes instead of one pair (C versus c^S) as in the heredity of the Siamese coloration. However, the same rules apply. The germ cells will transmit one of each pair. That is, the germ cells from the blue point parent will contain the genes Bd and those from the chocolate will contain the genes bD. Fusion of the germ cells will produce the F1 of BbDd. These will be seal point because B is dominant to b and D is dominant to d.

The interesting aspect is when the F1 are mated together. A mixed bag of germ cells are produced as the result of random combination of the two pairs of genes. When the germ cells are formed, chance comes into play, in that there is equal likelihood for gene B to enter the same germ cell as gene D or d. Similarly, gene b will have equal likelihood of combining with either D or d.

This means that the F1 will be producing the four kinds of germ cell, BD, Bd, dB, and bd, in equal numbers.

The inter-mating of the Black F1 will result in the random combination of these four kinds of germ cells. It is possible to detail in words how this is accomplished but it is easier and more explicit to demonstrate the process by a similar diagram to that of Fig. 1 for the recombination of the genes C and c^S. These diagrams are known as genetic checkerboards and are freely used as a quick and accurate method of explaining elementary genetics. The procedure is simplicity itself. A large square is drawn and subdivided into as many smaller squares as there are numbers of different germ cells. The latter are written across the top and down the left side of the large square, as shown in Fig. 3.

	BD	Bd	bD	bd
BD	BBDD Black	BBDd Black	BbDD Black	BbDD Black
Bd	BBDD Black	BBdd Choc Tabby	BbDd Black	Bbdd Choc Tabby
bD	BbDD Black	BbDd Black	bbDD Choc	bbDd Choc
bd	BbDd Black	Bbdd Blue Tabby	bbDD Choc	bbdd Lilac

Fig. 3. The expectations in the F2 generation from mating the seal Siamese F1 inter se from an initial mating between a blue Siamese and chocolate Siamese.

There will be 16 smaller squares. Inside of each smaller square are entered the gene symbols at the top of the column and at the side of the row in which each square resides. It only remains to write in the colour of the Siamese, which is determined by the genetic constitution of each square. This is indicated by knowing which gene is dominant to its partner. That is, B and D to b and d, respectively. In summary, there 9 seal points with the constitutions BBDD, BBDb, BbDD and BbDd, 3 blue points with BBdd and Bbdd, 3 chocolate with bbDD and bbDd and 1 bbdd. The solitary lilac point cannot be other than lilac because it does not possess any dominant genes!

The expectations for the backcross generation from mating the F1 to lilac point is instructive because it shows the direct relationship of the equal numbers of four different germ cells with the expectations for the four colour varieties of Siamese. The four colours black, blue, chocolate and lilac will assort in a 1:1:1:1 ratio. The results are derived from the fact that the lilac point can only produce germs cells carrying the recessive gene b and d. See Fig. 4 for details. Incidentally, cats with two recessive genes are often referred to as "double recessive".

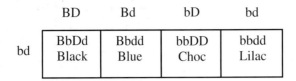

	BD	Bd	bD	bd
bd	BbDd Black	Bbdd Blue	bbDD Choc	bbdd Lilac

Fig. 4. The expectations in the backcross generation from mating the F1 seal Siamese from an initial mating between a blue Siamese and a chocolate Siamese to a lilac Siamese.

PHENOTYPE AND GENOTYPE

It is important to realize the difference between the appearance (phenotype) of an individual and its genes (genotype).The diagrams show that cats may be of the same phenotype but have different genotypes. Their similar appearance will belie the fact that they will breed differently. For example, the genotype BbDd is a black cat carrying two hidden recessive genes and will breed differently from a black without hidden genes or from one with only one hidden gene. Genetically, a cat without a hidden gene is known as a homozygote while a cat with a hidden gene is known as a heterozygote. It is usual to state which are the hidden genes in the following manner: a cat with the genotype BbDd would be described as "a black cat heterozygous for the genes b and d".

Table 1 lists the expected colour ratios of kittens for all of the possible matings between the four varieties of Siamese, both homozygotes (pure breeding for the colour) and heterozygotes (carrying the gene for the recessive colour). Note that lilac is produced by two genes (b and d): thus seal carrying lilac means the seal is heterozygous for both b and d; while a seal carrying brown or blue is heterozygous for either b or d, as the case may be, but not both. The other cases are more simple. Chocolate carrying 'lilac' is heterozygous for d, while blue carrying lilac is heterozygous for b. It would a useful exercise in elementary genetics for the reader to use the information of Figs. 3 and 4 to work out the expectations illustrated in Table 1 on the next page.

THE GENETIC IMPORTANCE OF TABBY POINTS

A significant event in the evolution of the Siamese varieties was the appearance of the tabby points. To understand how these are created, it is necessary to examine the genetics of the tabby pattern. The tabby coloration has two components: 1) the dark markings which, properly, are the tabby pattern, and 2) the greyish background. The dark markings need not concern us further, for it is the genetics of the background colour which is relevant.

The ground colour is known as agouti and it is produced by the black guard hairs being banded with yellow and tipped with black. Their presence, and the lie of the hairs, gives the coat its greyish colour. If the band were absent, the hairs would be completely black. A mutant gene has arisen from the basic agouti gene A which does just this. The mutant gene is denoted as non-agouti, symbolised by a – a fact that indicates that the gene is inherited as recessive to the agouti gene A. The effect of the genotype aa is to produce some of the various self-colours.

To be explicit, the genotype aaBBDD is the black, aabbDD is blue, aabbDD is chocolate and aabbdd is lilac. Add $c^s c^s$ to each of the genotypes (such as, aaBBDD$c^s c^s$ for the seal Siamese) and we have a more precise genotype for the four Siamese varieties. All of these have self-coloured points. Indeed, all of the varieties considered to date may be regarded as selfs. This being so, what will happen if the agouti gene A were to replace a, such as for instance, in AABBDD$c^s c^s$?

The answer is that the cat would be the seal tabby point Siamese. It should be obvious that four colours of tabby point Siamese are possible and this is indeed the situation. In brief, the genotypes

*Chocolate Point:
This Siamese displays
clearly defined
markings on the face,
ears and legs, while
maintaining a very
pale body colour.*

Photo: Paddy Cutts.

ABOVE: Seal Tabby Point:
Killdown Medea.

Photo: Paddy Cutts.

RIGHT: Seal Point:
Lalinda's Lady Jane,
imported into the UK by
Mary Dunhill, descended
from her US export,
Sumfun Banhari. In the
USA, this Seal Point
Siamese was registered as
Sumfun Banhari of Dahin
by her owner, John Dawe.

Photo: Paddy Cutts.

Lilac Point: Gr. Ch. Daunus Pascali, showing the muted colour which gives an ethereal appearance.

Photo: Paddy Cutts.

Cream Point: Ch. & Pr. Palantir Tom Bombadil.

Photo: Paddy Cutts.

Red Point: Ch. & Pr. Leolee Mr Apricot.

Photo: Paddy Cutts.

Blue point: These two Blue Points show excellent, large, pricked ears, which is most desirable is a show cat.

Photo: Paddy Cutts.

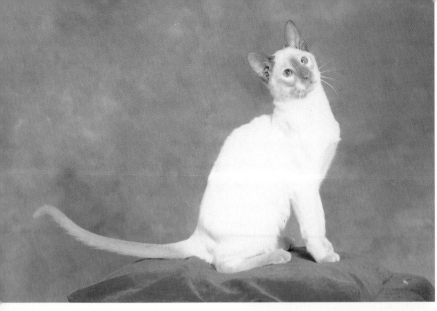

Cinnamon Point: Bluespice Cinnamon Ice.

Photo: Rita Ford.

Apple Head: Sir Chang, an American traditional type Tabby Point Siamese.

Photo: Marjorie Griswold.

Apricot Tabby Point: Unowhose Hocus Pocus.

Photo: Matthew Speight.

*RIGHT: Seal Tortie Point: Ch.
Cobweb Mist.*

Photo: Paddy Cutts.

*BELOW: Caramel Tabby Point:
Astromiam Pretty Opal.*

Photo: Paddy Cutts.

Lilac Tabby Point: Ch. Zachary Bat Girl.

Photo: Paddy Cutts.

Mating		Seal	Blue	Chocolate	Lilac
Seal	Seal	1			
Seal	Seal/b	1			
Seal	Seal/c	1			
Seal	Seal/l	1			
Seal	Blue	1			
Seal	Blue/l	1			
Seal	Choc	1			
Seal	Choc/l	1			
Seal	Lilac	1			
Seal/b	Seal/b	3	1		
Seal/b	Seal/c	1			
Seal/b	Seal/l	3	1		
Seal/b	Blue	1	1		
Seal/b	Blue/l	1	1		
Seal/b	Choc	1			
Seal/b	Choc/l	3	1		
Seal/b	Lilac	1	1		
Seal/c	Seal/b	1			
Seal/c	Seal/l	3		1	
Seal/c	Blue	1			
Seal/c	Blue/l	1		1	
Seal/c	Choc	1		1	
Seal/c	Choc/l	1		1	
Seal/c	Lilac	1		1	
Seal/l	Seal/l	9	3	3	1
Seal/l ·	Blue	1	1		
Seal/l	Blue/l	3	3	1	1
Seal/l	Choc	1		1	
Seal/l	Choc/l	3	1	3	1
Seal/l	Lilac	1	1	1	1
Blue	Blue		1		
Blue	Blue/l		1		
Blue	Choc	1			
Blue	Choc/l	1			
Blue	Lilac		1		
Blue/l	Blue/l		3		1
Blue/l	Choc	1		1	
Blue/l	Choc/l	1	1	1	1
Blue/l	Lilac		1		1
Choc	Choc			1	
Choc	Choc/l			1	
Choc	Lilac			1	
Choc/l	Choc/l			3	1
Choc/l	Lilac			1	1
Lilac	Lilac				1

Table 1.
Expected ratios for matings between seal, blue, chocolate and lilac varieties of Siamese.
Key:
Seal: Pure Seal
Seal/c: Seal carrying chocolate
Seal/b: Seal carrying blue
Seal/l: Seal carrying lilac
Choc: Pure Chocolate
Choc/l: Chocolate carrying lilac
Blue: Pure Blue
Blue/l: Blue carrying lilac
Lilac: Pure Lilac

are $AABBddc^Sc^S$ for the blue, $AAbbDDc^Sc^S$ for the chocolate, $AAbbc^Sc^S$ and $AAbbddc^Sc^S$ for the lilac. Observe that the varieties are engendered by the simple recombination of the normal and mutant genes. Normal, in this context, is a term used to denote the original, or non-mutant, gene. The recombination of genes is genetics at its most simple and some would say at its most exciting. With just three mutant genes, it is possible to create eight different varieties of Siamese.

To reiterate the principle of recombination of pairs of genes, consider how the blue tabby point could be created. The initial mating would be between a blue point and a seal tabby point. The F1 will be a tabby point of genotype $AaBBDdc^Sc^S$. The germ cells produced by the F1 will be AD, Ad, aD and ad. Fig. 5 shows how the expectations for the F2 can be derived. The expected colours and their ratios will be as follows: 9 seal tabby point, 3 seal point, 3 blue tabby point and 1 blue point. The reader may like to verify the expectations by working through the successive steps.

	AD	Ad	aD	ad
AD	AADD Tabby	AADd Tabby	AaDD Tabby	AaDd Tabby
Ad	AaDD Tabby	AAdd Blue Tabby	AaDd Tabby	Aadd Blue Tabby
aD	AaDD Tabby	AaDd Tabby	aaDD Black	aaDd Black
ad	AaDd Tabby	Aadd Blue Tabby	aaDD Black	aadd Blue

Fig. 5. The expectations in the F2 generation from mating the tabby point Siamese F1 inter se from an initial mating between a seal tabby point Siamese and a blue point Siamese.

Note that each of the germ cells from the F1 will contain the B gene, ABD, ABd, aBD and aBd, but, because the B gene is homozygous, it does not feature in working out the expectations. It is good practice to ignore all genes which are not directly relevant for an expose. In the same vein, in all of the diagrams, the gene c^S is not included in either the germ cells or genotypes, since it occurs in every one and may be taken for granted. All of the cats are Siamese and homozygous c^Sc^S.

EXTENDING THE GENETIC PRINCIPLES

The principle may be extended to a mating between varieties which differ in three pairs of genes. For example, imagine a mating between a seal tabby point and a lilac point. The relevant differences will be between the gene pairs A versus a, B versus b and D versus d. The F1 will have the genotype $AaBbDdc^Sc^S$ and will produce eight different germ cells. The F2 offspring will be expected in the ratios of 27 tabby point, 9 blue tabby point, 9 chocolate tabby point, 9 seal point, 3 lilac tabby point, 3 blue point, 3 chocolate point and 1 lilac point.

The derivation of these expectations will be left as an additional exercise in elementary genetics. A newcomer to genetics should have no compunction in using checkerboards for working out the expectation from matings between cats which are heterozygous for two or more genes. The method is quick and, in particular, accurate. As a check on the latter, the number of different germ cells from a parent is a multiple of two. This is true even if the parents differ in the number of heterozygous genes. Remember that each cat can have only two members of a pair of genes and the germ cells can only transmit one of each pair. It should be appreciated that a close approximation to the theoretical expectations will only be observed when a large number of offspring can be bred. Much effort was expended in the early days of genetics to confirm that the expected ratios would be obtained, using rapidly breeding animals such as mice and rats. This is not possible with slower breeding animals such the cat, with its small litters and expensive upkeep. Breeders of cats must expect wide variation in ratios for individual small litters. Summing over many litters, however, reveals a steady approach to the expected numbers. Practical breeding is very much a numbers game, like tossing a coin or dealing hands in a round at cards.

Suppose a seal point heterozygous for chocolate (BbDD) brown is mated to a seal point heterozygous for blue (BBDd). What will be the colour of the progeny? Yes, you are right: these will be seal point. The reason is the dominance of B and D to b and d, respectively. Details of the assortment of the genes are shown by Fig. 6. This is not a trivial exercise, for it illustrates how "hidden" genes are passed on unseen from generation to generation. It might be supposed that the seal point parents and offspring are homozygous whereas they are not; or, at least, only some of them are. A recessive gene may be passed on for several generations before a chance mating between two cats which are heterozygous for the same recessive reveals the presence of the gene.

	BD	BD	Bd	Bd
BD	BBDD Seal	BBDD Seal	BBDd Seal	BBDd Seal
BD	BBDD Seal	BBDD Seal	BBDd Seal	BBDd Seal
bD	BbDD Seal	BbDD Seal	BbDd Seal	BbDd Seal
bD	BbDD Seal	BbDD Seal	BbDd Seal	BbDd Seal

Fig. 6. The expectations in the F2 generation from mating a seal point heterozygous for chocolate to a seal point heterozygous for blue. Note how the respective recessive genes are passed on to half the progeny.

It is rarely feasible to carry through crosses involving differences between three or more genes pairs because of the large numbers of progeny which must be bred. With prolifically-breeding small animals, yes, it is possible, but with cats, the answer has to be no. With cats, the evolution of varieties within a breed has been a slow process and, it must be admitted, in many cases has been the result of chance appearance of recessive genes. If a more deliberate approach is adopted, the method is to proceed in stages.

For example, the procedure to produce the lilac point if the only Siamese available were seal point, blue tabby point and chocolate tabby point, would be in three stages. 1) To mate the seal point to blue tabby point to produce tabby point in the F1; whence blue point will be realized in the F2 at a probability of 1 in 16 kittens. 2) To mate the seal point to chocolate tabby point, to produce tabby point in the F1 and chocolate point in the F2 at the same probability. Finally, mate the extracted blue point and chocolate point to each other. The F1 will be seal point but the lilac point will be expected in the F2.

Fortunately, the Siamese is a popular breed of cat and most of the varieties are generally available and the above extended breeding programme may never be required. In stating that the F1 should be mated together to produce the F2, this does not necessarily mean that the mating is brother to sister. A stud cat could be mated to two different queens to produce the F1. Kittens may be selected from different litters as parents for the F2. This is half brother to sister mating, admittedly, but the degree of inbreeding is much less (in fact, it is half that of full brother to sister mating).

SEX-LINKED HEREDITY

A feature of feline genetics is a case of sex-linked heredity. An exception to the usual situation of the pairs of chromosomes being matched in size and shape is a special pair which determine sex. These are known as the X/Y pair. The X is a large chromosome and carries many genes. Contrarily, the companion to the X, the Y, is a relatively small chromosome with merely a few genes. The primary function of the Y is to induce the developing embryo to become a male.

The rule that all animals have two pairs of chromosomes still holds for the X and Y. Females have two X chromosome while the males have the X and Y. The germ cells of females can only transmit an X but those of the male will transmit either a X or a Y. The random fusion of the germ cells at conception will produce fertilized XX and XY eggs in equal numbers. The former will become females and the latter will become males in a 1:1 ratio. It is commonly said that the male determines the sex of the individual.

The sex-linked mutant gene of the cat is the orange O. The effect of the gene is to convert the pigment granules from the normal blackish-brown colour to yellow; the shape is also changed, from ovoid to spherical. These effects combine to produce the orange colours. The O gene is inherited as a dominant to the normal gene which is denoted by o. The gene is said to be sex-linked because it is on the X chromosome.

Male cats with but one X chromosome, can only be normal coloured (viz., tabby, black, etc.) with the genotype o, or red with the genotype O. On the other hand, females, with their two X chromosomes, can be normal coloured (genotype oo) or red (genotype OO). However, they also can have the genotype Oo and this is the tortoiseshell; a coat of normal (usually black or tabby) and orange. The heredity of O is rather more complex than usual because the sex of each parent must be taken into account.

Table 2 shows the expectations for the six possible matings which involve the O and o pair of genes. The derivation of expectations for two of the matings are diagrammed in Figs. 7 and 8. Specially note that the male can only transmit either gene O or o in half of his germ cells.

	O	o
o	OO Red Female	oo Tortie Female
Y	OY Red Male	oY Black Male

Fig. 7 *The expectations from mating between a male red point Siamese and female seal tortie point Siamese. Note that the male on the left of the checkerboard will only be transmitting the O gene in half of his germ cells. The other half will be transmitting a Y chromosome.*

	O	o
o	OO Tortie Female	oo Black Female
Y	OY Red Male	oY Black Male

Fig. 8. *The expectations from mating between a male seal point Siamese and female seal tortie point Siamese. Note that the male on the left of the checkerboard will only be transmitting the o gene in half of his germ cells. The other half will be transmitting a Y chromosome.*

Table 2. Expectations for matings between red/cream point and tortie/torbie Siamese.

Mating		Expected kittens	
Queen	Stud	Males	Males
Red	Red	Red	Red
Black	Red	Black	Tortie
Tortie	Red	Red	Red
		Black	Tortie
Tortie	Black	Red	Tortie
		Black	Black
Red	Black	Red	Tortie
Black	Black	Black	Black

Black is taken to mean non-red – that is, black, blue, chocolate, lilac, tabby, blue tabby, chocolate tabby, lilac tabby, etc. The genes which produce these varieties are inherited independently of red or tortie.

It was only a matter of time before the red point Siamese appeared on the scene by combining the orange and Siamese genes. The genotype is Oc^Sc^S and OOc^Sc^S for males and females, respectively. Incorporating the dilute gene d gives the cream point, with the genotype $Oddc^Sc^S$ and $OOddc^Sc^S$, according to sex.

If red and cream point Siamese are possible, so are tortie points and these may be one of four varieties, according to the colour of the non-red or non-cream part of the pattern. Therefore, there is the seal tortie point of genotype $aaBBDDOoc^Sc^S$, the blue of genotype $aaBBddOoc^Sc^S$, the chocolate $aabbDDOoc^Sc^S$ and the lilac $aabbddOoc^Sc^S$.

A complication of breeding red tabbies is that the O gene will mask the presence of the agouti gene A and the non-agouti gene a. Thus it is possible to have red tabbies of either genotypes AAOO, AaOO or aaOO (discussing females only for convenience). These red tabbies are indistinguishable in appearance. They may look identical but it is clear that they will breed differently. This is also true for the red point Siamese and has raised a problem: some people have expressed annoyance when their treasured seal point mated to a presumed red point has produced a seal tortie tabby point instead of the expected seal tortie point.

IDENTIFICATION BY BREEDING BEHAVIOUR

The remedy has been to distinguish carefully between the red point Siamese of genotype $aabbddOOc^Sc^S$ and red tabby point Siamese of genotype $AAbbddOOc^Sc^S$, despite the fact that they appear indistinguishable. The two varieties are separated by their breeding behaviour. Gene A is dominant to a, hence it is wise to presume that all red pointed Siamese are either $AABBDDOOc^Sc^S$ or $AaBBDDOOc^Sc^S$ until proven otherwise. In practice, this means descent from cats with proven red point parentage (by pedigree) or from seal tortie point queens. The latter is a little more definite, although there can be a problem about the number of kittens examined.

An identical situation arises for the cream pointed: these may be either $AABBddOOc^Sc^S$, $AaBBddOOc^Sc^S$ or $aabbDDOOc^Sc^S$. A similar procedure to the above has been adopted, that of registering all cream pointed as cream tabby point until proven otherwise. The criteria for being a cream point will be exactly as for the red point. Cream kittens bred from proven red point parents may be taken as cream points. Proven red point and proven cream point may be intermated without loss of status.

Although the impossibility of visual detection of red point and red tabby point Siamese has caused some concern, it may be mentioned that red pointed Siamese of genotypes $BBDDOOc^Sc^S$ and $bbDDOOc^Sc^S$ are indistinguishable. It is just possible for the latter to be a clearer colour but this can be unreliable. Cream pointed may carry either genes B or b, yet be identical in appearance. In all of the above cases, their breeding behaviour will reveal their true genetic nature.

EPISTASIS RELATIONSHIP

The masking by one member of a pair of genes of the effects of another pair of genes is not the same as the more usual dominance/recessive relationship. The latter applies between members of the same pair of genes. Thus, gene O masks the effects of both A and a, and both B and b. Masking is a sufficiently common occurrence to warrant a special term, known as epistasis.

The realization that some red pointed Siamese may be agouti under their red exteriors leads naturally to the conception of red tortie tabby points. These are recognizable because the tabby pattern is expressed in the non-red areas of the mosaic coat. These can occur in the usual four varieties; namely, seal as genotype $AABBDDOoc^Sc^S$, blue as $AABBddOoc^Sc^S$, chocolate as $AAbbDDOoc^Sc^S$ and lilac as $AAbbddOoc^Sc^S$. The blue and lilac will have cream-coloured areas instead of red. These Siamese could be called torbie in keeping with the frequent use of the term to designate the tabby tortoiseshell.

The black gene B has produced two known mutant genes, one of long standing, namely, the brown or chocolate b described earlier. Comparatively recently, a second mutant has been identified as the light brown gene b^l. The gene produces a distinctly lighter brown coloration and this effect is carried over for the points of the Siamese. These are a lighter shade than found in the chocolate point and the variety may be designated as the cinnamon point of genotype $aab^lb^lDDc^sc^s$. The dilute version has lighter points than the lilac and would be the fawn point of genotype $aab^lb^lddc^sc^s$.

There seems to be little to be gained in a detailed enumeration of all of the possible combinations of the cinnamon and fawn varieties. However, the cinnamon tabby and fawn tabby points may be singled out in the form of the genotypes $AAb^lb^lDDc^sc^s$ and $AAb^lb^lddc^sc^s$, respectively. The point is that it is possible to have corresponding self and tabby tortie versions. The principle involved is the substitution of gene b^l for gene b, with the expectation of a lightening for the points. This raises the question whether or not it may be possible to distinguish easily all of the versions. The Siamese gene initially lightens the points and now two other genes will be lightening them further. The most likely source of confusion will be between the lilac and fawn varieties.

The dominant dilute modifier gene Dm has the curious effect of lightening dilute coat colours (blue and lilac) but not those of dense colour (black and chocolate/brown). Blue is changed to a colour not unlike lilac, but lighter in tone, while lilac is changed to a still lighter tone. The former has become known as caramel while the latter has been named taupe. The genotypes for the two colours would be written as aaBBddDmDm and aaddddDmDm, respectively. The cream, of course, is a dilute colour which is further lightened by the addition of the Dm gene. The colour has been named apricot. There is no reason why these colours should not occur as Siamese; it only needs the addition of the c^sc^s genes. The problem will be similar to that posed above – whether or not the phenotypes of these light colours will be readily distinguishable.

Another gene which will cause problems of recognition when combined with Siamese, will be the dominant inhibitor gene I. The gene inhibits the formation of pigment or limits the amount of pigment in the hairs. Those areas of the coat or parts of the hair which are most affected are the lighter-pigmented areas between the tabby pattern and the light undercolour to the hair below the intensely pigmented tip. The outcome is the well known and popular Silver and Smoke long-haired breeds.

The Silver is a tabby, with the yellowish agouti areas of the coat replaced by white and a very light undercolour. The Smoke is a self coloured cat and is considerably more intensely pigmented than a tabby. In consequence, those parts of the coat which are most affected will be the lighter undercolour, to generate the unique "smoke" coloration. The undercolour can vary from a barely perceptible lightening to obviously white.

The seal smoke Siamese of genotype $aaBBDDIIc^sc^s$ has seal coloured points with light undercolour. The c^s gene tends to produce a lighter undercolour and the I gene will tend to emphasise the effect. If the amount of light undercolour is extensive, the seal smoke may be readily recognized but, if it is not, the variety may be difficult to separate from an ordinary Siamese. The differentiation will become progressively more difficult for the lighter colours; the blue smoke Siamese of genotype $aaBBddIIc^sc^s$, the chocolate smoke Siamese of genotype $aabbDDIIc^sc^s$ and the lilac smoke Siamese of genotype $aabbddIIc^sc^s$.

The seal silver Siamese of genotype $AABBDDIIc^sc^s$ will be very similar to the seal tabby Siamese. If anything, the problem of recognition will be probably greater than with the self varieties. The c^s gene tends to remove the yellow pigment from the points and all that the I gene will do is remove any traces which may remain and produce a less distinct tabby pattern. All of the tabby Siamese will be affected in this manner, some more than others. These varieties will possess the usual tabby Siamese genotypes with the addition of one or two inhibitor genes.

The combination of the inhibitor and orange genes will produce the "cameo" Siamese with the basic genotype IIOOc^{S}c^S. In all, both red and cream cameo pointed Siamese will be possible, as well as eight tortie and torbie cameos in the usual colours. It will be nigh impossible to distinguish between many of the varieties. Some may have a curiosity value but, in company with many of the varieties of previous paragraphs, will constitute a classification nightmare.

GENERAL GENETIC INHERITANCE

This chapter has focused on inheritance of colour but it should not be imagined that the topic is the "be all" of Siamese genetics. Health, reproduction, conformation and temperament are also important aspects of the well bred, superior, cat. All of these features are governed in part by heredity and should not be left to chance. Health may be regarded as the province of the vet, but it is wise to breed from the most robust and active animals. Weedy kittens should not be blamed on a bad start in life but to a more fundamental cause.

Stud cats should display a healthy interest in oestrus queens and have a low percentage of "missed" matings. This is a practical measure of fertility. The queen should be capable of producing and rearing a large litter with the minimum of assistance. The milk flow should be adequate. It is wise to be wary of queens which fail to come into heat or do so erratically, and those which have small litters. All of these features are determined in part by heredity, not one hundred per cent, of course, but substantially enough to be of concern.

Conformation in the Siamese has reached a high level and in the majority it is largely a case of guarding against deterioration. Some varieties are better than others in this respect and this is where a knowledge of colour inheritance is an advantage. The fact that the Siamese, as a breed, has a consistent breed conformation is a clear indication that it is inherited. The advice is to breed from cats with the better all-round conformation. The recommendation is to use a breeding policy based on the "Total Score" or "Breeding Index" method of selection.

Temperament definitely should not be neglected. The ideal is a placid, friendly and affectionate cat. Highly strung or nervous animals should not be tolerated, if only because they can be unpredictable. Undue aggressive behaviour to other cats or to people should not be tolerated in breeding studs or queens.

The Siamese is a popular breed and inbreeding should not be a problem. However, it may arise in particular strains if the inbreeding has been too close or has continued for too long. It may also arise if restrictions are placed on the mating of certain varieties. The effects of inbreeding are insidious, leading to inferior growth, poor health and low fertility. If the deterioration has not gone too far, the remedy is to introduce unrelated stock. Usually, this will produce an immediate improvement. Within recent years computer programmes have been developed by which the degree of inbreeding of a cat or a mating in prospect can be quickly and easily calculated without great genealogical expertise.

Table 3. Normal and mutant genes described in Siamese genetics.
Their names, symbols and effect of the gene.

Gene	Symbol	Effect
Agouti	A	Yellow band to the hairs.
Non-agouti	a	Absence of band to the hairs.
Black	B	Blackish-brown hair pigment granules.
Brown	b	Dark brown hair pigment granules.
Light brown	bl	Light brown hair pigment granules.
Full colour	C	Maximum production of pigment.
Burmese	c^b	Reduction in production of pigment.
Siamese	c^s	Greater reduction of pigment.
Dense	D	Normal packing of pigment granules.
Dilute	d	Abnormal clumping of pigment granules.
Dilute modifier	Dm	Lightens hair of dilute phenotypes.
Normal	dm	Normal dilute phenotype.
Inhibitor	I	Inhibits production of pigment granules.
Normal	i	Normal production of pigment granules.
Orange	O	Converts black/brown pigment granules to yellow.
Normal	o	Normal black/brown pigment granules.

Genetic terms used in the text

BACKCROSS	The generation from mating F1 to one of the parents.
CHECKERBOARD	Diagram for deriving the expectations of a mating.
CHROMOSOME	The carrier of the genes in the cell nucleus.
EPISTASIS	Where the effect of a gene masks the expression of members of another pair of genes.
DOMINANT	Where the effect of one member of a pair of genes is expressed in the F1.
F1	The first cross or generation..
F2	The second generation from mating F1 to F1.
GENE	The ultimate determinant of heredity.
GENE SYMBOL	Symbol of a gene for writing genotypes and for checkerboard diagrams.
GENOTYPE	Genetic constitution of a cat.
GERM CELL	The reproductive cell, male sperm and female ovum.
HETEROZYGOTE	Where the members of a gene pair in the genotype are different, as Aa.
HOMOZYGOTE	Where the members of a gene pair in the genotype are identical, as AA or aa.
MUTANT GENE	Mutant (altered) form of an original gene.
NORMAL GENE	The original gene present in the genotype of the cat.
PHENOTYPE	The appearance of the cat or expression of a gene.
RECESSIVE	Where the effect of one member of a pair of genes is not expressed in the F1.

Chapter Sixteen

BREEDING

RESPONSIBILITIES OF BREEDING

Breeding can be a fascinating hobby but it takes up a great deal of time and money. You must be clear why you want to do it. Numerous problems can beset even the most experienced breeder, let alone the unprepared novice or pet owner.There are so many things that can go wrong from the initial conception to finally seeing the kittens go to their new homes. How do you explain to your family that their treasured pet has died giving birth, or just after birth? Consider that a queen can become exhausted or go into uterine inertia (dystocia), let alone the panic and feeling of helplessness that envelops you, the owner. Consider also the possibility of coping with a young mother after a Caesarian operation and keeping her slightly anaesthetised kittens alive until she can look after them; the birth of dead kittens; or abnormal kittens, for example with cleft palates or umbilical hernias, having to be put to sleep.

FINDING HOMES

Most people have some difficulty in finding loving, permanent homes for their progeny. Unless you are a very well-known breeder whose kittens are booked in advance by others wanting their line, you will have to advertise and then hope you can find enough suitable people who actually want your kittens. It is not unheard of for a family to fall so much in love with the kittens that they have kept the whole litter as family pets. This happens especially when they find that advertisements fail to bring in buyers, or your friends back out at the last minute when they decide that they cannot take on the responsibility of looking after a kitten.

Even when you have found what seems to be a good home, families break up with divorce, or long-term illness or other changes in circumstances. You could find that you are asked to take back your kittens after they have left you – we had some come back after two years – or that they have been passed on to a rescue organisation.

THE COSTS

Many owners think that they can recoup the initial cost of their queen by allowing her to have one litter. However, you will need to think very carefully about all the intrinsic costs, such as the initial stud cat fee, and all the other costs of raising a litter to the approximate age of thirteen weeks, when the kittens will leave you for their new homes. These costs, including the initial vaccinations, registration fees and the occasional veterinary consultation, should help you conclude that breeding is not the path to take to increasing your bank balance; it is more likely to lead to a very healthy overdraft.

REGISTRATION OF THE BREEDING QUEEN

If you feel you can surmount all these obstacles, you will need to check the original agreement under which you bought your Siamese. Unless you actually bought the kitten for breeding, you may find her registered on the "non-active" register. You will then need to see if the breeder will agree to reverse this initial registration with the Governing Council of the Cat Fancy. The GCCF will not action this change without the correct form being signed by the breeder and the owner. If you were to decide to breed with a queen who is registered on the non-active register and can find a stud owner who will take a queen knowingly on these terms, you will be unable to register the kittens with the GCCF.

CONDITION OF THE BREEDING QUEEN

As well as checking the registration documents, and taking advice from the breeder of your cats where possible, you may want to see for yourself that she is "good enough" to have a litter. You may find that it is worthwhile visiting a cat show to see how she matches up to the exhibits. Her personality may be the most wonderful in the world but she may have genetic faults that are thought to be undesirable.

If she is apparently good for breeding, then you will need to assess whether she is in good health. You will need to check her vaccination record and make sure she is up to date. Some vets will suggest a booster if it is not the annual time of re-vaccination. This will confer greater protection on your queen and developing kittens, especially as her body will be under stress. It is also a good idea to give worming preparations as a preventative measure at this stage. One of your regular maintenance tasks should include regular clipping of claws. Nearly all matings are supervised and part of the procedure can become quite lively, to say the least. The stud owner will not thank you if he or she becomes clawed in the process.

BREEDING AGE

The Siamese breed is extremely precocious and a female will often start calling from the age of four to five months. At this age she is still a kitten needing time to mature and will not be regarded as an adult until the age of nine months at least. A few lines of Siamese do not fully mature until they are at least a year old. A queen should not be mated until she is at least ten months old and her breeding life can extend up to the age of seven to eight years of age. After this litters will not be quite as frequent.

Kittens make an enormous drain on the mother both physically and psychologically. She may start calling again as soon as her kittens are weaned but in fairness to the queen, she should be given a good rest between litters to rebuild her strength. Some breeders let their queens have a litter once a year, while others work on the frequency of three litters over a period of two years. During the first year of owning your queen you will be able to record her pattern of calling so that you can actually plan with confidence when you intend to let her have her litter of kittens. The calling pattern is individual to each cat and in a multi-cat household, breeders often diarise such a pattern rather than leave it to memory. Another factor determining breeding age is the actual date of your queen's birth.

THE CYCLICAL PATTERN OF BREEDING

Observations of stray and feral cats have identified a polyoestrus, or breeding cycle, which is strongly conditioned by our seasonal weather patterns and daylight hours. The dark, short days of the late autumn and early winter seasons dictate a period of anoestrus, when the breeding cycle shuts down. It slowly re-awakens after the shortest day of the year and the cat's reproductive system starts to prepare for activity. Generally speaking the first few calls are not strong; the peak of your queen's activity will probably occur during the spring and the summer months. These rules are at best a guide to this cycle because many Siamese are kept at home as housepets/breeding queens. Long hours of day light or even artifical light can affect the cycle and some housebound Siamese will not go through a period of anoestrus.

THE OESTRUS CYCLE
The term Oestrus indicates that the queen is calling. Other terms used by breeders are "heat cycle" or "in season".

The first stage – Pro-Oestrus: What actually happens physiologically to your Siamese during this oestrus cycle is that the cat's reproductive system is triggered into action by the longer daylight hours. This stage of the cycle is characterised by the queen becoming restless and extremely fussy and affectionate with her owner. Some Siamese at this juncture spray around the house and all queens will certainly use their litter tray with more frequency. They tend to become extremely active, usually near doors and windows, and will attempt to get out at the first possible opportunity. Some Siamese cats may release a slight discharge from their vulva which should be clear in colour.

The second stage – Oestrus: Within approximately two to four days of the Pro-Oestrus stage, your queen will be more receptive to the advances of a stud cat. Behaviour can be summarised by one word – agitation, hers and yours! She will roll around on your floor trying very hard to escape from confinement in your house and call very loudly. With her need to urinate more frequently and in her frustration as her call becomes stronger and often louder, she may totally miss her litter tray and spray onto your curtains, furniture and walls. She may even lose her appetite as nature takes over. If you touch her back at this stage, she will crouch in the mating position. Some Siamese vigorously swish their tails from side to side in the process of calling. A Siamese calling is an amazing sound which can vary from loud yowls to a form of barking.

TIMING OF MATING
This needs to be critically evaluated because cats do not ovulate in the same way as other animals. They are known as induced ovulators. In most cases the very act of mating triggers what can only be described as receptors within the queen's vagina, releasing luteinising hormone from the queen's pituitary gland, enabling ovulation to take place and preparing the lining of the queen's uterus to receive the fertilised eggs.

FINDING A SUITABLE STUD
There are various avenues that you can explore to find the stud cat of your choice. If you have joined a specialist breed club, the Secretary or one of the Committee members will know what ones are available in the area to which you are prepared to travel. The breeder of your queen may have a suitable stud you can use. This will obviously have advantages to the novice breeder; you will feel you can trust the owner and will know the hygiene conditions of the cattery. Otherwise you will be able to locate a stud by combing the advertisements in cat publications, or see a suitable advertisement in the current GCCF studbook. Most breeders are happy to accept enquiries and send out their stud's pedigree.

There are three types of stud agreements: "at open stud" generally means that there will be no restrictions on queens coming in, providing the queen's owner complies with any testing procedures required and that the pedigree line is suitable to the stud owner.

Some studs are kept at "limited" stud. This means the owner will decide whether or not to accept

*Stud cat's quarters
showing indoor
accommodation and a
suitable exercise area.*

Photo: Steve Franklin.

*A raised tail
indicates friendship,
but it also shows
that spraying may
be imminent.*

Photo: Paddy Cutts.

your queen. Other stud cats are kept at "closed" stud, which means that the owner will not allow anybody to use her stud except her own queens. Sometimes as a favour she may allow a close friend's cat in to her male. Some owners prefer to use a proven stud with a maiden queen rather than a stud who needs to prove himself and what genes he carries by his first litter. A few stud owners will sometimes charge a reduced fee to a queen's owner who uses the new stud for the first time.

THE HEALTH AND CONDITION OF THE STUD

Stud owners feel they owe it to their cat to keep him in the peak of condition and not to overwork him. They would certainly not appreciate a queen coming in and bringing him infections and viruses. It is quite likely that when you make a serious enquiry to a stud owner, you will be asked many questions about the health and also about the temperament of your queen. Most stud owners will not want to expose their stud cat to a queen who can be exceptionally aggressive in strong heat, especially when penned in the stud's quarters as a preliminary to mating. Very few stud owners like to be bitten by a strange cat – a cat bite is one of the most painful of injuries to endure!

It should be possible to visit your queen's chosen mate to see what he looks like. Ideally you should look at the condition of his coat and eyes, which will reveal a lot about his standard of health. Do not be put off by his facial appearance; older Siamese males tend to develop jowls which may make their face look rounder in spite of their wedge-shaped profile. It is also likely that an older Siamese's coat has darkened with age, particularly if he is a Seal Point Siamese or a Blue Point Siamese. You may be allowed to observe him as as he walks around his run. A well cared for Siamese stud cat will exhibit good muscle tone and stamina.

THE STUD CAT'S QUARTERS

Owners who keep entire male Siamese cats used for stud purposes agree that they should be kept in suitable surroundings but, very often, their ideas on the subject of housing are rather diverse. As most entire male cats will spray and strongly defend their territory, it is generally agreed that they need to be kept separate from other cats. One stud cat owner keeps her stud cat in a separate room within her house. She is able to control the smell of cat urine by adequate disinfection methods and he enjoys being able to hear the general day-to-day noises of a busy household. Also on cold, windy and rainy days she does have one major advantage over all owners who keep their stud cats in garden houses and runs – she only has to climb the stairs to see him rather than brave the elements. Other owners keep their stud cats in sheds that are adapted for this purpose and have a run to enable the male cat to exercise. A shed should have a window to provide air and enable the cat to see what is going on outside his area. The movement of birds flying around in the garden provides hours of entertainment.

Siamese are able to stand cold weather but there is a limit to what they can endure and there are heaters available that are thermostatically controlled to provide a suitable ambient temperature. Stud owners vary greatly with the type and size of accommodation provided for visiting queens. There is no wrong or right method in determining what is provided – all have their good points. Some breeders utilise a pen as queen's quarters, some have purpose-built units attached to the stud house, whilst others set aside an area within the stud house for the queen. The basic purpose of whatever method is used is providing safety for the queen until she is ready to accept the advances of the male cat.

Nowadays many breeders keep their own studs, partly because of the possible risk of infection to their queen when taking her out to stud, but also for convenience. This is fine, provided the stud owner has an adequate number of females to keep the male happy and contented. It is usually reckoned that three is the minimum. Very few stud cats remain active for the whole of their lives; many are neutered by the age of four or five years so that they can enjoy a family life.

THE STUD FEE AND CONTRACT

Another factor that will dictate your choice of stud cat is cost. Stud fees vary tremendously according to locality, popularity, type, colour, temperament, title and pedigree.

Some stud cat owners have other terms and conditions and may enter into a verbal or written contract requesting a kitten from the queen's owner in lieu of the stud fee. It is up to you whether you agree to this: it has been known for these type of agreements to end beautiful friendships, especially if you end up giving away a kitten who becomes an outstanding show winner. A written contract should spell out quite clearly the stud fee and the length of time that a queen will be kept by the stud owner to ensure mating has taken place. It is unreasonable to expect a stud owner to feed and look after your cat for a couple of weeks, unless this has been specifically agreed.

Further clauses usually cover other eventualities such as a failure to conceive or give live birth. Usually a free remating will be offered, subject to the usual testing procedures. The fee is paid when you pick up your queen. It is not usual to pay in advance. You will be given a copy of the stud cat's registration details and pedigree. If a written contract has been made then both parties will sign it, each keeping one copy for future reference. A caring stud owner will help a novice breeder sort out all these questions, as they are interested in ensuring that their stud cat sires sturdy healthy youngsters with loving personalities and free of defects. Their prefix and stud cat have reputations to keep, and if they feel that you would be better suited by finding another stud cat, then it is likely that you will be told.

MEDICAL TESTS

Nearly all breeders insist on the queen being tested before coming into stud. Very few breeders will accept an untested queen. The test most frequently requested is for FELV, otherwise known as Leukaemia. Some breeders are happy with a recent test whilst others ask for a test to be completed within the previous twenty-four hours of accepting a queen into their stud cat. This particular virus is acknowledged to cause more deaths within the cat population than any other. The vaccine can be given to your cat at the same time as those for Flu and Enteritis, but at a separate site on the body.

Another test is one that detects the presence of antibodies in the blood to the Feline Immunodeficiency Virus, otherwise known as FIV, or Feline Aids. It is a Lentivirus and was found to be part of the same group to which the human AIDS virus (HIV) belongs. The virus can only be passed from cat to cat, *not* human to cat.

The question of testing for Feline Infectious Peritonitis (FIP) is a rather controversial one, especially as the test only indicates exposure to the corona virus family, not the disease. It is believed that Feline Infectious Peritonitis is not as infectious as once thought but it still remains a most serious and fatal disease.

THE TIMING OF THE LITTER

You will need to think very carefully about the timing of your litter because the last thing you will want on your hands are unsold kittens over the summer vacation or the Christmas period. Probably the best time in which to sell kittens is between early September and early December, followed by late January up until May.

There is always the worry for breeders, of kittens being sold as potential Christmas presents and facing the stress of a household in great excitement and upheaval. The Christmas period is not the ideal time in which to introduce a young kitten or cat to a new home.

PRELIMINARIES TO MATING

About the second day into the oestrus cycle, contact the stud owner and say that you need to bring your queen in to stud. She will need to be transported in a very secure basket and taken into the queen's quarters, where she can settle down, see and smell her future mate and he can investigate her. The length of the courting period depends very much on the temperament of the two cats involved. A maiden queen can be quite nervous and need to be coaxed by the stud owner speaking to her quietly and stroking her. The owner's reward for this is often scratches or, at worst, a bite. An experienced queen, who has to contend with a very active male or first time stud cat, can react very differently.

An experienced stud owner will know when a bond has been established between the two parties and will supervise the first contact between them by opening the door to the queen's quarters very cautiously – standing nearby with a blanket or broom to separate the two cats if need be. Generally speaking, a queen in full call will attack the stud cat, who often reacts to this with a look of complete surprise and bewilderment, rather than the stud cat going for the queen, but there is always an exception to the rule.

MATING

Some queens can be difficult to mate, whilst others take being mated in their stride. On average, mating lasts for a period of four to five days. Stud owners will often let the queen and stud cat co-exist side by side during the daytime, with frequent periods of supervision to ensure mating has taken place, and then separate the two by night. If the stud owner is at work during the day, there tend to be more supervised matings in the evening, with the queen placed in secure surroundings during the daytime period.

The stud owner often has a washable piece of matting or carpet sample available in the stud's quarters, so that both stud and queen can get a firm grip. During the mating process, events can get so intense that the mat has been seen to move around with all the action. The stud cat will often walk carefully around the queen, sniffing her presence and making a few sounds. She will sometimes vocally acknowledge his presence, but will certainly adopt the mating position. This can be identified by the queen crouching on her front legs, her back held rigid in the shape of a concave curve, with her rear end raised (which is known as lordosis), paddling her back legs, with her tail raised to one side. He scrutinises her situation, often walking to her right and left sides in turn, sniffing her rear end and then when he sees his opportunity he makes a lunge for the back of her neck. He gets a grip on her by holding the scruff of her neck with his teeth, and then straddles her, coaxing her into an acceptable position by standing on one of her thighs, which causes her to elevate her rear end and push her tail aside.

He then quickly arches his back, lowers his rear end and enters her. Mating is completed in a few seconds, with the queen letting out a high-pitched scream, which can sound frightening to the looker-on. This is then followed by a growling sound as the queen rolls around on the floor. The stud cat, meanwhile, jumps out of the way as the queen will often fly at him with her claws, ready to fight him. Many stud owners have a shelf or chair placed in the stud quarters, on to which the stud cat can jump for sanctuary. After a few minutes the queen will settle down and both partners will wash and groom themselves. Soon she will let the stud cat approach her again, to re-commence the mating ritual. It only needs one mating for conception to take place but stud owners monitor several matings to make sure.

POST-MATING

After the queen has been mated, she will probably continue to call for several more days. During this period of "heat", fertilisation of the eggs will take place, approximately twenty-four hours after the mating, but studies have indicated that fertilisation can occur even up to fifty hours after mating. This is why it is wise, on collecting your queen, not to allow her outside the house, as she is still capable of being mated by the local tom-cat and having her eggs fertilised. There have been many instances of dual matings occurring. The stud owner will also have checked your queen's neck, because some stud cats, particularly young inexperienced males, will tend to grab the scruff of the neck in quite a rough manner. Sometimes this over-eagerness will result in your queen losing a little fur, or in a sore patch developing. If by any chance his teeth have broken the skin of your queen, you will need to check that no infection builds up; obviously if this does happen you will need to seek veterinary advice.

Chapter Seventeen

PREGNANCY AND BIRTH

If you are extremely impatient to know if your queen is pregnant, some Veterinary practices do have ultrasound machines which can diagnose pregnancy after approximately seventeen days. X-rays can determine pregnancy after about thirty-eight days, though this method has its pros and cons. On average the period of gestation is sixty-five days. Once you have a good idea when the birth is going to take place, you will be able to plan so that you will be on hand to assist.

THE STAGES OF PREGNANCY
The first twenty-eight days
Some, but not all, queens develop morning sickness about a week after fertilisation. At about three to four weeks, you should notice that her nipples have become slightly enlarged, with a rosy glow. This is known as "pinking". You will also see some changes to the character and look of your Siamese. Her coat will take on a very glossy sheen and she will look in the peak of condition. She will appear more content and happy, often purring herself to sleep.

   It is generally accepted that, if anything is going to go wrong in the development of the embryos, potential malformations will occur from around the twelfth to the eighteenth day of pregnancy. If your queen is unwell at any stage, then please seek help and advice before administering any form of drugs. During the latter part of this period, approximately from the sixteenth day onwards, developing kittens can be felt as if they were small ball-bearings less than half an inch long placed at regular intervals along the horns of the uterus. At this stage in their development they will already have the rudiments of a respiratory system. There is no need to change or supplement your queen's diet.

Twenty-eight to thirty-five days
You should not explore the sides of the body where the uterine horns are placed because you could cause damage. The kittens will be approximately one inch long and will have all their organs in place.

Thirty-five to forty-two days
The queen's abdomen will look quite swollen. Her nipples will be quite prominent and she will need extra food. The manufacturers who produce a life-cycle kitten diet suggest that, during the last trimester of pregnancy this diet should be fed free choice. For those breeders who like to feed a mixed diet, an extra meal of a very good quality protein food should be offered as well. If she is receiving a morning and evening meal, then giving her this at lunchtime will help to space out her meals. It is very difficult to draw a line between feeding an adequate amount to a pregnant queen and overfeeding, but you know her, and must judge accordingly. As long as she exhibits good muscle tone and not evident layers of fat, then you will have a very healthy, pregnant queen. The

foetuses will have grown to approximately two and a half inches long by this stage of gestation.

Forty-two to forty-nine days

The queen's daily intake of food will also need increasing again by another small meal of good quality protein, if you are already feeding her three meals a day. This includes fresh or canned meat, cheese, egg yolks and diluted evaporated milk which also contains minerals, and Vitamins A and D.

When your Siamese walks around it will look as if she is waddling. It is a good idea to give her some form of exercise and she will still maintain some enthusiasm for play. It is also an idea to keep a watch on her litter tray. You neither want to cope with diarrhoea nor, at the other extreme, constipation (which can be eased with a teaspoon or dropper of 2.5 ml of liquid paraffin or pure olive oil).

A little cod liver oil is an ideal source of Vitamin A (a lack of it is thought to be one of the reasons for kittens being born with cleft palates) and of Vitamin D; or a light sprinkling of a good quality vitamin and mineral powder on her food, or a vitamin tablet will achieve the same results. Your queen will seek a lot of reassurance and affection from you and will invite you to gently massage her tummy when she rolls over.

An expectant mother can experience a miscarriage which, if it is going to happen, will occur around the fifth or the sixth week, on the forty-fifth or forty-sixth day. You will either notice that she has passed foetuses on the floor of her area or in her bed or litter tray, or she will simply stop putting on weight. The latter is usually referred to as "kitten absorption", which occurs when the kittens liquefy and she re-absorbs them. Normally with a miscarriage there is bleeding, but if she keeps herself clean it is likely you will not notice this.

Obviously, if you notice any blood around this time, you will need to seek the help of your vet who may be able to give a hormone injection to prevent miscarriage. There are many causes of miscarriage; it could be a situation where the genes from both sides are mis-matched, often referred to as a "lethal factor", or it could be due to a simple uterine infection, excessive exercise in the early stages of pregnancy, stress or inadequate nutrition. If she does miscarry on one occasion, this does not necessarily mean your queen is unsuitable for future breeding.

Forty-nine to sixty days

At this stage your queen will start to hunt for what she considers to be the ideal spot for giving birth to her kittens. It is guaranteed that whatever place she chooses will not be your idea of a delivery room. If the kittening area is prepared in advance, then your queen will come to recognise that it is the right place in which to give birth and will happily accept any new items bought for the purpose. Although there are proprietary kittening boxes available we have tended to make up our own delivery boxes because of hygiene and cost. Use a very large, rigid box about two foot wide, two foot in height and about two foot six inches long. This should allow your queen to stretch out her feet against the sides, giving her the necessary support when in labour. A round hole should be made at one side, large enough to enable her to walk through without difficulty in her pregnant state, and the bottom should be at least five inches off the floor. This is so that the newly-born kittens will not be lying in draughts. Finally, you will need to make a lid for the top of the box for ease of access.

Preparation includes wiping the box with a cat-safe diluted disinfectant. After it has dried out, line the bottom with clean newspapers and cover these with old clean cloths that you can throw out after the birth. You could also use a heated pad, which can be placed at the bottom of the box. Its gentle temperature will encourage the queen to use her box to sleep in. Most pads are thermostatically controlled, otherwise set the temperature so that it is not too hot for the queen to sleep on. You should place some bedding over the pad to distribute the heat evenly.

Within the designated kittening area, place her litter tray so that she can easily reach it, together with her food and water bowls which should be placed close by but away from her litter tray. All her items need to be kept hygienically clean and there must always be an adequate supply of very fresh drinking water.

This stage of pregnancy and preparation involves a certain degree of cat maintenance. Check her nipples frequently and keep the areas surrounding them clean. Any specks of dirt can be wiped away and in doing this you will be keeping the area moist and clean as the skin tends to get dry at this time. There is usually a distinct area surrounding the nipples where the fur ends but if there are any overlapping long hairs, these can be trimmed away. She will find it difficult to keep her rear end clean after passing urine as well as faecal matter, as she will be so large. Drops of urine may crystallise on her vulva, causing itching, and in extreme cases, infection to pass through the vulva to the rest of the urogenital system. A quick wipe with a piece of cotton wool dampened with warm water, followed by a dry tissue, will relieve the problem.

This is the time to think about offering your queen further supplementation, in the form of minerals if you are feeding a mixed diet, as the growing kittens are depleting her reserves. It also seems wise to give some form of calcium supplementation, plus a certain amount of phosphorus, at this stage until the end of pregnancy. Homeopathic pharmacies are able to sell a calcium phosphorus solution for this purpose and can recommend the correct strength, providing you inform them of the stage of pregnancy of your queen. Another method of giving much needed calcium is through diluted evaporated milk. It is unwise to offer cow's milk: while this is an excellent source of calcium, it contains lactose that can upset your queen and give her diarrhoea. One word of warning: too much calcium is just as bad as too little – both can cause problems at parturition. Your vet can give you advice on this subject.

These last couple of weeks coincide with the growth of the unborn kittens reaching about four inches. You will notice that the queen's abdomen will look a little "lumpy" and, if you look carefully when she is resting, you should be able to see some signs of movement under her skin.

Sixty days to birth day

Some breeders will check the queen's temperature to see when the birth will be expected. The average temperature of a cat is 101°F or 38.5°C. When birth is due within twelve hours, the temperature drops to between 98-99°F or 36.5-37° Celsius. These figures are only a guide. It is best to get your queen accustomed to having her temperature taken, which is done through the rectum, well before pregnancy, as it can cause her distress if she is not used to it. If the temperature has actually risen by a couple of degrees above the normal level, you will need to contact your vet for help.

If the queen has not produced her kittens by the sixty-eighth day from the first day of mating, it would be wise to seek veterinary guidance. It is not unusual for a queen to carry her kittens as late as this provided there have been no other signs of birth such as contractions, and her temperature is normal. She should be eating normally. Warning signs to watch out for include bleeding or vaginal discharge before labour starts, and if this occurs, get your vet to check if the kittens are distressed in any way. Other negative signs may include diarrhoea and sickness, raised third eyelids, "open" coat, and any premature contractions. If there is any distress, a Caesarian operation may be advisable.

DELIVERY KIT

This needs to be prepared in advance and kept in an accessible place for when kittening begins. Items should include:

Blunt-topped scissors or artery forceps (latter available from your Veterinary Surgeon).

Unopened kitchen roll of paper.

Unopened box of tissues.

Dermisol solution or Betadine solution (available from your Veterinary Surgeon) or alcohol from the chemist.

Reel of white cotton.

Scales for accurate measurement of ounces/grams.

Food colouring.

Black rubbish bags.

Unopened jar of Vaseline or any other proprietary make of petroleum jelly.

Thin white surgical gloves.

Old, freshly washed bedding that you can throw away after the birth.

Cotton buds.

Artificial colostrum and cat's milk.

Sterile dropper or syringes.

Sterilising fluid or tablets for syringes and dropper if needed.

Heated pad if necessary.

Writing paper and pen.

Clock with second hand.

Your vet's telephone number if not already committed to memory.

A disinfectant hand-wash.

You may like to include a stiff drink for yourself in the list!

You may find that you will only need to use some of these items, and when you are attuned to the kittening process it is quite likely that your list of supplies will be much smaller. These items should be placed near the designated kittening area to be on hand when you need them.

FIRST STAGES OF LABOUR

Signs of impending birth include the drop in temperature. This will coincide with your queen indicating that she is no longer interested in her food, a small vaginal clear-coloured mucous discharge, and the ripping up of the newspaper you have so carefully laid down for her in the kittening area. A few queens will cry loudly, others will have a loud rhythmic purr, all will breathe a little faster. Some will be restless and pace up and down, others will make kneading motions with their paws. Some maiden queens can become quite frightened as the first kitten is about to be born. Some females will also make it clear that they want their owners with them during this process and will actually hold back until they are present. Others will get on with the process of birth unaided, with you just observing. Approximately twelve hours before the kittens are due, some queens will lie on their sides.

The clearest sign of all is uterine contractions. These occur when the first kitten starts its journey to life down the uterine horn to the cervix. They will become stronger as the intervals between them become shorter. If the queen is not ready to give birth, any contractions will cease after a few minutes. At this point sterilise some of the delivery kit, the scissors, forceps and lengths of cotton. Dry them in the air, then pick them up, wearing plastic gloves, and wrap them in clean paper towels in an accessible place. Try to make the birth as sterile as posssible, so wash your hands and use a nailbrush to clean under the nails with soap. Then dry them and rub with a disinfectant.

Unfortunately, there is no hard and fast rule as to how long the first stages of labour will last and it can indeed go on for several hours. Uterine contractions will increase in intensity and the stage of heavy labour can be recognised when the contractions cause the queen's whole body to heave. This is where the clock, pen and paper come into their own. You can make notes on the "peaking"

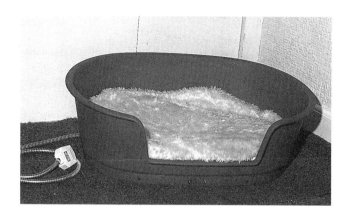

A heated electrical bed. This is a most useful piece of equipment for a nursing Siamese mother and her newborn kittens, providing a gentle heat under thermostatic control.

Photo: Paddy Cutts.

of contractions, which will eventually culminate with one about every thirty seconds. Call on your vet for help if, after an hour of heavy contractions no kitten has appeared; if the queen appears to be exhausted even before this hour has elapsed; or if she is passing bright red blood. A qualifying note should be added to the last point – that it is normal for some blood to be passed with uterine fluids, but the colour of this discharge should not be the same colour as your queen's undiluted blood. It is possible at this stage that you will be wiping away the blood and uterine fluids with paper towels and this will enable you to make an informed decision regarding the colour of the blood being passed.

NORMAL BIRTH

The queen, in most cases, will be lying on her side and will give birth in this position. A few queens have been known to give birth standing up. Following the onset of heavy contractions, the queen will start to strain and what can only be described as a bubble of filled fluid will be expelled. This will either come out whole or will break during labour. This should precede the birth of the first kitten which, as a guideline, should make its appearance within the next hour. Hopefully the first kitten will be born head-first, and with two or three further contractions the rest of the body follows. Each kitten is enclosed in an amniotic sac and is surrounded by a straw-coloured fluid. Sometimes the kitten is expelled complete in its sac, other times the sac is broken during its expulsion from the vulva. The fluid is then absorbed by the newspapers in the kittening box and these can be disposed of later with all the soiled bedding when clearing up.

THE BREATHING KITTEN

After birth the kitten will have an initial stretch and then should be moving and breathing. The mother will usually lick the membrane away and begin washing the kitten's face to remove fluid from the air passages. This starts when the kitten is just born and is still attached to its cord and placenta, which may still be in the mother's body. If this is the case, just wait for nature to take its course to pass the cord and placenta. You may need to help at the time of the kitten being born surrounded by the fluid in its amniotic sac. If this fluid is not removed, the kitten will not be able to breathe and can die. If there is no visible sign of the kitten breathing or cord and placenta being expelled, cut the cord as close to the queen's vulva as possible. Take great care. Do not cut it too close to the kitten's body. Rub the kitten gently with a rough piece of towelling or flannel to break the sac. You will need to wipe the fluid away from both nostrils and mouth, and brisk rubbing with a towel should help with the process of the kitten breathing. If there is still no discernible breathing, blow very gently into the kitten's nostrils, then hold the kitten head downwards, supporting the body very carefully and briskly rubbing all the time. The action of alternatively raising and lowering the kitten's forelegs can also cause air to fill the lungs. As a last resort, if the kitten still appears lifeless, place its body between your hands, its head nearest to your fingers. Then sling your hands in a downward movement to clear the respiratory passages of fluid. Out of all the methods listed one, at least, or a combination of two methods, should enable your kitten to cry loudly which will tell you that it is breathing normally.

Offer the kitten to its mother so she can lick away any bubbles that come from its mouth and nostrils and so that she can keep it warm. It is important not to let the newly-born kittens get cold at any time.This is a big contributing factor to kitten death at birth.

THE UMBILICAL CORD

The umbilical cord links the placenta to the kitten. This should be severed by the queen, who normally eats the placenta and cord up to a point of about three quarters of an inch to an inch of the body of the kitten. Ensure that the queen does not become too enthusiastic about eating the cord and sever it too close to the body of the kitten, which could cause a kitten to develop a hernia. Some queens do not sever the umbilical cord and this is where your sterilised fingers, scissors or forceps play their part. Some breeders use their fingers or scissors and gently pinch, then break or slightly tear the cord about an inch from the kitten's body. Usually a drop or two of blood is lost without causing the kitten any harm. We use forceps to clamp down in two to three places to squash the blood vessels within the cord and so stop the bleeding that can occur during cutting. After cutting, tie it with a piece of sterile cotton. Saturate the end with whatever sterilising medium you have chosen to prevent the passage of bacteria into the kitten's body, which can cause a range of infections, the most serious being peritonitis, which can be fatal. You will end up adopting the method that you find easiest to use; there is no right or wrong way

THE PLACENTA

The placenta, otherwise known as the afterbirth, is usually expelled with the next set of contractions. It looks like a small piece of liver and it attaches the developing kitten to the uterine horn. It is the means by which the kitten has received nourishment. With each kitten born there is a placenta, unless your queen has given birth to twins. The birth of twins is far from common and can be identified because they share a placenta. All placentas should be accounted for. Eating the placentas is a very natural process for the newly delivered mother and it will provide her with a very rich source of nutrients and hormones that can be utilised by her body to give her the immediate sustenance she needs. If you suspect that your queen may not have passed all her placentas, do not try to pull them out, because this could cause death by tearing her uterus. Your vet will give an injection of oxytocin to expel any remaining material which, if left internally, can cause serious infections and, in extreme circumstances, be fatal.

BREECH BIRTH

Not all kittens in a litter are born head-first; some may be born in a breech position, that is with the hind feet entering the world first. Breech births can take longer and in some cases may need help. Use the surgical gloves and smear the exposed part of the kitten and the vaginal wall with petroleum jelly. Often a breech birth at this point will have the body of the kitten wriggling with the head still inside the birth canal. If the whole of the body has not appeared, support what is showing with one hand and, with the following contraction, gently pull and the head will appear. Do not at any stage pull on the kitten's legs or tail.

DIFFICULT BIRTHS

Even though you will be extremely excited at the thought of your queen having her kittens, you will need to think about what you will need to do in the event of the birth becoming difficult. We experienced this last year for the very first time and know the feelings of panic and helplessness that can ensue. You may need to get to your vet in a hurry, once you realise something has gone wrong, or the births are very slow, and you may need the help of knowledgeable friends.

MOVING THE KITTENS

This is totally up to you. Some breeders try to keep the kittens as close as possible to the mother while she is giving birth to her second and subsequent kittens. There is one problem with this, however, if you are not able to watch all the time – that of the queen rolling onto and suffocating her kittens as she is straining against the sides of her kittening box with contractions.

We tend to remove newly born kittens from the queen when it is apparent that the births are not too far apart from each other. They are put in a separate heated bed which the queen can see and, when she shows an interest, the cover is turned back so she can see her kittens. If there is a waiting period between the appearance of her last kitten and the birth of the next, her youngsters are returned to her so the process of bonding can begin. Otherwise they should be returned to her as quickly as possible after the births have been completed.

If the queen shows signs of not wanting her kittens, there are some things you can do to stimulate her interest. The main trick is to get the kittens to absorb her smell and this can be done by letting them lie on some of the discarded soiled bedding of the birth. This will contain the smell of her uterine fluids and blood. Another method is to present the rear end of the kitten to the queen. If her maternal instinct is strong, there are very few queens who can resist a youngster's bottom waved under their nose. Another way is to try and transfer some of the mother's urine onto the kittens. This is not very easy to do as the mother will have concentrated on giving birth rather than using the litter tray.

CLEARING UP

Once the birth has finished, clear up all the soiled cloths and newspaper into a large black bin-liner. Re-sterilise, dry and put away the used implements such as the artery forceps. Give the kittening box a quick wipe over with a disinfectant spray and place fresh cloths of a close weave over the heated pad to provide a suitable temperature for the newly born kittens. The claws of newly born kittens appear quite prominent and, although they are soft, as the kittens blindly move around, their progress can be impeded if their claws become stuck in a loose-weave material.

Not all breeders use heated pads at this post-delivery stage. The general rule of thumb is that there should be no extra need for an additional source of heat for kittens born in the spring or summer months. Ideally the room in which the kittens are kept should be a constant 70°F or 21°C.

After all the kittens are delivered, the queen will start licking herself clean. If the queen ate all or some of the placentas, it is unlikely she will be hungry but in most cases she will be extremely thirsty. Don't expect her stomach to go down immediately after giving birth.

CHECKING FOR DEFECTS

As we gained more experience with litters of kittens, we soon learnt how to check for congenital defects. Luckily, we have had only one kitten that had to be put to sleep very quickly. It was born with a massive umbilical hernia, with many organs outside a hole in the stomach lining, and this could never be repaired in one so tiny. Most umbilical hernias are not as large as that one was and indeed this defect can be classed as quite a minor one, if there is only a small bulge by the navel. A veterinary surgeon will monitor the situation and most leave well alone until the cat is brought in to be neutered. Both jobs are then carried out under the application of one anaesthetic.

Another defect to look for is a cleft palate. When a kitten's mouth is opened the nasal cavity and the mouth cavity will appear as one. The kitten will experience great difficulty suckling and if you and your vet feel that the kitten has any chance of survival, then it will have to be hand-fed through a gastric tube until the repair operation can be done. In most cases the kitten will be put to sleep, as feeding by tube is a very specialist procedure and not one for the faint-hearted.

Other defects such as a club foot or club feet may not be too much of a problem to deal with but, again, you will need to take the advice of your vet. The condition, in most cases, is due to a leg or both hind legs being caught in an unnatural position during development or in the process of birth. If the "abnormality" is due to this reason, it could straighten out in time.

THE FIRST FEW DAYS

It is a most wonderful sight to see a happy mother rhythmically purring to herself as her young kittens blindly scramble for their chosen nipple. This, however, does not always happen automatically! Some kittens appear to have one main aim after birth, to find the milk bar as soon as possible. Other kittens seem to have been so overwhelmed by the process of birth that they would happily sleep their first few hours away. They have to be helped, and many an hour has been whiled away offering a sleepy kitten the choicest selection of nipples on the house until one finds favour. The third group of kittens appear to swim blindly over their mother's abdomen without using any of their senses to identify that the regularly spaced small lumps offer nourishment.

It is said that kittens are attracted to nipples by smell, so with this in mind we never wash the queen after birth. We will only intervene by squeezing a nipple to release some colostrum and gently opening a kitten's mouth to allow this liquid to drop onto the tongue. This usually works and within a couple of hours after the birth the mother can be left alone with all her kittens suckling and making kneading movements on her abdomen, which stimulates the flow of colostrum and, later, milk. For approximately the first two days of the kitten's life, the queen produces this colostrum, which is a slightly white opaque fluid which needs to be suckled by the kittens from birth because it gives them added immunity against bacterial infections.

FEEDING KITTENS IN AN EMERGENCY

This can be required should the mother become ill or simply reject her kittens. In most cases, she will bond with them later, whatever the reason for her initial rejection. It is best to keep in stock a proprietary feline dried milk. In an emergency, diluted evaporated milk can be given; the diluting water should have been boiled and allowed to cool. Do not use cow's milk under any circumstances. It can cause diarrhoea, which can be fatal in such young kittens, as they are unable to digest the lactose in it. Proprietary cat milks obviously contain less lactose but they are not really ideal for newly borns. The major point to bear in mind is not to force too much liquid down in one attempt, otherwise milk can get into the lungs which means the kitten will die from inhalation pneumonia. Also make sure that the temperature of the milk is not too hot – try dropping a few drops onto the sensitive part of your hand or inside arm to monitor it.

Do not drop milk into the kitten while it is lying on its back; make sure the kitten is on its stomach. Open its mouth and place the dropper at approximately a 45 degree angle to its mouth. The kitten will catch on very quickly to this new game. Don't flood the kitten's mouth with more milk than it can handle. A rhythm will soon be established between the two of you and the kitten will let you know when it has had enough; it will simply stop sucking. Return the kitten to its mother and she will clean her youngster to stimulate the process of defaecation. Some vets will show you how to insert a tube through the kitten's mouth which will go down directly into its stomach. This method is recognised to be the best feeding method. It should not be attempted without practical instruction as too rough handling can lead to internal damage. Just like a new-born baby, the kitten may need to expel wind. Place the kitten in an upright position against your shoulder and very gently rub or pat its back. If you have to adopt the full mothering role, tickle the young kitten's stomach and rear end with a cotton bud or cotton wool ball, which will encourage the flow of waste product.

A kitten, just like a newly born baby, has to have its feeding utensils kept scrupulously clean. All feeding equipment needs to be washed by hand in hot water with soap to loosen the milk debris, rinsed in fresh hot water and then plunged into a container of freshly prepared sterilising solution. For the next meal, the feeding implements are dropped into boiling water, removed and allowed to dry on a piece of paper kitchen towel. This is to prevent any of the sterilising solution from being ingested by the kitten with its milk.

IDENTIFICATION

Identification of each little Siamese individual is not very easy at this stage as they will all look fairly similar, with no colour points to guide you. They are all born white because they have developed inside their mother, whose body maintained a constant temperature. The colour points develop gradually after birth due to sensitivities in temperature. You probably won't be able to resist looking at them, providing the queen will let you and you will, on close examination, see very slight differences in the shape of the head and in size. Unless you have an exceptionally good picture memory for little individuals who will be constantly changing, one of the surest ways of identification can be made using food dyes. These are non-toxic to the mother. A very tiny dot of each colour can be made under one of the armpits of each kitten. The mother often misses out this area when she is licking her kittens.

Having identified your kittens, one of the next jobs is weighing them. Kittens can weigh from one and a half ounces in most extreme circumstances, to four and a half ounces. Three ounces is the average. Weight is determined by the sex of the kitten and the number of kittens in a litter. Weighing is a good idea, because any movement down the charted scale on graph paper can give you an early warning sign that something is going amiss. A loss of weight, or no gain for two days, should be the sign to seek veterinary help even if there are no other symptoms.

One of the "fun" parts of your queen having kittens is finding out what she has presented you with. Loosely pick up the tail and look at the rear end: most male kittens will have a very small bulge with two vertical dots; female kittens will have openings resembling an inverted exclamation mark. Nature can also play tricks on you at this stage; sometimes it can be very hard to determine whether the kitten is male or female in the early days. You have to be very patient and wait.

POTENTIAL PROBLEMS

In most cases you will not have to heed this section at all, as your queen gets on with the job of nursing and rearing her kittens.

Spotting: the queen will always lose a little bit of blood during the first few days after having her kittens. These spots are totally normal, part of the birth process, and they will dry to a fairly dark red colour.

Metritis: one problem which could reveal itself if there is a dark brown smelly discharge, is metritis, which is inflammation of the womb. If you call your vet quickly, all this condition needs is a course of antibiotics.

Mastitis: this can occur as soon as one week after kittening. It is quite a painful condition and appears when the mammary glands become swollen. In extreme cases, the abdomen appears to have its own breastplate of red armour. A course of antibiotics soon corrects the situation.

Rejection: in very rare circumstances a mother can reject one or all of her kittens. If she rejects one kitten you can assume there is something wrong with it and the mother has sensed a defect. She will indicate this by refusing to care for the kitten and may even smother it by lying on it. If a mother attempts to abandon all her kittens you will quickly need to call in the vet in case she has a problem. It could mean that she is producing no colostrum and an injection can solve this problem. A very unusual situation, but one that does occur, is that a first-time mother may end up by being totally frightened by the whole process of giving birth. If the kittens are not able to suck from a traumatised mother, her milk will dry up and you will end up being a foster mother or trying to find a foster mother for this litter. You can soothe an agitated mother by laying her down on her side frequently and gently talking to her whilst attempting to get her kittens to suckle. In extreme cases she may need a tranquilliser to calm her down.

FALSE PREGNANCIES

These do not occur often but can arise when a queen has been mated eventually after several calls. The physical cause underlying a false pregnancy is a growth on one or both ovaries. The queen will have gone through all the signs of pregnancy including an enlarged uterus, milk production, nest behaviour and, if you have any other kittens around the house, she will steal them or attempt to hurt their mother. If she has undergone a false pregnancy, mate her the next season providing she is in good health. If this mating ends in another false pregnancy, then approach your veterinary surgeon for help and advice.

Chapter Eighteen

KITTEN DEVELOPMENT

It is advisable to handle the kittens daily from birth to acquaint them with human contact, providing the mother is happy for you to do so. Even though the kittens cannot see their owners, talking to them and their mother stimulates the animal/human bond. Some breeders do not encourage their friends to see the kittens during the early weeks of development to minimise any risk of infection.

THE FIRST WEEK
Appearance: Siamese kittens are born with their eyes closed and their ears folded down. Once their fur dries, their overall body colour appears white. The kittens will not look like their mother at all. Towards the end of the first week, the very first sign of colour begins to show at the edge of the ears, which is the coolest area of the kitten. The darker colours reveal themselves first – seal, blue, and chocolate – followed by the other colours, but at this stage all colours will be hard to identify, especially if you are expecting more than one colour to appear in your litter. The remaining length of umbilical cord will remain attached to the kittens for the first few days but this shrivels, darkens in colour and gradually falls off during the first week. You should take care not to pull off the umbilical cord as this could lead to a hernia.
Movement: The kittens spend their time sleeping and feeding and will show a distinct preference for a favourite nipple. When awake, they do not crawl far away from the mother, and crawling takes on a wobbly stance as they move on their legs for the first time.
Weight: the weight of a newly-born kitten averages between three and five ounces (ninety to one hundred and forty grams). It is advisable to check the weight of each kitten at regular intervals.
Calling again: If the queen is restless while calling she may have to be restrained into her pen, so that she will continue to nurse her kittens. Any thoughts of mating should be delayed in the mother's best interests until her kittens are safely reared and she has reached the peak of condition again.
Warmth: keep the kittens warm – but remember too hot is as bad as too cold.

THE SECOND WEEK
Appearance: The fur on the tail develops a little colour but this often takes on an indeterminate "tone" of the darker colours and a "tint" of the lighter colours. Faint shadows of colour will appear on the nose and paws as well. It will still be very difficult to identify the colours. During the second week the kittens' eyes start to open. This happens gradually over a few days, so do not expect all kittens to open their eyes at the same time. Don't force the eyes open; this could cause damage. As soon the eyes are open, you will need to be on your guard against eye infections.

Bacteria can be passed into a young kitten's eyes when they are not fully open by the mother washing her young. If you see anything which would indicate infection, such as a yellowish crystal crust along the eyelids, or a whitish/yellowish secretion, do not pull the eye lids apart with your fingers. Soak the area with dampened cottonwool that is impregnated with a warmed home-made saline solution at frequent intervals. If the pus is a very definite colour, your vet may prescribe antibiotic drops or cream. It is important that kittens are not subject to bright lights until their eyes are fully open. All the umbilical cords should have dried up and fallen off by this time.

Movement: the kittens will still be alternating between sleeping and crawling in a very wobbly fashion, keeping close to their mother.

Weight: an average weight increase is in the order of half an ounce daily for each kitten, so that by the second week they should have doubled their birth weight.

THE THIRD WEEK

Appearance: the markings on the ears, nose and tail will slightly darken in colour but still be fairly indistinguishable. Their teeth will have started to develop.

Movement: the kittens will be crawling and attempting to take their first staggering steps, keeping close to their mother. Some kittens will attempt to walk out of their bed and explore the area outside.

Weight: weight gain should continue steadily.

THE FOURTH TO SIXTH WEEKS: THE WEANING PROCESS

Appearance: the colour markings on the ears, face, nose and tail deepen. To all intents and purposes the kittens will be recognisable as Siamese.

Movement: At this point move the mother and kittens into a larger space in order to provide a safe play area for fast-moving kittens and another area for the mother to which she can retire and have a well earned break. The kittens will begin scrambling around exploring new sights and sounds. They start to play with each other and may climb a "baby" scratching post if there is one. If you take them out of the pen to let them run about your room, watch out for hidden dangers, such as live electical wires, flowers and leaves, and loose ornaments.

Be careful how you pick up the kittens. They will now be quite heavy and will need support. Pick a kitten up by putting one hand under its chest and use the other hand to support its rear end and weight. You may wonder why the mother still carries her kittens by what appears to be the scruff of the neck. In fact she is picking up the kitten by the whole of its neck, which fits neatly across her semi-open mouth in between her canine and other teeth. Kittens will not have been trained to relieve themselves in a litter tray and it is quite possible you may find a wet patch on your favourite chair after they have climbed on to it.

Weight: weight gain should continue steadily during this critical weaning period.

The Weaning Process: the mother will still keep her kittens clean but this will not be as intensive as during the first three weeks. Make sure that the new kitten area is free from draughts, has an easily washable floor surface and be prepared for frequent changes of bedding. The mother will leave the kittens for short periods of time, due to a change in the level of her hormones. This change from her intensive care will give you an idea as to when to commence the weaning process. Another factor to look out for is the condition of the mother and the quality of her milk. Not every litter at the age of four weeks is ready to be weaned, but this can be tested by offering the kittens some very finely minced chicken breast. Even if some of the litter show some interest in licking the new food, they should not be taken away from their mother. Each breeder commences the weaning phase at a pace to suit them.

The weaning phase lasts approximately three to four weeks. The start can be very messy and it is usually best to wear an apron or take some other measure to prevent splashes of weaning formula ending up over you. Dip a clean finger into a milk-cereal mix and encourage the kitten to lick the mixture off your clean finger. If the kitten is reluctant then a little food can be smeared onto its muzzle to encourage it to lick. This often works and then the finger-licking stage can be used. It only takes a day or two to get the kitten used to licking your finger or a spoon.The next stage is to lower your finger or spoon to the surface of the food in the saucer; the kitten will follow suit by lowering its head and will soon be licking the surface of the food in the saucer all by itself. There is no specific length to this process; some Siamese learn very quickly but there is always one in a litter who takes a little longer than most. Clean drinking water should be provided at all times and, unless you use a weighted bowl, you can guarantee that the water will be knocked over with the kittens' attempts at playing together. If you want to give a milk preparation, use evaporated milk diluted with cooled boiled water, or one of the proprietary feline milk powders, which are obtainable from your vet and from some pet shops. Whatever brand you use, always follow the manufacturers' instructions. Introductions can be made to minced white fish (make sure that all bones are removed), minced chicken or a little rabbit to get them used to different textures and smells of food. Don't forget that the mother will appreciate all these tit-bits too! She has the job of raising the kittens.

It is also advisable to give the kittens a clean litter tray. Make sure that the litter is completely digestible and has no chemicals sprayed on to it – many kittens at this weaning stage will actually eat their litter. To avoid this happening, some breeders start litter tray training by placing a pad made up of kitchen towels in the kitten litter tray with a sample of the mother's used litter to give the kitten a hint. Sometimes the mother carries a kitten to the litter tray and leaves it there. Being curious though, most kittens usually find their own way to the litter tray and urination and defaecation commences with the weaning process. It is such a funny sight to see a little kitten registering surprise on its face when it uses its litter tray properly for the first time. If a kitten is a little slow in learning how to use its litter tray, do not "rub its nose in it", just be patient and if you see it scratching around in its pen, just pick it up and put it on its tray. It will eventually learn.

Vaccinations: some breeders will give a flu-only vaccine to their kittens at the age of six weeks to confer some extra immunity. This is a good idea if the kittens are from a multi-cat household.

Diarrhoea: one of the more common problems you may experience with your litter is diarrhoea. It can be the the result of a mild stomach upset or a serious infection. If you think that the kitten is suffering from a minor infection, cutting out a meal may help. You will need to examine the kitten carefully to look for other symptoms if further bouts of diarrhoea set in during the day. Other symptoms can include an open "staring" coat. Take the kitten's temperature, if you have been trained to do it and have a sterilised thermometer handy. The kitten may appear lethargic and sorry for itself. It can even whimper or cry if in pain. Pinch the coat with two fingers at the base of the kitten's neck and if it does not immediately spring back, it means the kitten is becoming dehydrated. If any of these symptoms are present, get veterinary help immediately.

The fading kitten syndrome: there is no particular symptom underlying this condition, but over a period of time, from about three weeks onward, the kitten will appear lethargic, weakened and suffering from an undetermined malaise. Any general veterinary treatment proves unsuccessful and the kitten literally fades away.

THE SIXTH TO EIGHTH WEEKS

Appearance: by the end of the eighth week you should have a clearer idea of the colour of the points of the kittens to enable you to fill in your GCCF kitten registration form correctly. The

Kittens love suckling their mother and will often continue beyond the ideal age, unless stopped!

Photo: Paddy Cutts.

kittens will also have a full set of milk teeth. Their whiskers should be longer and standing proud of the mouth. These tend to be brittle and will break during boisterous play but they soon grow again

Movement: the kittens will be extremely active. Their mother will spend some time with them to clean them and probably sleep with them but she will have longer periods on her own. Socialise the kittens constantly by speaking gently to them, and stroke and gently fondle them with your hands. Any rougher play can result in them growing up to be rough with their new owners, who will probably object to deep scratches on their hands.

Weight: the kittens will have been weaned steadily onto solid food and should by this stage be "eating you out of house and home". Always make sure that each kitten gets its fair share of food daily. They should be taking four small meals daily and will enjoy small quantities of grated cheese as a "treat", scrambled egg, a small drink of diluted evaporated milk and minced cooked fish or chicken. Offering kittens uncooked meat should be avoided. They should be eating mostly solid food and at about eight weeks it is safe to introduce one of the dried kitten life-cycle diets that are available. The kitten's teeth will have developed sufficiently to be able to chew and break up the triangular pieces of biscuit that are available.

You will have to make up your mind as to when you will finish the weaning process. The best guide comes from the mother herself. If she repeatedly leaves the kittens while they are trying to suckle from her and they have been gaining weight steadily and eating solid food for two weeks at least, then it is time to keep the two parties apart. You will need to be careful that your kittens are not weaned away from their mother too early; they may become ill as a result and lose momentum. After the mother has been separated from the kittens, her nipples become full of milk. Keep a very close watch on her and make sure no other member of the feline household accepts a tipple from the milk bar. Her milk production should stop fairly quickly and the swelling around her nipples should go down. If she develops hard areas around her nipples which are hot to the touch, then take her immediately to the veterinary surgeon, as it will be likely she has developed mastitis. After milk production has ceased she can return to her kittens but ensure she makes no attempt to carry on feeding them. If this happens then they should not be left together. One of the reasons for this is that you do not want to pass on potential "wool chewers" or kittens suckling any other item in their new homes.

THE EIGHTH TO TENTH WEEKS

Appearance: the points continue to darken and you will be more sure of the colours of your kittens. To all intents and purposes they will look like miniature Siamese cats with an excessive abundance of energy. You will be more sure of their individual characters as they develop. At around nine weeks you should see enough to be able to make a preliminary assessment on the "type" and colour of each kitten – whether the kitten is show quality, breeding quality or pet quality.

Weight The weight gain should be steady, with kittens weighing approximately two to two-and-a-half pounds. They should by now be eating four meals a day.

Vaccinations: at the age of nine weeks, kittens usually receive the first of two vaccinations against Flu and Enteritis. Some breeders also ask for the first of the Leukaemia course of injections. There is a Chlamydia vaccine available and this can either be injected into your kittens at your request or on advice from your veterinary surgeon if he knows there is a problem in your household.

Worming and de-fleaing: at the time of the first vaccination, if you have not already done so, ask your veterinary surgeon for worming preparations against roundworms and·tapeworms. Always check the mother for fleas or flea dirt in her coat and that of her kittens.

Advertising: if you have not been able to sell your kittens by word of mouth or recommendation, you will need to think about advertising and the best medium. Some breeders will advertise well before this stage, others will wait for the kittens to receive their first vaccination before they advertise.

Registration: This must be done through the Governing body of your country.

THE TENTH TO TWELFTH WEEKS

Appearance: the kittens at this stage will be growing very quickly and in most cases their points and masks will be clearly emphasized. What is known as the "ugly duckling" stage of development coincides with these weeks, with part of the body looking 'gangly' and some parts, like ears, looking out of proportion with the rest of the body. Some larger kittens may start to shed their milk teeth and will chew whatever is available, including your fingers. It is possible that the eye colour will still be changing to a more defined blue and this may carry on for the next few weeks until it stabilises into its adult colour.

Weight: by the twelfth week, the kittens will weigh between three and four pounds. There is no hard and fast rule about weight; the main point to remember is that they need to be lively, happy, healthy and without infection.

Vaccination: the second part of the two-part vaccination programme will be carried out by your vet, who in most cases undertakes a final check for good health and any possible defects. It is recommended that kittens should not be passed on to their new homes until five days and preferably seven have elapsed after the second vaccination. This is to give the kitten a chance to develop total immunity from the second round of injections before being faced with the stress of a new home.

*Seal Tabby Point:
This kitten is
ready to leave for
its new home.*

*Photo:
Paddy Cutts.*

THE THIRTEENTH WEEK

By this week the kittens will be small versions of adult Siamese, with colour points developed, fully weaned, extremely active and very, very lovable.

Departure time: rather than have all the kittens leaving home on the same day, try and stagger their departure for the sake of their mother. This gives her a chance to adjust to the loss of her kittens slowly. After a couple of weeks, she will have lost interest and will no doubt be calling for a new mate. The departure of kittens can be quite an emotional time. We have brought these kittens into the world by planning the original mating and we feel a responsibility towards them for the rest of their lives.

Chapter Nineteen

RECENT DEVELOPMENTS

October 20th 1993 was the date when Preliminary recognition was given to three "new" Siamese colours, Cinnamon, Fawn and Caramel points and their associated varieties. This meant that Show Managers could offer Siamese Assessment classes, so cats of these colours were able to obtain Merit Certificates which would be needed for future promotion.

However, Siamese cats and kittens of these "new" colours have been around for many years, often registered as other colours. For example, a fawn could be registered as lilac and a cinnamon as chocolate. A "lilac based" caramel may be registered as lilac, a "blue based" caramel may be registered as blue. Some of these "misregistered" cats have even obtained titles in competition, becoming Champion, Premier and the Grand equivalents.

As with all colours there are variations of shade; the Dutch line produces a "foxier", redder shade of Cinnamon than the slightly darker toned English lines. To understand the history of the new colours, it is necessary to understand the history of other breeds, since the colours developed more in the other breeds – mainly Oriental – than in Siamese themselves.

CINNAMON AND FAWN

Cinnamon and Fawn Siamese have a diverse history which can be traced back to the Sorrel (Red) Abyssinians at the beginning of this century. It is known that before the First World War, a Mr Brookes owned a rather unusual cat described as a 'warm brown of colour' and very beautiful to observe.

Two breeders, Maria Falkena, who developed Cinnamon and Fawn varieties of Siamese and Orientals in Holland, and Dorothy Winsor who developed Sorrel Abyssinians in England, regularly corresponded during the 1960s. They concluded that Mr Brookes' cat was responsible for the "red gene" in Abyssinians and Maria Falkena thought that this cat was the first spontaneous Cinnamon.

THE ENGLISH DEVELOPMENT

An early letter from Dorothy Winsor to Maria Falkena mentioned what may be regarded as the earliest English breeding experiment with the colour Cinnamon.

Mrs Winsor had a cat she described as a "chestnut blotched tabby" with a "creamy fawn" background colour who was mated by her Abyssinian stud cat. She was most surprised that the coat patterns and colours of the resulting litter contained "black ticking" on a "fawn" (oatmeal) background and some "red". Further litters revealed similar results.

The next recorded development with Cinnamons in England concerned Roy and Maureen Silson, who bred what is now regarded as the first known Oriental (previously known as Foreign)

An accidental mating with the Chinchilla breed provided the beginning of new varieties of Siamese.

Photo: Paddy Cutts.

Bluespice Cinnamon Ice born in the first Scottish Siamese and Oriental Cinnamon litter of kittens.

Photo: Rita Ford.

Heijac Magic Crystal: The Cinnamon Point has now been recognised for showing under GCCF rules.

Photo: Angela Bearman.

Cinnamon, Southview Pavane, in May 1971. She was actually registered as Havana, since Cinnamon was not then recognised. Pavane's parents were Kernow Gerza and Kernow Koptos, bred by Pam Evely. These cats were produced from a mating between her Sorrel Abyssinian stud, Tranby Red Tutankhamen, and her Seal Point Siamese queen, Annelida Fair Maid.

The Silsons were more interested in investigating this "red colour" than in breeding the Cinnamon and Fawn varieties in Siamese and Oriental lines, which were, in fact, a by-product. This mating introduced the long-hair gene into these lines which can be seen in the Somali (long-haired Abyssinian) breed. Tranby Red Tutankhamen was found to carry the long-hair gene.

The story of the developing Cinnamon and Fawn Siamese varieties was further complicated by Maureen Silson's interest in the Recessive White gene. She imported a Recessive White cat named Anart's Miiko from the USA. (A Recessive White has the Siamese phenotype but it carries the blue-eyed Albino gene instead of the Siamese gene. In the USA it is also known as an Albino.) Anart's Miiko became part of her breeding investigation with the result that some cats inherited not only cinnamon but also the long-hair and recessive white genes.

In mid-1975, the GCCF was concerned about the breeding of Recessive Whites. No further registrations were accepted of these or of cats bred from Recessive Whites until 1979, when it was decided they could be registered on the Experimental Register. This meant that cats registered could not be shown in competition but only put on exhibition. Any carriers of this gene would be registered on the Supplementary Register and their registration document would be overstamped: "This cat is thought to carry the Recessive White gene and is not recommended for breeding."

The next two noteworthy breeders were Tony and Sheila Clayton, Siavana prefix, who were followed by Barry and Shirley Walters, Antiquity prefix, Angela Sayer, Solitaire prefix, and Glenda Worthy, Sayonara prefix.

The Claytons actively bred and exhibited Cinnamons during this period in an attempt to create interest. One cat they exhibited was Siavana Pranayama and in a leaflet they announced that a mating had taken place which could produce the first dilute Cinnamon, expected to be a very soft "pinkish-fawn" colour. Their stud boy was Siavana Kama, whose antecedents not only went back to the original Abyssinian x Seal Point Siamese mating, but also included Burmese, through Ramree Effie Lump, a Blue Burmese.

The exhibition leaflet also contained an appeal to breeders who would be interested in developing the Cinnamon and Fawn colours. They invited owners of Havanas, Oriental (then Foreign) Lilac, Chocolate and Lilac Point Siamese to join them in a breeding programme. As both parents have to carry the light brown gene to produce Cinnamon and Fawn, the proposed breeding group would have to draw up an outcross breeding programme. A setback materialised when breeders found it difficult to sell kittens whose registration documents were overstamped with their genetic possibilities. As a result many lost interest and some Siavana cats were sent abroad. The Havana, Int. Ch. Siavana Charlie Brown went to Holland and participated in the breeding of Maria Falkena's Cinnamon & Fawn Van Mariendaal lines. There are apparently British records in existence which indicate that Siavana Charlie Brown sired Recessive Whites whilst in England but the Dutch Registration Societies appear to have no similar records.

However, fortunately for the development of Cinnamon and Fawn, a few breeders carried on with their lines and the gene pool slowly expanded. A Havana, Champion Siavana Fetiche, passed on the Cinnamon gene to his daughter, Ch. Ailsa Madellena, and her descendants, thereby founding Janet Waterhouse's Kambuku line. These are among the antecedents behind the first GCCF registered Cinnamon Point Siamese kittens, Sukoota Cream Fudge and Sukoota Chocolate Nutmeg, bred by Mrs Patricia Legge.

Angela Sayer used another Cinnamon carrier, Rian Firefox who sired Cinnamon and Cinnamon-carrying short-haired kittens with registrations overstamped: "May carry the long hair gene". The Solitaire line produced the first GCCF registered Cinnamon Tabby Point Siamese, Solitaire Spinelle, and the first GCCF registered Fawn Tabby Points, Solitaire Sparkler and Solitaire Spindrift.

Glenda Worthy wanted to obtain Cinnamon in her lines and she had tried mating her Chocolate Point Siamese queen to the Clayton's Havana, Ch. Southview Duakylin, but without success. Not one to be beaten, she was then offered a kitten from the mating of Southview Duakylin to Siavana Topsy, who was an Oriental Cinnamon. This kitten, Siavana Picot, was mated to outcross lines without the Cinnamon gene in order to bring in fresh blood lines. One of these matings was to a Chocolate Point Siamese, Sayonara Champagne Fizz and this produced Champion Sayonara Bucksfizz, "Stevie", a Havana whose name features in most Cinnamon and Fawn lines current today. Sadly this grand cat died in October 1994.

Sayonara Cinnafoot, owned by Mrs J. Jarrett, achieved the first Merit to be awarded to a Cinnamon Point Siamese at the Breed 32 Show in May 1994. He was sired by Felic Calico Printz, an Oriental Classic Tabby, and his dam was Apri Fantasia, a Cinnamon Point Siamese. In the late 1980s and early 1990s many other breeders have developed Cinnamon and Fawn lines.

Sharon Walker's Apri line produced Cinnamon and Fawn Pointed Siamese during the 1980s. Some made their way to the Netherlands and now feature in many Dutch Cinnamon pedigrees including those of Mrs Hetty Berntrop. The Apri line is descended from the Kambuku and Sayonara lines.

Other Cinnamon and Fawn lines to note include the Rexlizian prefix of Elizabeth Tomlinson whose Cinnamon lines are derived from two sources, one being the Sunjade line with Sunjade Brandysnap, an Oriental Cinnamon. He was bred by Elizabeth Wildon whose Cinnamon line is descended from Antiquity Amber. Elizabeth Tomlinson's other breeding lines are descended from the Greysbrook, Salste and Sayonara lines.

The Whipplewind line of Jenny Parsley is descended from a litter sister to Antiquity Amber, Antiquity Martini Ripple (a Havana) and the Greysbrook line.

Julia May's prefix is Palantir and she has bred, among others, the first and only (to date) GCCF registered Cinnamon Tortie Point Siamese, Palantir Hylytes.

Angela Bearman and her husband own a Cinnamon Point Siamese, Heijac Magic Crystal, born on June 1st 1990. The Heijac Cinnamon line of Jack and Heidi Stoker also traces its descent from the Sayonara and Apri lines.

Many lines have now eliminated the Recessive White overstamping. Some breeders have also carried out test matings with their cats to remove the overstamping for the long-hair gene.

Sue Barnett, prefix Sisophon, was asked by the Oriental Cat Association to exhibit her kitten, Sisophon Bilbo Baggins, a Cinnamon Tabby Point Siamese, at the 1987 Supreme Cat Show. Both his parents carried the Siamese gene through the Solitaire line.

In late 1993 the first ever Siamese and Oriental Cinnamon litter of kittens was born, in Scotland, and included a Cinnamon Point Siamese called Bluespice Cinnamon Ice, known to his friends as Toofee. He brings a great deal of joy to the residents of a nursing home for the elderly in Dumbarton where his owner, Moira Kim, is a nursing sister. Bluespice Cinnamon Ice was bred by Mrs Rita Ford, and both his parents, who carry the Siamese gene, are Oriental Cinnamons, Sunjade Brandysnap (sire) and Rexlizian Doughnut (dam).

THE DUTCH DEVELOPMENT

In the late 1950s, Maria Falkena did not know about Dorothy Winsor's work in developing "Red" (Sorrel) Abyssinians until she wrote to her asking for a "normal" Abyssinian kitten. Dorothy Winsor had none available, but later was able to export to Maria the first 'Red' Abyssinian to appear in Europe, Tranby Dalila, 23a (originally registered as breed number 26, Any Other Variety), born December 20th 1961.

When the Falkenas first saw Dalila they realised, like their English counterparts, that her colour bore no resemblance to the "orange" of their Red Tabby who was called Vosje. Dorothy Winsor informed them of an English geneticist's pronouncement on the colour as being "just another source of red".

In 1962, Dorothy bred another male "red" Abyssinian kitten, Tranby Red Sothis. He was originally registered as 26 (Any Other Variety), born April 2nd 1962, and he followed Tranby Dalila into the Netherlands to live with Maria Falkena.

Dalila was mated to another Abyssinian, Int. Ch. Nigella Simba, who did not carry the "red gene". One of the resultant kittens was registered as Iris van Mariendaal. She would carry her mother Dalila's "red" gene.

Following a discussion on the subject of colour with Mr Doeksen, the Chairman of Felikat, a test-mating was arranged between Iris van Mariendaal, 23, and Int. Ch. Crossways Heritor, 29, who was the first Havana stud cat in the Netherlands. He had been bred by Mrs Joan Judd in England. Maria Falkena knew it was her chance to find out if her theory regarding Dalila's ticked tabby coat was a red shade or, as she thought, some kind of brown shade.

This mating produced three kittens on March 8th 1964 who looked quite dark at birth. One was less dark in colour than the others – it "looked brownish somehow"; but if the "orange" gene had been present this litter would have included torties, black or brown kittens.

The Dutch Cat Fancy in the 1960s considered these kittens as "mongrels" but they were still registered in the "hulpstamboek". The "brownish" kitten, Choco-Prince van Mariendaal was kept

A Twinkle Star's litter, including a Cinnamon Tabby Point, sired by Salste Blake out of Twinkle Star's Fonda.

Photo: Yvonne Craane.

The first Van Mariendaal Cinnamon Point Siamese litter with Oriental Cinnamon siblings.

Photo: Maria Falkena.

by Maria Falkena. His colour and coat pattern of "brownish" ticking was not recognised, so he was registered as an experimental Abyssinian. Maria Falkena considers Choco-Prince van Mariendaal to be the true ancestor of the Cinnamon and Fawn Pointed Siamese varieties and their Oriental cousins. As a result of Choco-Prince van Mariendaal's birth many Dutch breeders concluded that the colour "red" of the Abyssinian was in fact a shade of brown.

We can now conclude that the gene referred to as "red" previously is what we now call Cinnamon, or "light brown". The gene referred to as "orange" produces the true "gingery" shade of red associated with Red Point Siamese. However, the Dutch story took on an unusual twist when Maria Falkena had two hybrid kittens born on July 3rd, 1962. Their mother, Soedi, was a Sudan Wild Cat, "Afrikaanse steppenkat". Maria Falkena only saw Soedi once, she was unable to buy her and eventually Soedi went to live at the Amsterdam Zoo. Maria Falkena remembers that Soedi "was spotted all over, but in a vague way, black spots on a sandy-coloured underground. She was very shy."

The father of these two kittens was an unregistered red moggie, Karel, described on pedigrees as a "red-tabby korth", breed number 19. Considering the two female hybrid kitten's voices, they were registered as Ruby R (Renato) Tibaldi, and Sylvi M Callas, after the opera singers. This was also appropriate since they were the descendants of Soedi whose Latin classification was Felis

Choco-Spot van Mariendaal.

Photo: C.A. Adriaanse.

Silvestris Rubida. Maria Falkena felt it was only natural that they should be called Silvi and **Rubi**.

They were two years old when they were mated to Int. Ch. Tranby Red Sothis. This was partly curiosity, to find out if there was any common relationship between the two Soedi-hybrids and the Abyssinian breed, the latter of which was subject at that time to a great deal of discussion regarding its origins. Both the Sudan Wild Cat and Abyssinian breeds were part of the "Felis Sylvestris" classification. Another more practical reason was that he was the only male in the house!

The results confirmed her theory. One of the kittens from Ruby was registered as Hortensia van Mariendaal, whose phenotype resembled that of an Oriental Ticked Tabby and she went to live with the Boekhorst family with a promise that later she could be bred back into the Van Mariendaal line. A female kitten from Silvi, Mimi van Mariendaal stayed with Maria Falkena. The interest in the wild spotted coat remained with Maria Falkena and in the early 1960s she thought that mating together the two lines carrying the genes of the Sudanese Wild Cat would produce kittens with spotted coats resembling their progenitor, Soedi.

Mimi van Mariendaal was mated to Choco-Prince van Mariendaal and in February 1966 one of the kittens produced from this mating was a "light brown" (Cinnamon) ticked tabby coat with only a spotted tummy. She was registered as Choco Satin van Mariendaal.

As promised, Hortensia van Mariendaal was mated back into the Van Mariendaal line. One of the kittens born on April 7th 1966 was Monkitty van de Boekhorst, the great grand-daughter of Soedi, the Sudanese Wild Cat.

The Siamese gene came into the Dutch Cinnamon line with the import from Finland of the first Lilac Point Siamese stud cat in the Netherlands, Polaris Lila Liekki. Maria Falkena thought Liekki was extremely beautiful and it was from him that Monkitty van de Boekhorst produced the warm brown spotted Choco Spot van Mariendaal who carried the Siamese gene. He appears in many Dutch pedigrees and became a very well known stud cat in Holland.

Choco Spot van Mariendaal was shown in Amsterdam and Maria Falkena felt sure that breeders and public alike would love him. However, she recorded that nobody even looked at him and the British judge who assessed him reported: "This is just a mongrel and should not be exhibited."

However, the gene pool now had the right combination to produce the Cinnamon and Fawn Siamese varieties.

Choco Satin van Mariendaal and Choco Spot van Mariendaal were mated and the kittens born on May 16th 1968 became very well known in the Netherlands. There were two Havanas, Pinar van Mariendaal and Josefine van Mariendaal, and a Cinnamon Spotted male, Spotty Go Go van Mariendaal, who Maria Falkena thought was one of the most beautiful cats she had ever owned. His spots were small and round and were this wonderful light brown colour. Josefine and Pinar were judged "nice type but lack colour", which was an unusual comment, as their warm brown coats showed they carried the Cinnamon gene.

To improve on the Havana colour, Josefine was mated to another of Maria Falkena's imports, Gaines Co Co, a Chocolate Point Siamese from America who did not carry Cinnamon. This mating produced a Havana, Josef van Mariendaal, who became Maria Falkena's first International Champion. Although several years had gone by since Maria Falkena had commenced her breeding investigations, the colours had still not been officially recognised by Dutch cat clubs and associations. Siamese and Oriental Cinnamon and Fawn kittens born were registered as AOC 26 and many were sold as pets.

Mr M. Weilinga brought his Havana female, Pistache des Montes Dores, to be mated by Choco Spot van Mariendaal in February 1969. She was a Belgian import and a great grand-daughter of Beaumanor Tammi, a Seal Point Siamese who was owned by Mary Dunnill. The name Cinnamon actually was "born" after the Weilinga family, prefix Frankendael, compared the colour to Cinnamon biscuits!

From this mating arrived Bel'in Casa van Frankendael who was born on May 1st 1969. She was kept by Maria Falkena and contributed greatly to the breeding of Cinnamon and Fawn Siamese varieties.

Ten years went by and it was not until 1979 that Mrs Stibbe-Leineman, prefix De Mont Eyk, described her litter of Havana kittens as containing two males whose colour she likened to "blonde Havanas". On researching her pedigrees she discovered the story behind Maria Falkena's hard work in developing the Cinnamon and Fawn colours.

By chance, Maria Falkena heard of an Oriental Cinnamon stud boy, Catty Castle's Singa Mas, who lived with the van Eck family in Veenendaal which was very close to her home. He was the son of Ch. Siavana Charlie Brown, a Havana exported from England.

Maria arranged with the van Eck family to accept a Havana of her breeding, Akeleia van Mariendaal, born on March 2nd 1978, for a mating with Catty Castle's Singa Mas.

Little did she know it but this mating was to create breeding history. Nestle Crunch van Mariendaal, who was born on January 25th, 1980 became the first officially recognised Dutch Cinnamon Point Siamese. The mating incorporated the parallel development of the English Cinnamons (Southview and Siavana prefixes) and Maria Falkena's own Dutch line. It also confirmed that the two lines carried the Cinnamon gene.

Mrs Stibbe-Leineman pushed hard for the recognition of the Cinnamons and wrote an article for the Newsletter, *Kattenwereld*, the periodical of the Dutch Club, Nederlandse Kattenfokkers Vereniging (Independent Dutch Society of Cat Friends).

Maria Falkena then received a call from the Chairperson, Inneka Zegers, asking her to bring along Cinnamons of two different lines to a "club match" so that they could be recognised. On January 25th 1980, the same day as Nestle Crunch van Mariendaal was born, the colour Cinnamon was recognised both in the Oriental and Siamese Pointed varieties.

The dilute shade of Cinnamon, Fawn, was recognised by the Independent Society of Cat Friends at the instigation of Yvonne Craane, prefix Twinkle Star's, and Inneka Zegers on 13 November 1982. Very soon after this date, Yvonne Craane's Twinkle Star's Fonda, an Oriental Fawn, became a Champion and her colour today is still that of a very beautiful pink mushroom.

LINKING OF THE VAN MARIENDAAL AND TWINKLE STAR'S LINE

Turning back the wheel of history to the early 1960s, Yvonne Craane and her mother, Mrs Tina Mulder-Craane, had specialised in breeding Havanas and Oriental Lilacs. Their pedigree lines had been improved by importing Havanas and Siamese from England. Their cats have been regular winners at Dutch and International Cat Shows. During the mid 1970s, Yvonne Craane developed an additional interest in Torties, which resulted in the birth on November 22nd 1977 of Gr. Int. Ch. Twinkle Star's Torka.

Torka became the foundation of the Twinkle Star's Oriental Torties. Through the mating in 1981 of Torka's daughter, Int. Ch. Twinkle Star's Tortina, with Yvonne Craane's Oriental Cinnamon stud, Int. Ch. Muscato van Mariendaal, the Cinnamon gene was introduced into the Siamese/Oriental Twinkle Star's line with the birth of Oriental Chocolate Tortie, Twinkle Star's Andromeda. Muscato van Mariendaal died in April 1994.

THE SALSTE CONNECTION

A few years later, in 1986, Sayonara Cinnamon Tigress, who had been bred by Glenda Worthy and owned by me, became the first GCCF registered Oriental Cinnamon Tabby.

In 1987 she had her first litter of kittens, including two Oriental Cinnamon Spotted Tabby boys and one Oriental Cinnamon girl. One of the boys, Salste Blake, went to Holland and during the early months of 1988 he mated many of the females in Yvonne Craane's house.

The result was twenty-three kittens, all born within a few days of each other. Yvonne found that Salste Blake carried the Siamese gene and, mated to Ch. Twinkle Star's Fonda (the Oriental Fawn who Yvonne Cranne already knew carried the Siamese gene), he sired Cinnamon and Fawn Tabby Points born on August 1st 1988.

One of the Oriental Cinnamon boys from this mating stood out as having inherited the Dutch shade of Cinnamon from his mother, together with a sound coat, and so Salste Blake was neutered in favour of his son, Int. Ch. Twinkle Star's Regilio. It was only after Regilio had sired numerous litters of kittens that Yvonne Craane found she had lost the Siamese gene that had come in with Salste Blake.

One of the earlier matings of Regilio was to Twinkle Star's Gemma, a Lilac Point Siamese. This

Twinkle Star's Kaneel Scarlett, Oriental Cinnamon Tortoiseshell, Twinkle Star's Kaneel Regilia, Oriental Cinnamon (UK imports from Holland), with Arrianrhod Dorabella, a Blue Tabby Point Siamese.

Photo: Steve Franklin.

mating produced three kittens, one of whom was an Oriental Cinnamon and registered as Twinkle Star's Kaneel Regilia. I imported her into the UK with her half-sister, Twinkle Star's Kaneel Scarlett, an Oriental Cinnamon Tortoiseshell, the daughter of Twinkle Star's Andromeda.

In the future, descendants of both girls and my Kerrimon Somefun Jamie, a pure 24 series Seal Point Siamese stud boy, will be returned to Holland to enable Yvonne Craane to continue breeding Cinnamon and Fawn Pointed Siamese and Orientals under her Twinkle Star's prefix.

CARAMEL AND APRICOT

Caramel and Apricot are produced by a gene called the "dilute modifier" gene rather than a separate gene for the colour. This gene is now recognised to be dominant, but it can only be fully expressed when a cat owning the dilute modifier gene, plus at least one gene for dilute (even if it does not show it), is mated to a cat that is blue, lilac, fawn or cream or to a cat that is chocolate, black/seal, cinnamon or red but carrying the gene for blue.

It appears there are two routes by which the dilute modifier gene passed into the Siamese breed. One route is very well documented, while the other route can only be put down to pure conjecture

THE SCINTILLA LINE – APRICOT

From 1962 Pat Turner had been involved in breeding what were termed in those days "unclassified" colours. Her involvement with the inhibitor gene (which gives rise to the silver and smoke pointed varieties of Siamese and Orientals) led to her identifying the action of the dilute modifier gene that produces Caramel and Apricot.

Ten cats that needed rehoming were passed to Pat Turner. Among them were two Marisarni Chinchillas, Marisarni Retara and her sister, and a Chocolate Point Siamese, Marisarni Dandino. Marisarni Retara had given birth to kittens sired by Marisarni Dandino and one of the two kittens in the litter was described by Pat Turner as a Shaded Silver. She was registered under the Any Other Variety (AOV) breed number of 26 as Scintasilva Sue. In terms of breeding she can be described as the F1 generation and when she matured she was mated to Ch. Pitapat Zeno, 32a, a Red Point Siamese who carried blue.

Out of this came a BC1 (first backcross) generation queen, Scintilla Serene Sunset (Sevena), who again was registered as AOV but, in reality, was a heterozygous Oriental Tortie Shaded Silver, known today as breed number 43es. Pat Turner found out in her breeding investigations that Serena carried "blue, chocolate, Siamese pointing, non-inhibitor, blotched (classic tabby)," and that, when mated to Ch. Darling Red Rufus, a Red Point Siamese, she would produce a totally new colour, described by Pat Turner as Apricot.

In 1973 Apricot appeared again in self and smoke varieties when Pat Turner mated Scintilla Serene Sunset to Taurus Kay Kavalier, who was a Lilac Point Siamese. These kittens were registered by the GCCF as Apricot.

Scintilla Serene Sunset had a litter sister who was registered as Scintilla Pastel Pansy, who participated in Pat Turner's breeding programme. She was later owned by Alice Law, prefix Nasyla. Pansy was the dam of Scintilla Honey Frost who was registered as a Cream Smoke but was thought by Pat Turner to be an Apricot Smoke. He also sired Apricot Smoke kittens when mated to an Oriental Black Tortoiseshell in 1974. Interestingly enough, Pat still thought of Apricot as a variation of the red colour in Siamese already recognised by GCCF.

Over the years, Apricot series kittens have continued to be born, and there is now an awakening interest in breeding the Apricot series with the Siamese pattern. A lovely example of an Apricot Tabby Point Siamese was born in 1993 and registered as Unowhose Hocus Pocus. This Siamese was born in a litter of Oriental Apricot and Caramel kittens and bred by Rick and Di Speight.

The GCCF has not as yet granted Preliminary Recognition to the Apricot Pointed Siamese series. Kittens will be registered by the GCCF but with the registration slip endorsed "This cat may not be shown".

THE SCINTILLA LINE – CARAMEL

The colour of Caramel in the Siamese patterns was recognised by GCCF on October 20th 1993 and given Preliminary Status, with Cinnamon and Fawn colours. In 1974 Pat Turner was trying to prove whether Scintilla Serene Sunset carried the long-hair gene from her Chinchilla heritage. Serena was mated to a new stud cat, the long-haired Southview Trappist, bred by Roy and Maureen Silson. He was also descended from the imported USA Recessive White, Anart's Miiko, who features in the history of the Cinnamon and Fawn Pointed Siamese varieties. In the litter were two kittens of a colour that would be eventually recognised as Caramel, one of whom was registered as Scintilla Dresden Rosa.

Interested parties such as the geneticist Roy Robinson, the Dytes, Maureen Silson and Julia May gathered at Pat Turner's home in Eastbourne to try and determine the genetic heritage of Pat's breeding investigation – whether the Caramel Scintilla Dresden Rosa had inherited her colour from her mother or whether her father AND her mother both carried the blue-eyed albino gene. (A Siamese carrying the blue-eyed Albino gene is called Dandinese.)

Maureen Silson had brought with her what was regarded as a Chocolate Point Dondinese and the two exhibits were compared for tones of colour. Pat Turner remembers that Scintilla Dresden Rosa had a slightly more opaque look to her coat colour. The kitten's coat colour was also compared to the colours of Chocolate, Lilac and Blue.

Some time after this meeting a Burmese whose coat colour was similar to that of Scintilla Dresden Rosa was brought to Pat Turner for her opinion on its colour. The conclusion that Scintilla Dresden Rosa was the same colour as the Burmese was not formed until both Peter Dyte and Pat Turner had the opportunity to see both cats.

The Coopers registered their Burmese as Lilac to avoid any dissension about a new colour amongst Burmese breeders. It is now known, however, that the dilute modifier gene was passed down in some lines in the Burmese breed.

Pat Turner decided that she would only register Scintilla Dresden Rosa when her points colour

Caramel Point Siamese: Shelemay Pye Wacket and Shelemay Merlin, a Lilac Point Siamese, descended from Adixism Rural Felicity and Salste Haldane Prince.

Photo: Dr. Andrew Boag.

had fully developed so that she could be registered under a suitable descriptive colour name. Test matings did eventually prove that Scintilla Dresden Rosa's colour was not a Chocolate colour diluted by Recessive White.

It appeared that the GCCF Siamese Registrar must have been labouring under great difficulty with these "new" colours suddenly materialising without what appeared to be any definite foundations. Fortunately, Pat Turner is a very respected geneticist and any threats of inspection that reached her on the active "cat fancy grapevine" appeared to be without foundation and she received her registration certificate.

She did maintain that at least her kittens were registered correctly whereas the Burmese breeders registered their similarly coloured kittens under the most suitable recognised breed number and colour description!

By the time Pat Turner received her registration certificate from the Siamese Registrar, she realised in hindsight that she had in fact bred thirty-seven other kittens whose coat colour was due to the dilute modifier gene. All of these kittens had one common factor, they were descended from Scintasilva Sue. When she realised that Scintasilva Sue was the common denominator, she then researched the Chinchilla antecedents of this little cat and came up with the theory that the gene she had identified as the dilute modifier gene had been passed through the USA imports of the Bonavia Chinchilla line into the Marisarni breeding line. She did not believe that the gene had come through Marisarni Dandino.

In 1975 Pat Turner bred Scintilla Serene Sunset to her half-brother Nasyla Mink Moonlight in an attempt to breed paler Tipped Silvers. This mating produced eight kittens, one of whom was registered as Scintilla Kaffy Ole, an Oriental Caramel. Another kitten, Scintilla Hazy Sprite was exported to Germany to Heidi Stamm, prefix Tai-Bagheeras. Even though she was not Caramel herself, it became evident that she carried the dilute modifier gene. She became the foundation cat behind the Dutch and German Caramel Pointed Siamese and Orientals. More important for Pat Turner, this mating confirmed that Caramel could be produced without the Recessive White gene.

A further test mating was carried out in 1975 using Scintilla Dresden Rosa to the Lilac Point Siamese, Taurus Kay Kavalier, and the kittens, two Blue Point Siamese, one Caramel Point and one Lilac Point Siamese, proved without doubt that Caramel was not produced by a combination of Chocolate Point Siamese and Recessive White. The Siamese Registrar registered the Caramel Point Siamese with Pat Turner's chosen name of Scintilla Roseanna.

The breeding investigation for Caramel continued in 1976 and Scintilla Serene Sunset was mated to a Chocolate Point Siamese. One of the kittens, Scintilla Rosario, was a most interesting combination. He was actually a Seal Silver Tabby Point Siamese (although registered as a Dove Point) and later proved to be a carrier of the dilute modifier gene.

Eventually Scintilla Roseanna and Scintilla Dresden Rosa were neutered, partly because of the difficulties being experienced with the registration of descendants with Recessive White ancestry. Scintilla Rosetta, the daughter of Scintilla Roseanna, was by now the only Caramel Siamese descendant left from the Southview Trappist/Recessive White lines.

So Pat Turner stopped breeding with that part of her line and concentrated with the line that had produced Scintilla Rosario, the Seal Silver Tabby Point Siamese who carried the dilute modifier gene. He was mated to Scintilla April Blessing, a Foreign White who had Lilac Point Siamese ancestry, and from this came Scintilla Koffee Kreme who was then bred to a grand-daughter of Scintilla Serene Sunset. This produced an Oriental Caramel Silver Spotted male, Scintilla Muted Mink.

Pat Turner felt that she had adequately demonstrated that Caramel was not dependent on the blue-eyed albino gene resulting in Recessive White cats. As a result of a difference in opinion,

Scintilla Rosetta was sent abroad and her pedigree was accepted for future registrations with an alternative registration body. Having moved to a smaller house, Pat Turner did not carry on with such a large breeding programme. She became involved with the development of the Oriental Silver and Smoke breeding programme and the occasional birth of a Caramel Point Siamese or an Oriental Caramel variety was largely a by-product of her other breeding interests.

In 1981 her Oriental (Foreign) Blue, Amoureuse Melody, was mated to Scintilla Muted Mink and so Scintilla Pastelle Royale, a Caramel Silver Tabby Pointed Siamese, appeared.

Little did Pat Turner know how important he would be in keeping her Caramel line going. During 1981 she discovered that her cats had succumbed to the Leukaemia virus and tragically by the end of 1982, Scintilla Pastelle Royale was the only survivor. He had grown up in complete isolation and all the precautions that had been taken to prevent the passing of the virus into his stud house had proved worthwhile.

Scintilla Pastelle Royale sired two Caramel Tabby Point Siamese, Scintilla Caradon, and Scintilla Caramellian who was later used as a stud cat and mated once to Scintilla Caramelodots – who also has an interesting history. She was an Oriental Caramel Silver Spotted Tabby bred by Pat Turner out of the Oriental Black Smoke, Tai Bagheeras Barbarian, given to her by her friend Heidi Stamm of Germany. Pat was most surprised to see this kitten appear and when she researched the lines off the 5-generation pedigree with which she had been supplied she found the Tai Bagheeras line had carried the dilute modifier gene through all those generations, from Scintilla Hazy Sprite and ultimately back to Scintasilva Sue.

Scintilla Caramelodots went to Barbara Castle who bred from her and produced Caramel Pointed Siamese and Caramel Tabby Pointed Siamese, as well as the Oriental Caramel and Caramel Silver varieties.

OTHER SIAMESE LINES

In 1986, a Siamese known as Astromiam Pretty Opal, born on July 15th 1985, was seen by Pat Turner and pronounced to be a Caramel Tabby Point Siamese, not a Lilac Tabby Point as she was registered.

After the birth of Opal's kittens, her owner decided that she wanted to concentrate on breeding the Oriental Cinnamon varieties and Opal was offered to me on condition that she should not be bred to an Oriental Blue or a Blue Point Siamese. This condition was adhered to throughout Opal's breeding life.

We first had to re-register Astromiam Pretty Opal with the knowledge and agreement of her breeder, Mrs Bernice Martin. Her registration details were changed from a Lilac Tabby Point Siamese to a Caramel Tabby Point Siamese and she became one of the earliest Caramel Tabby Point Siamese to be registered.

On July 25th 1987 Opal gave birth to her first litter by Orissa Extra Edition, an Oriental Lilac Ticked Tabby bred by Angela Morse. Not long after her kittens were born, Barbara Castle, prefix Shelemay, came over to help identify their colours. One was an Oriental Lilac, two were Oriental Caramel Spotted Tabbies, and the fourth was an Oriental Caramel Ticked Tabby. It was hoped that some Caramel or Caramel Tabby Pointed Siamese would appear, but this did not happen.

Not long after this, Oriental Caramel were given Preliminary Recognition, and Salste Carmel, the Oriental Caramel Ticked Tabby, became the first Caramel of any Oriental variety to obtain a Merit.

Still hoping for a Caramel Tabby Point Siamese to resemble Astromiam Pretty Opal, her second litter with us was born on April 25th 1988. In that litter was the first GCCF registered Oriental Caramel, Salste Haldane Prince, who went to live with Barbara Castle. During his brief stud career

Turevooh Jeu Desprit: The only British Caramel Tortie Point born to date.

Photo: Vic Grant.

Astromiam Pretty Opal, a Caramel Tabby Point, with her daughter, Salste Carmel, an Oriental Caramel Ticked Tabby, and Salste Mr Mistoffelees, an Oriental Caramel Silver Ticked Tabby.

Photo: Steve Franklin.

he sired a few Caramel and Caramel Tabby Pointed Siamese. After the birth of Salste Haldane Prince, Pat Turner told me about some Siamese lines that she had suspected of producing Caramels over the years. These lines were not related in any way to her Scintilla Caramel lines. Mary Dunnill and I became interested in researching Salste Haldane Prince's Caramel Siamese antecedents together with other known Caramel Siamese lines. Since the mid 1980s many more pedigree lines have produced Caramels and Apricots in the Siamese Pointed varieties as well as the Oriental varieties. The first and only GCCF registered Caramel Tortie Point Siamese born to date is Turevooh Jeu Desprit, bred by Alison Turtill.

POSSIBLE USA CARAMELS

Sometimes breeders have referred to Caramel as being the colour of Indigo (assumed by some to be blue-based Caramel) and it was interesting to read Vera Nelson's comments in her *Siamese Cat Book* , published in 1976, that she had seen a colour of Siamese that bore no relation to any published Standard.

She wrote about a Siamese with almost "purplish" points, which were much darker than those found on Blue Point Siamese. She referred to this one as an oddity as she had not seen other Siamese with this colouration being shown. The only other information she gave regarding this Siamese was that its pedigree contained Seal Point Siamese, Blue Point Siamese and Chocolate Point Siamese.

It is known that the dilute modifier gene is hypostatic to Seal and Chocolate: this means that these two colours can hide the presence of this gene. The dilute modifier gene works on blue, lilac or fawn colours to produce Caramel, so perhaps the cat referred to by Vera Nelson was an early example of a Caramel Pointed Siamese living in the States.

SILVER POINTED SIAMESE VARIETIES

This chapter would not be complete without mentioning other unrecognised varieties of Siamese. Silver tabby points have been around for many years and Pat Turner wrote in the well-known *Book of the Cat*, that the first Lilac Tabby Point Siamese were in fact Lilac Silver Tabby Point Siamese. One of the most recent to be born (amongst a litter of Shaded Orientals on February 22nd 1994) is Amenra Lalique, a Caramel Silver Tabby Point Siamese who excels in type and colour. She was bred by Carol Ward and was placed on exhibition at the 1994 Oriental Cat Association Show for interested fanciers to view.

The Silver varieties consist of smokes and shadeds, Silver Tabbies and Silver Tortie Tabbies. It is now known that the gene responsible for Silver is the inhibitor gene, given this name because it inhibits the standard colour of the points by suppressing part of the colouring matter contained in the hairs and replacing it with Silver. To produce the Silver pointed Siamese varieties either parent should possess the inhibitor gene; it is not needed from both sire and dam. Neither is it carried from past generations like some other genes; it has to be present in the current mating.

It cannot be predicted whether kittens will have the same degree of Silver as one or both of their parents when Silvers are mated, since the inhibitor gene varies in the amount of Silver it leaves in the coat with each generation. It was once thought that the effect of Silver within the coat was due to the Chinchilla gene (the heritage of some Siamese and Oriental lines), but the results of breeding investigations determined otherwise after 1970.

The Silver-pointed Siamese versions are produced as a by-product of Oriental matings. Breeders of Silver pointed varieties are often inclined to re-register their progeny when adult, as they say it can sometimes be difficult to know at the kitten stage which varieties have picked up the Silver gene from one or both Silver parents.

The future development of the Cinnamon, Fawn and Caramel varieties and the presently unrecognised Apricot and Silver Pointed varieties of Siamese depends on whether breeders are attracted by these colours and are prepared to work with them.